HERMES
Literature, Science, Philosophy

HERMES
LITERATURE, SCIENCE, PHILOSOPHY

by MICHEL SERRES
Edited by Josué V. Harari
& David F. Bell

 THE JOHNS HOPKINS UNIVERSITY PRESS
BALTIMORE & LONDON

844.914
Serres

This book has been brought to publication with the generous assistance of the Andrew W. Mellon Foundation.

The Johns Hopkins University Press, Baltimore, Maryland 21218
The Johns Hopkins Press Ltd., London

`

Library of Congress Cataloging in Publication Data

Serres, Michel.
    Hermes: literature, science, philosophy.

    Includes index.
    Contents: The apparition of Hermes, Don Juan—
Knowledge in the classical age—Michelet, the soup
—Language and space, from Oedipus to Zola—[etc.]
    I. Harari, Josué V.   II. Bell, David F.
III. Title.
PQ2679.E679A2 1981   844'.914   81-47601
ISBN 0-8018-2454-0   AACR2

Contents

     v

Editors' Note

Hermes: Literature, Science, Philosophy is conceived as a first step in the publication of Michel Serres's works. In order to help familiarize American readers with Serres's original mode of thinking and writing, we have opted for a book that would include a selection of his most representative and most readable essays. *Hermes* illustrates the full range of Serres's diverse and complex interests as well as the coherence of purpose in his thinking; it does not attempt to establish the kind of progression, continuity (in the narrow sense of the word), and unity that readers might expect from the anthologized work of an author. But *Hermes* should make abundantly clear how Serres's writing is interdisciplinary at all levels, tracing themes across the domains of literature, philosophy, science, and painting, borrowing their various techniques, and translating them into an original view of the world of knowledge.

Our introductory remarks follow these same lines. We do not wish to claim that *Hermes* resolves in any definitive manner questions that have never before been formulated. Nor do we intend to follow step by step the progression or development of Serres's thought, precisely because the idea of linear progress and development is fundamentally antithetical to his method of thinking. Serres's work is not to be understood as a systematic enumeration of new directions of knowledge or research; it assumes instead the form of an excursion or expedition (*randonnée*—the connotations of impetuosity and chance contained in the French term are important) with necessary pauses at certain crossroads. We shall explore one series of such pauses; Ilya Prigogine and Isabelle Stengers will analyze another in their important essay that appears in the postface.

A remark concerning the "language" of the present volume is in order. We would like to thank the friends who translated many of the essays: Susan Willey (chapter 1), Suzanne Guerlac (chapter 3), Marilyn Sides (chapters 5 and 6), Mark Anderson (chapters 7 and 8), and Lawrence Schehr (chapter 9 and the postface). In translating the other essays in the book and revising the above translations we have elected to choose intelligible English renderings, perhaps at the cost of sacrificing some of Serres's unusual syntax and stylistic effects. But the reader familiar with contemporary critical writing knows that the French language allows stylistic and syntactic "aberrations" that cannot always be produced or reproduced in English.

This book has benefited from the continuous advice of Wilda Anderson, Martine Bell, and William Sisler. Our most sincere appreciation goes to them for their support.

Introduction
Journal à plusieurs voies
by Josué V. Harari
& David F. Bell

There is no royal road to learning.
— Euclid

In 1966, Richard Feynman, the distinguished professor of physics at the California Institute of Technology, who had just been awarded the Nobel prize the year before, gave a lecture to the American Association of Teachers of Physics. The subject of his lecture was "What Is Science?" Undoubtedly when a paper boasts such a title and is delivered by a Nobel prize-winner there is an underlying expectation that the world will finally hear the answers to some, if not all, of the outstanding questions concerning the nature of science and scientific inquiry. One would naturally expect Feynman to offer the most serious remarks, arguments, and demonstrations couched in the most difficult terminology in order to present a tableau of the different conceptions of science, past and present, and to conclude with his own conception of the field. But this was not at all the case! Feynman spoke of his childhood and explained, among other things, how his father taught him the rules of logic and of set theory by playing with old bathroom tiles of various colors. But let us listen to him as he tells how he discovered an application of one of the most difficult principles of analytic geometry—the problem of intersection:

> When I was at Cornell, I was rather fascinated by the student body, which seems to me was a dilute mixture of some sensible people in a big mass of dumb people studying home economics. . . . I used to sit in the cafeteria with the students and eat and try to overhear their conversations and see if there was one intelligent word coming out.

ix

You can imagine my surprise when I discovered a tremendous thing, it seemed to me.

> I listened to a conversation between two girls, and one was explaining that if you want to make a straight line, you see, you go over a certain number to the right for each row you go up, that is, if you go over each time the same amount when you go up a row, you make a straight line. A deep principle of analytic geometry! . . .
> She went on and said, "Suppose you have another line coming in from the other side, and you want to figure out where they are going to intersect. Suppose on one line you go over two to the right for every one you go up, and the other line goes over three to the right for every one that it goes up, and they start twenty steps apart," etc. — I was flabbergasted. She figured out where the intersection was! It turned out that one girl was explaining to the other how to knit argyle socks.[1]

There would be much to say concerning the profundity of this style of thought. A few remarks, however, will suffice here to establish the context of Serres's own style of work.

Serres also chooses to recount mythical anecdotes—such as those the ancient Greeks used to exchange; he chooses to speak playfully of fictions, to participate in the conversations of La Fontaine's animals, to share in the festive meals of country and city rats, to listen to the nightingale's or the grasshopper's song or to the arguments of the wolf and the lamb. Elsewhere he tells fantastic tales about locomotives or about extraordinary journeys as in Jules Verne, Stevenson, or the *Adventures of Tintin*—after all, is Tintin not the greatest modern anthropologist, the chateau of Moulinsart the center of the world, and the opera singer Castafiore the illustration of parasited communication and intercepted messages?[2]

In Serres's work, the discrete charms of knowledge go hand in hand with anecdotes and memories, stories and myths, tales and encounters— and all of this belongs to the realm of *literature*. Instead of inflicting upon the reader the customary *pensum* of the scientist or philosopher, Serres chats about literature! Intellectual con game of a scientific philosopher? Again, as it was for Feynman, the answer is decidedly no. Literature represents for Serres a *Journal à plusieurs voies,* the personal log-book of a

[1] Richard P. Feynman, "What Is Science?," *The Physics Teacher* 7, no. 6 (1969):314-15.
[2] La Fontaine's *Fables* are discussed in *Le Parasite* (Paris: Grasset, 1980) and in the essay "La Fontaine and Descartes: Knowledge in the Classical Age" included in this volume; the locomotive is a reference to Serres's discussion of Zola's *La Bête humaine* in his *Feux et signaux de brume: Zola* (Paris: Grasset, 1975); the extraordinary journeys are of course the subject of his *Jouvences: Sur Jules Verne* (Paris: Minuit, 1974); and Madame Castafiore is the central character of *Les Bijoux de la Castafiore* (which belongs to the cycle of *The Adventures of Tintin*) that is the subject of Serres's essay "Rires: Les Bijoux distraits ou la cantatrice sauve" in *Hermès II: L'Interférence* (Paris: Minuit, 1972).

poet-philosopher of science who speaks with many voices and journeys across many paths (journal and journey do share the same root), all of which lead to *sophia*—wisdom and knowledge. We shall attempt to outline the routes to this knowledge in the pages that follow by focusing on certain themes—stories, anecdotes, tales, etc. —that run through Serres's work and by identifying the *points of exchange* and the *conditions of passage* that regulate these themes.

Thesis

"Serres's major interest is the parallel development of scientific, philosophical, and literary trends. In a very simplified manner, one might say that Serres always runs counter to the prevalent notion of the two cultures —scientific and humanistic—between which no communication is possible. In Serres's view 'criticism is a generalized physics,' and whether knowledge is written in philosophical, literary, or scientific language it nevertheless articulates a common set of problems that transcends academic disciplines and artificial boundaries." These remarks by René Girard express succinctly both the principal thesis and the program (with its "method") that Serres has set forth in his work begun in 1968 with *Le Système de Leibniz et ses modèles mathématiques* and presently including a dozen books published during the past decade.

Understood globally, the thesis is simple: it consists in positing that there exists a passage (or passages) between the exact sciences on the one hand and the sciences of man on the other. This thesis in itself is not new. Since the pre-Socratics and Plato, there have always been attempts to link these two domains, to overcome an unfruitful division. However, in order to pass from the exact sciences to the sciences of man, one does not simply open a door and cross the street, to use one of Serres's images. This passage, metaphorically compared to the glacial labyrinth that unites the Atlantic to the Pacific, is not as simple as the classification of knowledge would lead one to believe.

> The passage is rare and narrow. . . . From the sciences of man to the exact sciences, or inversely, the path does not cross a homogeneous and empty space. Usually the passage is closed, either by land masses or by ice floes, or perhaps by the fact that one becomes lost. And if the passage is open, it follows a path that is difficult to gauge.[3]

Such an itinerary is complicated for at least two reasons. The first involves the very *nature* of knowledge. Our textbooks teach us very early

---

[3] *Hermès V: Le Passage du Nord-Ouest* (Paris: Minuit, 1980), p. 18.

on to separate those who study the humanities from those who manipulate slide rules, those who work with letters and texts from those who use numbers, those concerned with interpersonal relations from those concerned with the physical world. We have now institutionalized this separation in our universities by distinguishing between the faculty of arts (or letters, or humanities) and the faculty of sciences. We have thus complemented conceptual categories and exclusions with physical and architectural configurations that mirror and reinforce divisions: walls, partitions, separate university faculties and libraries. An effort to think in unconventional modes meets not only with conceptual and linguistic difficulties, but with topographical ones as well. As a result of this situation, we ordinarily conceive of two populations: the scientists without culture (educated but not "cultivated") and the humanists without scientific knowledge (cultivated but not "educated"). And the gulf between these two populations continues to grow.

The second obstacle blocking the passage or transport between the two cultures results from the *evolution* of modern knowledge. The increasing complexity of the problems to be solved calls for more and more specialization — more divisions and separations developing into territories, disciplines, and branches of knowledge or, one might say, into schools, sects, and research groups. Indeed, modern science has acquired its effectiveness precisely because scientific work is organized today along the lines of a growing specialization of knowledge. The tendency to divide in order to conquer has brought science to a critical point at which it is slowly becoming more of a trade the scientist practices than a *scientia* whose object is knowledge. This transformation of the nature of scientific inquiry also involves a change in our conception of scientific objectivity. The history of science in Western society teaches us that science evolved by slowly distancing itself from lived experience. It developed on the basis of a process of experimentation that is defined as objective, as excluding all subjectivity. Fortunately we are presently rather far removed from the period of naive scientificity during which subjectivity was considered to be the domain of illusion and objective knowledge to be the sole expression of truth. We know now that our subjectivity is not an illusion to be overcome, but that it is another part of reality, no less important than any other part. That is why it is an urgent task for a thinker like Serres to find a way to reinsert the subjective domain into modern scientific discourse.

Philosophy accomplishes this operation. There is no need to remind the reader that philosophy is not science (although the two were synonymous until the eighteenth century), but rather, as its etymology shows, that it is the love (*philia*) of wisdom and knowledge (*sophia*). We seem to have forgotten this basic definition: philosophy must not be thought of as

xiii / Journal à plusieurs voies

against science, but rather *with* science (perhaps even beyond science if one is to adopt Aristotle's or Descartes's definition of philosophy as a meta-physics). As such, philosophy aims at formulating and explaining the meaning of the structure of the universe in relation to man, to his inner and social life. But in his search for solutions to the conflictual questions he faces, the philosopher in no way seeks simply to imitate the scientist in an attempt to occupy the entire cultural arena. The role of the philosopher is not to conquer a territory, but "to attempt *to see on a large scale,* to be in full possession of a multiple, and sometimes connected intellection."[4] This remark by Serres calls for an explanation that necessitates a detour.

Until recently, science had convinced us that in the classification of the spaces of knowledge the local was included in the global, in other words, that a path always existed between one local configuration and another, that from local configurations one could always move without break or interruption to a more encompassing global configuration. Clearly this assumption implied a homogeneous space of knowledge ruled entirely by a single scientific or universal truth that guaranteed the validity of the operation of passage. Such a space differs qualitatively from a more complex space in which the passage from one local singularity to another would always require an arduous effort. Rather than a universal truth, in the more complex case one would have a kind of truth that functions only in the context of local pockets, a truth that is always local, distributed haphazardly in a plurality of spaces. The space of knowledge, indeed, space itself, would not be homogeneous or rigidly bound together, it would be "in tatters."

> No, the real is not cut up into regular patterns, it is sporadic, spaces and times with straits and passes. . . . Therefore I assume there are fluctuating tatters; I am looking for the passage among these complicated cuttings. I believe, I see that the state of things consists of islands sown in archipelagoes on the noisy, poorly-understood disorder of the sea, . . . the emergence of sporadic rationalities that are not evidently nor easily linked. Passages exist, I know, I have drawn some of them in certain works using certain operators. . . . But I cannot generalize, obstructions are manifest and counter-examples abound.[5]

[4] Ibid., p. 24, emphasis added.

[5] Ibid., pp. 23-24. Predictably the problematic of spaces belongs to an epistemology that conceives of reality, time, and history in a radically different way. For instance, why is it that our logos posits the real as rational, that is, as a single common space within which everything takes place? According to Serres, philosophy represses the problem of spaces in favor of linear time because "time [is] the most immediate and simplest esthetic projection of ordered structure. With time, the esthetic is in order and those in political power are quite pleased. Spaces are repressed because they are possibly, better yet, certainly, disorderly. . . . Reason,

From this point of view, the philosophical truth consists in seeing that the universality of a model is not probable. What is evident, on the contrary, is the cohabitation of different systems of thought (hence of multiple models and truths), which form any number of unique discourses, each justified by a set of chosen coordinates and by underlying presuppositions. Rigor and coherence are regional. Thus universality and the global can only be conceived in a mode that recognizes the predominance of regionality and the local.

> Each domain [of modernity], in its own systematicity, circulates an autonomous type of truth; each domain has a philosophy of the relations of its truth to its system and of the circulation along these relations. In addition, it exhibits unique types of openings onto other domains that make it a regional epistemology of the system of science.... One must resolutely open a new epistemological spectrum and read the colors that our prejudices had previously erased. Logic contains one theory of science (or several), but mathematics surely contains another one, and most likely several. Information theory is consciously developing one also, just as are sociology and child psychology. In this coherent, but open world, each province is a world and has its world, so that epistemology (which is dead as long as it remains outside) becomes pluralized and relativized, within the system.[6]

"To see on a large scale, to be in full possession of a multiple, and sometimes connected intellection" means to understand that the foundation of knowledge presupposes neither *one* philosophical discourse nor *one* scientific discourse, but only regional epistemologies.[7] Multiplication, regionalization, localization: to see on a large scale thus means to attempt to travel through as much space as possible, as one does at sea when one goes from island to island searching for "Northwest passages" between different spaces. This journey of Serres's through multiple times, spaces,

---

the political powers that be, prefer order rather than disorder, time rather than space, history rather than multiplicities" (*Feux et signaux de brume*, p. 164). The development of languages, cultures, societies and histories is a function of this choice. Against homogeneous, metric, and ordered time, Serres opts for a concept of time that is multivectorial, complex, and distributed stochastically — yesterday, elsewhere, now here, now there, at unpredictable times and places. This is the time of Lucretius and the time of entropy. This model carries with it the discourse of a new history, one that would be neither in a straight nor a curved line, but rather that would be aleatory and stochastic. History is ergodic: the organizing principle of its order is not primordial, but is the result of the sufficient repetition of certain effects of chance that thus produces forms of regularity.

    [6] *Hermès II*, pp. 31-32.

    [7] "We have to change laws. Henceforth the global does not necessarily produce a local equivalent, and the local itself contains a law that does not always and everywhere reproduce the global" (*Hermès V*, p. 75).

and cultural formations suggests the contours of a general program we shall outline as we proceed in this essay.

Program

One should perhaps begin by recalling Serres's personal itinerary. Educated as a philosopher, Serres says that he began by studying geometry as Plato recommended. Afterwards, he continued in more concrete domains: physics, biology, and the sciences of man. In this last area he became especially interested in anthropology, more specifically, in the history of religions. There he encountered Georges Dumézil's work as well as that of Mircea Eliade and perhaps more fundamentally that of René Girard.[8] Thus Serres's itinerary is encyclopedic, covering the three great modes of knowledge: philosophic, scientific, and mythic.

If we now move to Michel Serres's bibliography, we immediately encounter again his encyclopedic concerns. There are five volumes of collected essays, *Hermès I* to *V*, one book-length essay, *Le Parasite*, dealing with the conditions for an epistemology of human relations based on the logic of the excluded third man (*le tiers exclu*), and finally four books dealing with specific authors—*Le Système de Leibniz* (1968), *Jouvences: Sur Jules Verne* (1974), *Feux et signaux de brume: Zola* (1975), and *La Naissance de la physique dans le texte de Lucrèce* (1978). Four book-length studies treat four authors each of whom is in his own way a system-builder: Leibniz constructs a metaphysical system out of mathematics, Zola constructs a genetic system, Verne a mythical geography, and Lucretius a physics. There is another common denominator: scientific thought plays an important role in the work of each of the four authors. Leibniz in the classical period and Lucretius in antiquity are scientific philosophers; Zola and Verne are nineteenth-century novelists well versed in science, what one might call philosophical scientists. Moreover, all four are thinkers of totality, in other words, they speak an encyclopedic discourse that attempts to describe the world in its totality. Hence Serres's interest in them and our use of them to construct our reading of Serres.

De Rerum Natura, which is about the birth of physics, has its basis in the natural universe and is descriptive of this universe. The atomists held that there is first of all the primal chaos, disorder *before* order. It is against this background that Lucretius writes a (non-Platonic and non-

---

[8] We can see the influence of comparative religion in Serres's work on Lucretius and Verne. The kinship with René Girard's thinking is more evident in Serres's later essays. See *Hermès V* and, in the present volume, "Origin of Geometry."

Aristotelian) story of the beginnings of the universe. It is a story in which physics neither represses (through experimentation) nor manipulates nature. Lucretian physics is a science of caresses whose logic is fluid and multiple rather than binary and whose models are taken from nature: rain, clouds, vortices, cyclones. It is a science that creates a harmony of the ideal, the theoretical, and the experiential. Physics translates the world, and the world demonstrates physics. Let us retain this last point: Lucretius's global system is not conceived as a preface to a theory, but as a preface to the world. Lucretian science teaches "naively," without separating itself from things. "The best model is the thing itself, or the object as it exists. The discourse [of declination] tells of its constitution."[9] Whence the following theorem:

Theorem 1: In order for there to be an encyclopedic totality, this totality must be constituted as a theory providing access not only to a field of knowledge but to the world as well. (An encyclopedia that omits any of the multiple dimensions of knowledge is a false encyclopedia at the very moment of its realization: this explains, in Serres's view, the repeated failure of all philosophers of totality.)

Against the Lucretian science of discovery, multiplicity, and fluidity, Leibniz constructs between 1666 (*De Arte Combinatoria*) and 1686 (*The Discourse on Metaphysics*) his own system of the world. Leibniz brings together all the modalities of the encyclopedic knowledge that characterize the seventeenth century: he is a jurist, a mathematician, a philosopher, and a theologian. Leibniz replaces the disorder of the world with a model of exact knowledge. His metaphysics uses the most rigorous and coherent elements of his mathematical knowledge to express the ideal of order in the classical age. Now, in order to produce this order, it was also necessary to formulate the concept of law, in other words, to invent an image and guarantor of stability.[10] But legislation signifies closure—law, order, stability, closure. And Serres asks, "In whose interest is it to lay down a law of history if not in the interest of whoever wishes to stop time? Of course it is in the best interests of whoever pursues power in economics, politics, or philosophy to close off genesis. . . . The law is a

[9]*La Naissance de la physique dans le texte de Lucrèce* (Paris: Minuit, 1977), p. 202. The *clinamen* is the operator that marks the passage from the theoretical to the practical: it is the birth of existence. Things come into existence due to the tiny deviations of atoms from laminar flow, the *écart à l'équilibre.*

[10]The passage order-law-stability historically marks the origin of an obsession with finding a law that would render the entire universe stable, an obsession that runs from the classical age through Newton and Laplace.

theft."[11] The theoretical necessity for order thus results in a political exigency. The dream of classical rationality becomes the political nightmare of our modern era. All the institutions created by the seventeenth century are there ready to govern nature and the world. They are strategies of domination whereby science itself becomes nothing more than a martial art: "These [scientific] epistemologies are not innocent: at the critical tribunal they are calling for executions. They are policies promulgated by military strategists. To know is to kill, to rely on death . . ." (p. 28).[12]

Metaphysics, positioned above and dominating because it can think in universals, brings about a general mobilization. "Knowledge in the Classical Age," included in the present volume, artfully describes the process by which metaphysics succeeds in occupying the entire intellectual sphere in a movement that resembles a conquest or a military invasion: "Metaphysics is operatory, it is the strategic set without which physics and the exact sciences are nothing but partial and dispersed tactics" (p. 27). Thus the classical ideal of order—through metaphysics and its subordinate sciences—becomes not an epistemology of knowledge but one of power relationships: "The most general knowledge that can be formed, the most exact, the most faithful, and the most effective, can be deciphered by a military model. The discourse on method is a science of war."[13] To sum up the preceding remarks, let us emphasize that a) Leibniz, in his attempt to provide a clear and ordered version of the world, speaks the classical paradigm in its purest form, b) beginning with the classical age the world is conceived in terms of law, and c) unlike the gentle Lucretian science, the classical *episteme* became one of death. Whence:

Theorem 2: Any theoretical exigency is inextricably linked to a moral or political exigency. (Theory always borders on terror—something that has always been known in academic circles that engage exclusively in theory.) From this follow two corollaries:

2.1: A philosophy is not purely and simply the result of a free choice; it always results from a double necessity, theoretical on the one hand, moral and political on the other hand.

2.2: The theory of science is akin to the theory of domination. Knowledge, including scientific knowledge, is always finalized by political practice: "To know is to engage in a practice implicated in the ideology of command and obedience."[14]

[11] *Hermès IV: La Distribution* (Paris: Minuit, 1977), p. 37.
[12] All references to the present volume will be indicated in parentheses by page number.
[13] *Hermès IV*, p. 289.
[14] *Hermès III: La Traduction* (Paris: Minuit, 1974), p 85.

After Lucretius and Leibniz, Zola speaks of the world as his predecessors spoke, with concepts belonging to *his* world. Against the metaphysical sequence that remains focused on the Cartesian couple of being and movement, Zola announces the construction of motors, a physical sequence based on reservoir, circulation, and entropy. Zola attempts to illustrate this change through the analysis of the natural and social history of a family: the Rougon-Macquart.

Zola's fiction is particularly interesting because it speaks at the same time the two supposedly antithetical languages of myth and science. Zola pursues a mythical trajectory with repeated (and often renewed) use of motifs such as the labyrinth, the weaver, the well, the bridge, and, especially, the mythical tree. Like the Greeks, Zola approaches his society through genealogy: the Rougon-Macquart family tree is the map of his itinerary. Zola, however, is writing in the nineteenth century. Putting his text into its context, one discovers that genealogy is rewritten as genetics. This is most evident in Zola's *Le Docteur Pascal.* The *incipit* of the novel immediately establishes Pascal's study as a laboratory in which he develops through genetic experimentation the genealogy of the Rougon-Macquart family. But the genealogical tree upon which Pascal is working is more than just a family record. It is an organon that structures the space of experimental knowledge: "Point by point the tree passes through the traditional classification of the sciences. It spreads throughout the encyclopedia. . . ."[15] Moreover, lest we forget, the nineteenth century saw the development of motors and the theory describing them.

> The region serving as a reference [for genealogy] seems to be the theory of heredity [genetics], however, the latter in turn refers to another region. The fundamental science with respect to which genetics remains secondary is rather difficult to discover, was difficult for the scientists of the period to discover, but the novelist Zola discovered it explicitly—it is there, burning, in his narrative. Zola uses genetics but designates the foundation of its conditions and of its subsequent progress. *It is impossible to qualify this insight as anything less than a scientific discovery.*[16]

This fundamental scientific discovery is thermodynamics. The genealogy of the Rougon-Macquart thus becomes a genetic treatise that is itself the materialization of a cosmology of heat—a steam engine.[17] The story of the Rougon-Macquart family can be explained according to Carnot's theory, that is, according to the two sources, one hot and the other cold—sex and death. Exit mechanics, enter thermodynamics.

[15] *Feux et signaux de brume*, p. 40.
[16] Ibid., pp. 17-18.
[17] Ibid., see especially chapter 2 on *Le Docteur Pascal*, pp. 59-128. Further on in this essay we discuss the methodological premises upon which this equivalence is established.

One must emphasize two important points in Serres's *Zola*. First, in the nineteenth century science was not constituted (contrary to what scientists suggested) outside other cultural formations; instead it participated fully in them. "When genetics broke new ground, and this was the case during Zola's life, it encountered within culture all the archaic solutions to the problems of family relations. Thus the discovery referred to two foundations: one consisted of epistemological conditions (and the narrative found that one) and the other of the culture in which the discovery takes place (and the system became lodged in myth)."[18] Secondly, not only does science *not* exclude myth, but in certain cases it can be enriched by myth: "the unexpected and disturbing result: the science in question is diffused along paths belonging to myth. It is grasped as myth, it becomes myth."[19]

Theorem 3: There is no hierarchy of cultural formations. "It is not, it has never been the case that science is on one side and myth on the other. In a given myth, millennial tradition, or barbarous thought, the proportion of relevant science is probably as great as the proportion of mythology that envelops any given science."[20] From which one may draw the following corollaries:

3.1: Science is a cultural formation equivalent to any other. Thus one passes from the cultural formation called "science" to any and all cultural formations. Take the case of the emergence of thermodynamics, for instance, when the old Cartesian machine is replaced by the motor. At the precise moment at which the motor "overtakes" thermodynamics it traverses all the other formations. Henceforth, it becomes the universal model of knowledge in the nineteenth century, a construct that always functions in the same way in all cultural domains—from Marx to Freud, from Nietzsche to Bergson, or from Zola to Turner:

> This is indeed what happens. Read Carnot starting on page one. Now read Marx, Freud, Zola, Michelet, Nietzsche, Bergson, and so on. The reservoir is actually spoken of everywhere, or if not the reservoir, its equivalent. But it accompanies this equivalent with great regularity. The great encyclopedia and the library, the earth and primitive fecundity, capital and accumulation, concentration in general, the sea, the prebiotic Soup, the legacies of heredity, the relatively closed topography in which instincts, the id, and the unconscious are brought together. Each particular theoretical motor forms its reservoir, names it, and fills it with what a motor needs. I had an artifact, a constructed object: the motor. Carnot calls it the universal motor. I could not find a word, here it is: reservoir. . . .

[18] Ibid., p. 18.
[19] Ibid.
[20] *Hermès III*, p. 258.

Question: in the last century, who did not reinvent the reservoir?[21]

3.2: There is no "natural" hierarchy within the sciences. At any given moment, one scientific discourse may fall silent to give another scientific discourse or mythology a chance to speak. (In some cases mythology may even express or explain the emergence of a new field of knowledge. This happens for instance in the nineteenth century with the emergence of topology. [See footnote 44.])

Serres's demonstration regarding Verne combines many of the patterns revealed in the three previous authors. In the first place, the Vernian voyage is encyclopedic, "cycle of cycles, in the sense in which Hegel maintained that the Encyclopedia was a circle of circles."[22] It is also a geographical dictionary that contains "the complete set of codified types of knowledge. From the navigation of ships to cooking, from optics to astronomy, [Verne] reviews the science and technology of [his] period."[23] Verne, like Zola, is well versed in science, and his intention is to draw up the balance sheet of all the known sciences and techniques by traveling across the cycle of human knowledge.

But Verne, contrary to Zola, lags behind the science of his time. Thus for him science plays a role quite different from the one it plays in Zola's work. Science is only the pretext for the journey. It is through this journey, which ultimately turns against the science that supports it, that we find the object — the three objects — of Serres's analysis.

What immediately appears at the level of the themes in Verne's fictional journey is the positivist dream that nothing in the world escapes or can escape knowledge. The journey displays encyclopedically and in its purest form the quasi-totality of knowledge contained in Auguste Comte's positivist program:

> The positivist map is methodically covered, including even sociology, with the same insistance on terrestrial and celestial mechanics, on biology, taxonomies, and milieu, with the same fascination for combinations and circularity. In the end, *The Extraordinary Voyages* are like a *Course in Positive Philosophy* for the common man. Same cartography of knowledge, same ideology of knowing.[24]

However, the belief in the progress of science that made readers of the period avid consumers of the scientific discoveries that journeys provided

[21] *Hermès IV,* pp. 60-61.
[22] *Jouvences,* p. 111.
[23] Ibid., p. 13.
[24] Ibid., pp. 12-13.

does not fully explain Verne's fascination for the latter. Serres offers a second explanation when he suggests that since the *Odyssey*, our imagination has been subjected, whether we like it or not, to the archaic laws of myth. "The sacred mythic and religious words are spoken at the same time and in the same breath as those of science and of journeys. . . . Verne represents the resurgence *volens nolens* . . .of a fantastic flow of myths."[25] Here the combination of positivist and mythical material provides Serres with another opportunity to illustrate his favorite thesis: myth informs science, it comes before and leads into scientific knowledge. In Verne's case, myth serves as the framework of the history of the positivist sciences. However, the realization that myth is at the origin of scientific advances and can be inextricably tied up with science is used by Serres to undermine the main positivist axiom describing scientific knowledge as a progress toward a greater truth. Instead, Serres offers the view he had already sketched in his *Leibniz*, namely, that progress can only be conceived as a series of indefinitely differentiable local cycles. "For any given process there are regional evolutions, partial accelerations, temporary regressions, alterances, equilibriums, finite transformations. The notion [of progress] is plural or pluralistic. . . ."[26]

The third aspect of the Vernian journey is the most important. The experience of the traveler consisting of a series of moves in space produces a phenomenon of a new order, one by which geography overtakes knowledge: "Our geography invades the planet. This is the second voyage, the reappropriation through knowledge. Geography is nothing else, its birth is there, at the moment at which knowledge becomes universal, in spatial terms and not by virtue of any right."[27] Thus, space and knowledge are conceived and recounted in the same way. Space makes an inventory of the adventures of knowledge, omitting nothing; knowledge traces a cartography of known lands, omitting nothing. The minute filling in of terrestrial reaches and the exhaustive account of cycles of knowledge are one and the same operation and permit *The Extraordinary Voyages* to establish the difficult relationship between the spatial or geographic model and the model of knowledge as encyclopedia. The (re)emergence of this language of paths, routes, movements, planes, and maps, this spatial language of the writing of the world (geo-graphy), marks the moment of passage toward a new epistemology.

Theorem 4: "Science is the totality of the world's legends. The world is the space of their inscription. To read and to journey are one and the same act."[28]

---

[25] Ibid., pp. 16-17.
[26] *Le Système de Leibniz et ses modèles mathématiques,* 2 vols. (Paris: P.U.F., 1968), 1:284.
[27] *Jouvences,* p. 12.
[28] Ibid., p. 14.

One must therefore conceive of a philosophy that would no longer be
founded on the classification and ordering of concepts and disciplines,
but that would set out from an epistemology of journeys, forging new
relations between man and the world: "The landscape contains pits,
faults, folds, plains, valleys, wells, and chimneys, solids like the earth and
fluids like the sea. The metaphor is geophysical here; it could be mathematical. In any case, the model is complex. Here and there, locally, I
identify fractures or discontinuities, elsewhere, on the contrary, relations
and bridges."[29] How does Serres render the relation of the world to
science and of space to knowledge more explicit? Verne provides the
paradigm: *by means of the voyage, the sum of all displacements.* Displacements on the ocean, on the sea, on the globe: *The Extraordinary Voyages.*
Displacements on the space of myth: "Language and Space: From Oedipus
to Zola." Displacements on the transversal of declination: Lucretius's
physics of fluids. Displacements on the family tree in search of hereditary
taints: Zola's *Le Docteur Pascal.* Displacements on the circulation of
energies along the Carnot cycle: Zola again, but also "Michelet: The
Soup" and "Turner Translates Carnot." Displacements on the slopes of
geometry, in applied sciences, and in political utopias: Leibniz's *Meditationes,* Descartes's *Regulae,* La Fontaine's *Fables* ("Knowledge in the
Classical Age"), Thales's theater of representation ("Mathematics and
Philosophy"), or Plato's *Statesman* ("The Origin of Geometry"), among
many other examples.

All of the above displacements are isomorphic, since they all belong to
pluralized spaces each constituted in a complex way and each related to
the other according to a multiple set of relations. As a result, circulation
both *along and among* those displacements cannot be conceived as a high
road, but only as a multiplicity of paths. What counts in this space constituted of fragmented local spaces is less the circumscription of a region
than the circulation along and among paths. And what holds for space in
general holds for the space of knowledge as well. Here one encounters
again the configuration of the encyclopedia, a space in which invention
develops precisely according to the art of passage and circulation.[30] To
know is thus to navigate between local fragments of space, to reject techniques of classification and separation in order to look for units of circulation along and among displacements. To know is to adopt the comparative and pluralistic epistemology of the journey, to implement a philo-

[29] *La Naissance de la physique,* p. 200.
[30] "Invention develops according to an *ars interveniendi*; intersection is heuristic, and
progress is an intercrossing" (*Hermès II,* p. 13).

sophy of transport over one of fixity in order to counter the dogmatism of unified and systematic knowledge.

The new space—spaces—of knowledge thus defined calls for a philosophy of communication that expresses at the same time the totality of the theoretical world of the encyclopedia and the totality of the world as it is: "Exchange as the law of the theoretical universe, the transport of concepts and their complexity, the intersection and overlapping of domains . . . represent, express, reproduce perhaps the very tissue in which objects, things themselves, are immersed—the all-encompassing and diabolically complex network of inter-information. Communication asserts itself once again at the end of a circuit that renews theory."[31] In order to produce this complex network of communication, it is necessary to find everywhere and in all their variety the units of circulation that express the fields of our reality. The ultimate goal: to fulfill the conditions for the broadest possible communication.

Let us turn our attention away from the domains of myth and literature and speak for a moment about contemporary science, more particularly, about the field of information theory. This move should come as no surprise to the reader. After all, Serres's itinerary from Lucretius to Verne and from *Hermès I* to *Hermès V* traces the transmission, transformation, and multiplication of messages through diverse spaces of communication. Twentieth-century science in turn reformulates the same concerns when it discovers that all our knowledge (classical as well as modern), even the limits of this knowledge, is of the order of the message. Modern knowledge expresses itself and is understood in terms of codes—whether in the domain of the unconscious considered to be structured like a language (pp. 80-81), or in the domain of the life sciences, which teach us that the transmission of life is a function of the genetic code (pp. 72-79), or in the domain of the experimental sciences such as physics and chemistry in which codes are essential. Modern science is thus specifically concerned with the study of all aspects of the transmission and propagation of messages—information, noise, redundancy. (Literary criticism understands these same problems in terms of theories of code, language, writing, and translation.) In this respect, information theory is all the more relevant, since it is located at the crossroads of all fields of contemporary knowledge.

> What is mathematics if not the language that assures a perfect communication free of noise? What is experimentation in general if not

---

[31] Ibid., p. 15.

an informational as well as an energetic evaluation of the laboratory?
What is a living system if not an island of negentropy, an open and
temporary vortex that emits and receives flows of energy and information? What is a language, a text, history itself with its traces and
marks if not objects of which the theory of information defines the
functioning?[32]

Information theory is thus one more translation of the same problem:
it is a modern version of the broader—and older—problem of communication. Information theory assumes its place within Serres's program as
one particular case, that of the circulation of signals, within the problematic of general circulation.

> Information theory follows directly from thermodynamics. It studies
> the transmission of messages, the speed of their propagation, their
> probability, their redundancy . . . Now, Lucretius had already said
> that atoms are letters and their elementary family an alphabet, as if
> things were words and phenomena sentences. According to Aristotle,
> the Greek materialists had also said the same thing. This discourse so
> impressed Descartes that he related it without understanding it as
> well as Leibniz did. The atomism of signals had never been separated
> from materiality. Without its original coagulum, no one would have
> understood anything in any case. When the modern period passed
> from propulsive energies in the macrocosm to the tiny energies in-
> scribed in messages, the identification of negentropy and information
> was a gesture that history awaited. Neither surprising nor particularly
> new.[33]

Serres's program: to identify all the elements of the global network of
communication. In order to constitute this network, Serres first had to
demonstrate that the beginning of the world, or rather, that the very idea
of beginnings is coeval with the establishment of a network of codes in
circulation. The creation of the world, the creation of order, the creation
of life, the transformational motor, and the informational motor are all
operations of coding. The *clinamen* is the first coding element, Leibniz's
god, the universal coder; Carnot's engine codes bidirectionally (hot and
cold), philosophy has a dual value code (good-bad, true-false)—one could
continue from one field of knowledge to another. It is always a question
of one and the same operation: to translate the several voices of the
"language" of the world's disorder into different languages, to translate
one language into another, to pass from one vocabulary to another, and

---

[32] *Hermès IV*, p. 287.
[33] Ibid., pp. 55-56.

thus to establish a world-encompassing network of communication. Serres's program of "beginnings" brings this out dramatically.[34]

Beginnings of	Conditions of possibility	Science	Works/Essays
the world	disorder	physics	*Naissance de la physique* "Science & Religion"
knowledge	order	metaphysics	*Système de Leibniz* "Knowledge in the Classical Age" "Mathematics & Philosophy" "Origin of Geometry"
life	mixture	genetics	*Feux et signaux de brume* "Michelet: The Soup"
energy	circulation	thermo-dynamics	*Feux et signaux de brume* "Turner Translates Carnot"
space	tatters	geography/topology	*Jouvences* "Language and Space"
signals	noise	information theory	*Le Parasite* "Platonic Dialogue" "Origin of Language"

In order to constitute the network of communication among these multiple beginnings (and domains of knowledge), one must establish corridors of communication across spaces and times, cultural formations and texts. How does one enter into communication? How does one activate a successful communication? Serres explains in his "Platonic Dialogue" the process by which a successful dialogue, a quasi-perfect communication can be set up. Correct transmission seems to require two contradictory conditions. On the one hand, it necessitates the presence of

[34] In the five beginnings of the program given here, one might perceive a variation of Bachelard's "psychoanalysis" of the four elements combined with his *Poetics of Space*. But in fact, a thorough study of Bachelard's and Serres's epistemologies would show how different the two systems of thought are. It should be noted, nevertheless, that Serres does suggest at one point that Bachelard's unscientific writings on the poetic elements might well have been moving unwittingly toward post-Bachelardian developments in epistemology. "Could it be that Bachelard's most scholarly and learned works are the ones treating the poetic elements? Might one not find there, albeit in the mode of negation and refusal, the prophecy of a new *Nouvel Esprit Scientifique*?" (*Hermès II*, p. 78).

noise, since the meaning of a message takes shape *only* against a background noise. On the other hand, it requires the total exclusion of precisely what it needs to include, namely, background noise. Here is Serres's elaborate solution to the dilemma:

> Such communication [dialogue] is a sort of game played by two interlocutors considered as united against the phenomena of interference and confusion, or against individuals with some stake in interrupting communication. These interlocutors are in no way opposed, as in the traditional conception of the dialectic game; on the contrary, they are on the same side, tied together by a mutual interest: they battle together against noise. . . . They exchange roles sufficiently often for us to view them as struggling together against a common enemy. *To hold a dialogue is to suppose a third man and to seek to exclude him;* a successful communication is the exclusion of the third man. The most profound dialectical problem is not the Other, who is only a variety—or a variation—of the Same, it is the problem of the third man. (pp. 66-67)

Hence two wills to communicate presuppose a third will opposing them that must be eliminated. In order to decide the difference between message and noise, there must always be an alliance of two against one, the third man being responsible for both noise and successful communication. By his inclusion in the circuit, he blurs the message and renders it unintelligible; by his exclusion, he renders it intelligible and assures its transmission. Serres calls this included/excluded third man the *demon*. These remarks on the communicative function were written by Serres in 1966. In 1980, Serres published his book-length essay entitled *Le Parasite.* He could just as easily have called it *The Demon* or *The Third Man.*

Precisely what is a parasite? It is an operator that interrupts a system of exchange. The abusive guest partakes of the host's meal, consumes food, and gives only words, conversation, in return. The biological parasite enters an organism's body and absorbs substances meant for the host organism. Noise occurs between two positions in an informational circuit and disrupts messages exchanged between them (noise or static in information theory in English is translated as *parasite* in French). Thus the parasite first presents itself in a negative guise: it is viewed as a malfunction, an error, or a noise within a given system. Its appearance elicits a strategy of exclusion. Epistemologically, the system appears as primary, and the parasite as an unhappy addition that it would be best to expel. Such an approach, however, misses the fact that the parasite, like the demon and the third man, is an integral part of the system. By experiencing a perturbation and subsequently integrating it, the system passes from a simple to a more complex stage. Thus, by virtue of its power to perturb, the parasite ultimately constitutes, like the *clinamen* and the demon, the *condition of possibility of the system*. In this way the parasite attests from within order the primacy of disorder; it produces by way of disorder a more complex order.

Theorem 5: Order is not the law of things but their exception.

For Serres, to think the concept of disorder does not mean to establish a dialogue between two symmetrical ontologies but rather to rethink the relations between order and disorder in such a way as to show how everything begins, ends, and begins again according to a universal principle of disorder. Consequently, it is necessary to rethink the world not in terms of its laws and its regularities, but rather in terms of perturbations and turbulences, in order to bring out its multiple forms, uneven structures, and fluctuating organizations.[35] One must rethink the physical universe of the *clinamen*, the transformational universe of thermodynamics, and the informational universe of noise according to a founding disorder and its power to modify reality and to render it in all its complexity.

One last remark is necessary here about what might be the most suggestive aspect of *The Parasite*. It pertains to the problem of human relations. Many recent discussions concerning social structures have tended to emphasize the problematic of exchange. Human interaction is seen as reciprocal, as a process of give and take in which one has to pay in kind for what one receives. The introduction of the notion of parasite puts into question the crypto-egalitarian ideology of exchange.

> The parasite invents something new. It intercepts energy and pays for it with information. It intercepts roast beef and pays for it with stories. These would be two ways of writing the new contract. The parasite establishes an agreement that is unfair, at least in terms of previous accounting methods; it constructs a new balance sheet. It expresses a logic that was considered irrational until now, it expresses a new epistemology, another theory of equilibrium.[36]

Men are not equal. The elementary theory of human relations is a function of the parasitic position from which one can take without having to

---

[35] Implicit in this conception of reality is a criticism of the problematic of representation. Serres conceives of it as an operation that reduces the multiplicity of reality to rational sequences and controllable consequences. The unitary space of representation is thus viewed as a geometry of violence: "Violence is one of the two or three tools that permit us to insert the local into the global, to force it to express the universal law, to make reality ultimately rational. In fact, as in geometry, what passes for a universal globality is only an inordinately distended [local] variety. Representation is nothing but this distension, swelling, or inflation. One can still say to those who are too violent: you are ignorant of, you are forgetting geometry" (*Jouvences*, p. 75).

[36] *Le Parasite*, p. 51.

repay the debt. At the origin of human relations one finds the irreversible logic of exchange without return: always take, never give back. And behind this anthropology, the parasite. In its absence, a homogeneous stasis of balanced exchanges existed, characterized by the perfect reversibility of all processes—paradise, without time or history. However, the parasite violates the system of exchange by taking without returning; it introduces an element of irreversibility and thus marks the commencement of duration, history, and social organization. The parasite exchanges paradise for a problematic of beginnings, namely, the beginnings of human relations. The odyssey of all of the human sciences, techniques, and social relations opens one more space of circulation within Serres's global network.

Beginnings	Conditions of possibility	Science	Works/Essays
of human and social relations	(irreversible) exchange	anthropology/ economics/ politics	Le Parasite "The Apparition of Hermes: Dom Juan"

To recapitulate: Serres's work often worries traditional scholars and philosophers, or else it is strategically kept at a distance. This does not, however, amount to saying that his program is not legitimate. After all, the question of order and disorder is not a new question, it dates from the beginning of history. The great philosophical and theological systems that we know have always been built around this relation, privileging order over disorder. In the traditional perspective, to posit disorder as primordial is absurd; but in the context of recent scientific inquiry, it becomes possible.[37] This permits a reappraisal of Lucretius, who was among the first to bring out the productive characteristics of perturbation. His concerns are those of contemporary science: large numbers, chance, reversible and irreversible times, open systems, the emergence of messages from noise, and so forth—in short, the emergence of order

[37]See François Jacob, La Logique du vivant (Paris: Gallimard, 1970); Jacques Monod, Le Husard et la nécessité (Paris: Seuil, 1970); René Thom, Stabilité structurelle et morphogenèse (Reading, Mass.: Benjamin, 1973); Henri Atlan, L'Organisation biologique et la théorie de l'information (Paris: Hermann, 1972); idem, Entre le cristal et la fumée: Essai sur l'organisation du vivant (Paris: Seuil, 1979); Ilya Prigogine, From Being to Becoming (San Francisco: Addison Wesley, 1980); Ilya Prigogine and Isabelle Stengers, La Nouvelle Alliance avec la nature (Paris: Gallimard, 1979).

from all sorts of perturbations. Serres is correct: Lucretius is our contemporary, in the sense that he occupies the same space we do. And so
are Zola, Verne, Michelet, Turner, and so many others.

The problem of order and disorder becomes one of mixture and separation when one attempts to define and partition fields of knowledge. One
must not ask why the poet Lucretius had a mathematical rigor superior
to that of the mathematicians of his time, or how Zola, a man of letters,
could have been one step ahead of the physics of his age. One must think
of Lucretius and Zola as speaking the languages of their cultures: not
only do they use the known results of their predecessors, but they also
participate in — and anticipate — the discoveries of their contemporaries.
The texts of Lucretius and Zola are born in spaces of communication
among several domains. Legend, myth, history, philosophy, and science
share common boundaries. It is futile to attempt to distinguish between
what signifies science in Lucretius's text and what still belongs to myth;
in reaching for the scientific model, one stumbles upon the mythical
structure and vice versa. Nor is it worthwhile to isolate what is specifically
literary in Zola's text; one inevitably encounters a narrative that functions
like a motor. Serres's point is clear. The domains of myth, science, and
literature oscillate frantically back and forth into one another, so that the
idea of ever distinguishing between them becomes more and more
chimerical.

Finally, there is an analogy between Serres's problematic of founding
disorder and the manner in which he puts it into practice in his work.
Serres never speaks of disorder in a disordered fashion. Rather, he speaks
of disorder in a *rigorously* disordered fashion. Serres's theoretical program
is encyclopedic; it cannot be thought of as a system or a taxonomy. Clear
and precise divisions are replaced by the play of interferences and inter-
references. The traditional idea of evolution toward progress becomes
instead a journey among intersections, nodes, and regionalizations. Serres
does not offer an epistemology that would represent the possible totaliza-
tion and unity of knowledge. To conceive of an encyclopedic epistemology means to think of knowledge not in terms of order and mastery,
but in terms of chance and invention. Invention itself is a function of a
quantitative model: it multiplies the quantity of knowledge. Invention is
an inventory, in other words, a multiplicity of phenomena and types of
knowledge comparable to the Lucretian chaos. The gesture through which
Serres invents is the same as that through which Lucretius produces the
world.

In order for Serres's discourse to measure up to the world of which he
speaks, it must be multiple. It is a discourse that undertakes many
journeys following complex itineraries across multiple spaces that in-

terfere with each other—a discourse "in which polymorphism remains irreducible."[38] The simple, the distinct, and the monosemic are no longer acceptable values of this discourse; they are replaced by concepts and logics of fuzziness, complexity, and polyvalence. True, science has been our culture for two thousand years, but it is a culture whose knowledge has perhaps reached its limits. Myth and fable, philosophy and literature go beyond these limits. Fables provide a more complete knowledge than geometry, philosophy a more fluctuating one than mathematics, and literature a more complex one than that of exact sciences. Indeed, *Hermes* privileges literature. It should be no surprise that from the very first paragraph of the book, Serres plunges the reader into a text of Molière: "Don Juan is the first hero of modernity both numerically and functionally. . . . He qualifies in a third way . . . as a scientific observer of society" (p. 3). There is no theoretical preamble to the demonstration. Theory is a worldly practice: abstract concepts and scientific notions are elicited *directly* from the adventures of the ladies' man. Seducer, scientific observer, and learned reader of literature: Serres assumes his multiple identities as he works through a myriad of inter(re)ferences to create a culture, a history, and a memory.

Anti-method

Since the beginning of this essay, we have attempted to point to a certain number of themes that organize Serres's conception of science, philosophy, and myth. It is possible to arrange these themes around one figure: that of Hermes. There is much to say concerning Serres's "methodological" itinerary if one approaches it from the perspective of Hermes's mythical journey. Who is Hermes and what is his role in Greek mythology?

The dictionary tells us that Hermes is a Greek god known for his cunning and his ingenuity. There are many myths concerning his youth. For instance, Hermes demonstrates an extraordinary precocity and a power of invention from the very day of his birth. He steals and hides Apollo's herd, invents the lyre using strings made of cow's gut stretched across a tortoise shell, and later exchanges the instrument for Apollo's herd. As he grows up, Hermes appears as protector of heroes. Some of the most salient mythic episodes tell how Hermes saves Zeus in his struggle against the monster Typhon and how he intervenes twice to save

[38] *Hermès IV*, p. 288.

Ulysses from Calypso's and Circe's holds. Among his many attributes, Hermes is considered to be the god of commerce—and of theft. He is the god of music and the patron of orators and also the inventor of weights and measures. He is the protector of boundaries and the guide of travelers (his statue could be found at crossroads in antiquity). One of his functions as guide is to lead dead souls to Hades. Hermes watches over shepherds, often he is represented carrying a lamb on his shoulders. He is later called Hermes Trismegistus (the thrice greatest) by the ancient Egyptians who identify him as the founder of alchemy (hermeticism) and many other sciences. Legend attributes the paternity of several children to Hermes, among them Autolycus, Ulysses's grandfather. According to certain traditions Hermes begot Pan with the unfaithful Penelope.

Hermes and myth. The notion of divinity in antiquity has a precise meaning: for the Greeks a god is a figure by which one explains a version of the origin of the world. This explanation is recounted by a myth. Myth is thus the first explanatory principle formulated by men. Hermes participates in the first system of knowledge about the world: cosmogony. And he plays a very particular role.

We know that a myth is constructed following the model of a genealogy, in other words, as a system that justifies both the transmission and the conservation of principles, but also their differentiation (through a process of branching off). We must remember that Hermes is the god who reassembles Zeus's mutilated body and saves his life from the monster Typhon, who had taken Zeus's tendons and had hidden them before Hermes stole them back and succeeded in reattaching them to Zeus's body. Interestingly, Typhon is also the progeny of Chronos, the father Zeus had dethroned. Chronos gives birth to the demon in order to dethrone Zeus and replace him. The two brothers fight on mount Kasion at the confines of Egypt and Syria. Typhon wins the first battle. This creates the possibility of a monstrous bifurcation on the graph of the family tree, a catastrophic genealogical deviation. The father of the universe, Zeus, lies helpless, his body mutilated, without tendons, and motionless. (In Zeus's wandering parts the discourse of myth links the genealogical imperative with a spatial problematic; the *discours* of myth is also a *parcours*.)[39] In this mutilation is inscribed the ultimate blockage of all

---

[39]There is an inescapable comparison to be made between Zeus and Oedipus. Both faced the same fate at birth (destruction by the father), both suffer forms of "tendonitis" (resulting in physical paralysis for the one and a permanent limp for the other), and finally, both illustrate problems of circulation (blockage in the case of Zeus, bifurcation and closure—incest —in the case of Oedipus). In relation to this last point one can see how the law of mythical narrative links the discourse of genealogy with a discourse on space. Regarding Oedipus,

circulation. It signifies the silencing of the genealogical imperative and with it the end of mythical discourse. Hermes reassembles the god of procreation: this is an act of rejoining of mythical communication as well. Zeus fights back and wins. Genealogy reassumes its course; it reactivates myth, which in turn renews the tree of knowledge and science. Thus Hermes is the reconnector of an explanatory system—myth—that plays a crucial role in Serres's epistemology.

Hermes and philosophy. In its polemic with nature, our knowledge is defined as a function of laws inscribed in a logic of force and violence, of discipline and death. Bacon and Descartes invent rules by which they can dominate nature, thus perpetuating the mythical language of the god of war. "The totality of our practices and of our culture has fallen into the bloody hands of Mars. Since there is no antistrategic strategy that is not itself a strategy, the god of war is always triumphant."[40] Serres links his point of view with the work of Georges Dumézil. For Dumézil, politics, power, and force belong to the domain of Mars and Jupiter, production and life to that of Quirinus, the god of agriculture. The same opposition exists between Dionysus, the god of violence and destructive madness, and Apollo, the god of inspiration, divination, and music. Hermes's position in this opposition is clear: in their double role as protectors of shepherds and farmers, Hermes and Quirinus complement each other; and by their reciprocal talents in the fields of divination and music Hermes and Apollo are twins. Mythology in antiquity confirms this vision of Hermes as "philosopher." Through his qualities of inspiration, invention, innovation, and independence, Hermes represents the best that philosophy has to offer when it is concerned with the preservation of qualities inherent *to life*—the nonthanatocratic solution.

Hermes and science. The ancestor of Ulysses is a voyager who, mythology tells us, had learned the art of foretelling the future using small

---

Serres asks whether the fact that Oedipus kills Laius at a crossroads is significant. "One can say that Oedipus kills Laius at this place, and miss the place, and thus repress the place of the repressed; or one can say instead that this place is such that Oedipus kills his father there, that it is a point so catastrophic and so confined that he must kill father and mother to go past it. To be the son or to place oneself at the crossroads: two bifurcations and two catastrophes that the myth joins together by its very word" (p. 47). The law of the mythical narrative is traced on the ground itself. Incest can be considered an aberrant path on the graph of the family tree that turns back upon itself toward a previous bifurcation to which it connects again. In other words, it reconnects two divergent zones and causes a catastrophe. The same could be said of the two roads that meet at a point so narrow that Oedipus cannot avoid murdering his father; and the discourse of myth thus links together topology and the Law.
[40] *Hermès IV*, p. 290.

pebbles. Like Tom Thumb, he deciphers the future through signs traced on the ground: geo-grapher of space, Hermes is also the protector of boundaries. All of his displacements are related to the problem of space. He calls attention to the myriad spaces in which we live; he is constantly on the move—messenger, herald—guiding the living and the dead respectively along and across spaces. Hermes, philosopher of *plural* spaces. We know how much this conception of space is crucial to Serres's epistemology: "To break forever with every strategy: the nonthanatocratic solution is to fragment space,"[41] and thus to opt for local versus global solutions . . .

But the guide keeps moving; he connects, disconnects, and reconnects the endless variety of spaces he traverses. At some point the protector of boundaries links up with Penelope; Hermes turns weaver of spaces: "Mythical discourse undertakes a weaving together, a junction, a connection of places that are closed, isolated, inviolable, inaccessible, dangerous, or mortal—disconnected, in any case. Once the weaving together is accomplished, one can speak of science."[42] The formation of a unified space achieved by the connecting powers of myth results in the emergence of science. Hermes the weaver is at the crossroads, not only of the many routes and spaces, but also of myth and science. Mythology reminds us here that Hermes learned the art of divination from Apollo, Pythagoras's father, himself the father of geometric idealities. Before him Hermes had already invented measure. Hermes, god of weights and measures, of mathematics, of the science of measure, proportion, relation, and scale. The "Greek miracle," mathematics, is a gift of the god of science: Hermes Trismegistus.

Hermes and literature. We have just seen how the birth of rationality and science signals the end of myth in its original form. However, when this happens, the problem of space—of pluralized spaces—does not vanish purely and simply, it is merely displaced. If on the one hand, the weaving together of disparate spaces accomplished by myth results in the birth of science, on the other hand, it creates a new field in which the work of connecting and disconnecting will continue, namely, *literature.* "Narrative, exiled from the locus of *muthos* where the logos was born, continues to disconnect the connected and to link together what is separated. What we call literature is the infinite pursuit of this work in progress."[43] In this respect, the legend of Ulysses is the first work of

[41] Ibid.
[42] *Feux et signaux de brume,* p. 169.
[43] Ibid.

literature to establish a close proximity among journeys, mythology, and techniques. Ulysses's journey represents an act of reformulation and renewal of myth as well as one of access to the direct knowledge of things, to a science of the world. The consultation of oracles and the practice of an experimental physics belong to the same structural scheme. The world of knowledge and the world of symbols give up their secrets in the same mode: Calypso teaches Ulysses the art of navigation by teaching him to read the stars, and conversely, the magic art of Circe is deciphered and undone through the "chemical experiment" of the *moly* plant. Thus the encyclopedia of all journeys, the sum of mythical knowledge, and the experimental practices of the Greek world converge in one work: *The Odyssey*. Space, myth, and technique have become literature.

Twice in his wanderings Ulysses is hopelessly stranded, twice the narrative of the *Odyssey* starts faltering, twice Hermes appears—to break Calypso's and Circe's magic—in order to revitalize the narrative. Ulysses departs and with him literature sets off again. How does one reinsert mythic speech into the concert of voices science diffuses? Hermes's magic solution: *literature*. Great texts of literature are saturated with mythical elements; we see time and again in these texts that "once the scientific contents are filtered out, a residue remains in which a circulational game organizes reformulations of mythical material" (p. 42). Hermes: myth, science, literature.[44]

The medium is the message. Hermes is the divine herald, the messenger of the gods. The travelers' guide and leader of souls must know the terrain over which he journeys, the shortcuts, the landmarks, the many paths. He must be able to decode the map, the dangers that topography hides. If he represents ingenuity and ruse, it is because these qualities are necessary in order to carry messages and to conserve them. It is not enough to know how to decode, one must also know how to hide, to disguise the code. Hermes manipulates Calypso ("the one who hides"); he knows how to manipulate languages since he is the god of orators and also the god of thieves. He can therefore cheat in an exchange, cover his tracks as he does when he steals Apollo's cows, lie and steal if necessary in order to deliver a message. Need one recall how central the notion of message is for Serres and contemporary science? Hermes: precursor of information theory!

[44]The question of why mythical elements can reappear massively in a text of literature with scientific concerns is discussed in detail in *Feux et signaux de brume*. In the case of Zola, Serres's response to the problem is historical. He contends that in the nineteenth century the reappearance of myth as an authentic discourse is linked to the emergence of topology as a new mathematical science. (See his discussion in "Language and Space: From Oedipus to Zola," p. 53). Thus Zola's text is emblematic of the power of literature to bridge the distance between two seemingly divergent discourses: topology and myth.

Hermes is not the god of political power, but of commerce and of theft, thus, of unfair exchange. The tricky Ulysses ate at Alkinoos's table paying for the banquet with words; he told of his adventures in exchange for good food. His ancestor Hermes payed for Apollo's cows with music (his lyre) and, according to mythology, later exchanged a little more noise (his flute) for Apollo's golden staff and for information (Apollo taught him the art of divination). Hermes is the father of eloquence, patron of orators, musician, master of words, noise, and wind. What does a parasite do? He takes and gives nothing in exchange, or rather, gives words, noise, wind. Don Juan, worthy heir of Hermes, understood this principle very well—he called it *variations on the tobacco theme*: "Do not return tobacco for tobacco, that is, goods for goods. . . . Give instead words for goods" (p. 5). The god of devious and deviated circulation, Psychopomp by name, chats with Don Juan while accompanying him to hell and is overheard saying: "Exchange is not what is most important, original, or fundamental. . . . I don't know how to say it: the relation in the form of a simple, irreversible arrow, *without anything in return*, has taken its place."[45] Hermes: messenger, exchanger, parasite.

The medium is the "method." The presence of Hermes is not limited only to the objects of Serres's study, he is constantly present in Serres's very writing, both at the level of structure and of style.

In order to grasp the complexity of the organization of Serres's work, one could quote him paraphrasing Norbert Wiener's description of contemporary information theory: "It is orthogonal to classification. More than a new domain, it is a crossing; more than a region, it is a mode of communication, an exchanger of concepts. . . . It is in the position of a railway junction."[46] And indeed, what is Serres's work if not a kind of encyclopedia—a series of crossings of varying length, a mosaic of knowledge made up of borrowings, detours, codes, and messages that cross each other, creating unforeseeable connections and nodes. One must renounce venturing into Serres's work or attempting to understand it if one does not follow in Hermes's footsteps.

But if the separation of knowledge into regions, formations, or disciplines is no longer applicable, then knowledge must be reformulated on new bases, new practical and theoretical operators must be discovered, and new operations must be defined. As we have seen, Serres calls these operations interference, translation, distribution, and they all converge toward the idea of communication. A recapitulation of Serres's meth-

[45] *Le Parasite*, p. 12.
[46] *Hermès II*, p. 29.

odological itinerary would show the place of these hermetic operators within his project.

Hermès I recounts the birth of communication. *Hermès II* develops a method that analyzes the means by which messages interfere with and refer to each other. *Hermès III* translates messages and evaluates their transformations. *Hermès IV* marks the end of the stable systems of classical science. The message becomes chaotic and scattered. *La Distribution* is another name for disorder: water, steam, fuel constitute fluctuating groups. *Hermès V* outlines the passages among these fluctuating groups, between the universality of form and the individuality of circumstances. The method of passage is that of the journey. Hermes calls this journey a *randonnée*,[47] an expedition filled with random discoveries that exploits the varieties of spaces and times.

The balance sheet of our present *randonnée* reconstitutes Serres's discourse on anti-method.[48] His aim is not to establish immediate relations between different domains, to mix philosophical with scientific contents, or to discover farfetched analogies. Convergences and alliances take place not by similarity and analogy, but through a formal set of operations of interference, transformation, and passage. Thus to speak of borrowing or of importing and exporting between domains is to miss Serres's point. It is to confuse the common idea of a critical grid with the much more fundamental notion of identical structure. The idea of a grid implies the imposition of external categories upon the text, whereas Serres is looking for formal equivalences—isomorphisms. The thermodynamic problematic in a novel such as Zola's *Le Docteur Pascal* is not simply a matter of applying a reading grid to a text, but it is precisely the structure of the text itself that is in question. The narrative does not function *like* a motor, it *is* a motor; thermodynamics is part of its very textuality. In this example, Serres argues that in the nineteenth century, language and hence literature are simply energies like other energy in that they fall under the descriptive powers of thermodynamics enlarged into information theory: "Little by little written or spoken language becomes an energy like any other, and narrative becomes a trivial motor. Hence we find repeated translation of cardinal categories: difference, closure, supplement, and

---

[47] *Randonnée* means excursion, journey, or expedition, and etymologically it is related to the English "random" through its Old French root *randon.*

[48] In Serres's work, method is found in the construction of models and in their applications and variations according to mathematical operations. Method is the illustration of a given type of knowledge through the set of results that the method can produce. But the term method itself is problematic because it suggests the notion of repetition and predictability—a method that anyone can apply. Method implies also mastery and closure, both of which are detrimental to invention. On the contrary, Serres's method invents: it is thus an *anti-method.*

so forth all the way through to dissemination, a concept precisely foreseen by the second principle of thermodynamics."[49]

According to the same principles of interference, translation, and passage, Carnot's machine appears in Turner's paintings or in the second chapter of Bergson's *Creative Evolution*; Descartes's *Metaphysical Meditations* surfaces in La Fontaine's fable "The Wolf and the Lamb," Lagrange's and Laplace's mechanics and geometry in Auguste Comte's positivism, the passage from disorder to declination in the "invention" of the compass by Panurge; Marcel Mauss's ethnology emerges in Don Juan's language of seduction; and so on.

Finally, Serres's taste for exploration can be found not only at the level of all the regions of knowledge he traverses—mythology, geometry, philosophy, geography, mechanics, thermodynamics, biology, cybernetics—but also throughout the multiple, hermetic, and unpredictable registers of his language. The philosopher speaks in turn the language of dockers, locksmiths, mechanics, geometers, geographers, painters, sailors—the list could be extended. In following Serres in his linguistic journeys, one is touched by the magic wand of Circe and the seductive charms of Calypso: vocabularies diverge and bifurcate, are transformed and concealed, and finally disappear precisely when one begins to appreciate their savor. Reading Serres is like a treat the outcome of which cannot be predicted. Serres himself, summing up the uncertainty of life and work, once said, "Banquets do not always end in a foreseeable fashion. One day, tomorrow, soon, one leaves life abruptly, as one leaves the table—without having finished."

Isn't this par for the (main) course of any *randonnée*?

Serres's Major Works

Le Système de Leibniz et ses modèles mathématiques. 2 vols. Paris: Presses Universitaires de France, 1968.

> Deals with the systematicity of Leibniz's thought and situates Leibniz within the history of science. Serres maintains that Leibniz, along with Desargues and Pascal, is at the heart of a philosophical and mathematical revolution that develops the question of a multicentered, infinite, complex universe.

[49]*Feux et signaux de brume,* p. 65. Let us not miss the allusion to contemporary theories of textuality and specifically to the Derridean problematic: what appears to be a new problematic is in fact the reactivation of an already existing one going back to the beginning of the development of thermodynamics.

Hermès. Paris: Minuit, 1968-

Vol. I: *La Communication,* 1968.

"Tells of the birth of the idea of communication, its blind emergence, through a series of articles written over a period of six years," as Serres remarks in the opening lines of the book. In texts on Descartes, Leibniz, Plato, Jules Verne, Michelet, Molière, and others, communication is seen as voyage/translation/exchange, and Serres initiates a series of reflections under the sign of Hermes, god of paths and crossroads, messengers and merchants.

Vol. II: *L'Interférence,* 1972.

An extended reflection on Leibniz describing a new scientific spirit that could be defined as a philosophy of transport, that is, of intersection, intervention, interception. Serres confronts the Bachelardian legacy and sets himself off from it.

Vol. III: *La Traduction,* 1974.

Texts on epistemology and the history of science from the classical age to the present. Essays on Descartes, Leibniz, Comte, François Jacob, and Jacques Monod cover topics ranging from mathematics to biochemistry. Included are three texts on painting that reveal the impact of science and technology in the esthetic domain.

Vol. IV: *La Distribution,* 1977.

Communication theory, thermodynamics, and topology intermingle in texts on Nietzsche, Boltzmann, Bergson, Michelet, Zola, Barbey d'Aurevilly, and others. Nineteenth-century thinkers are studied in terms of relations among the sciences of the period.

Vol. V: *Le Passage du Nord-Ouest,* 1980.

The immensely complicated maze of the Northwest Passage, full of dead ends and blocked paths, serves as a figure describing the bridge from the humanities to the exact sciences. Communication between the two disciplines, though possible and vital, is always difficult and unique. A notable essay on Musil develops this thesis.

Jouvences: Sur Jules Verne. Paris: Minuit, 1974.

A voyage through Verne using various scientific operators to rediscover Verne's texts. Serres demonstrates that literature is a reservoir of knowledge that scientists and mathematicians can ill afford to ignore.

Esthétiques sur Carpaccio. Paris: Hermann, 1975.

Using the alphabet of forms and chromatics, Serres remains resolutely in the margins of official art criticism in order to discover a Carpaccio freed from the discourse of a pious iconology.

Feux et signaux de brume: Zola. Paris: Grasset, 1975.

Never have the relations between Zola's *Rougon-Macquart* novels and the scientific developments of the second half of the nineteenth century been so convincingly analyzed. Serres argues that science in Zola's novels is not to be found in Zola's frustrated positivism, but in the narrative and thematic structures of the novels themselves. The *Rougon-Macquart* series is viewed as a convergence of literature, science, and myth.

La Naissance de la physique dans le texte de Lucrèce: Fleuves et turbulences. Paris: Minuit, 1977.

Serres argues that Lucretius's *De Rerum Natura* is a valid treatise in physics when interpreted within the framework of fluid dynamics. Vortices, turbulences, and the *clinamen* as described by Lucretius become the starting points for an extended reflection on history and on a possible new scientific spirit that would eschew the domination of nature by man, seeking instead a peaceful pact with nature.

Le Parasite. Paris: Grasset, 1980.

The parasite may be defined as an overbearing guest, an organism that lives off another organism, or a noise in a channel of communication. Weaving these different definitions together, Serres studies La Fontaine, Molière, Rousseau, Plato, and others, in order to establish an epistemology of human relations.

Genèse: Récits métaphysiques. Paris: Grasset, 1981.

Explores the notion of multiplicity and demonstrates the difficulties raised by the attempt to treat it in traditional philosophical or scientific terms. Multiplicity is linked to noise and can provide a new approach to the problem of history. Balzac, Beaumarchais, Corneille, and Georges Dumézil offer points of departure for Serres's reflections.

Serres's work is the object of a special issue of *Critique,* no. 380 (1979), entitled "Interférences et turbulences," which includes contributions by Shoshana Felman, René Girard, Ilya Prigogine and Isabelle Stengers, Pierre Pachet, Claude Mouchard, and Michel Pierssens as well as a list of Serres's publications.

I

LITERATURE &
SCIENCE

1 ▲ ▲▲

The Apparition
of Hermes: Dom Juan

A statue is an art object or a ritual icon. In the classical era it also becomes an automaton, an anatomical model, a laboratory device, a mechanical model of the living being. Condillac models his imaginary experiment after a statue, and before Condillac there is the Cartesian robot. The Commander's statue is a machine, Don Juan's death a machination: Molière will die no differently, trapped between footlights and stage machinery. The arithmetic atheism of the "grand seigneur, méchant homme" triumphs in the last scene with the realization that *deus est machina*.[1] The quintessential ladies' man is a man of ideas, the first hero of modernity. None of that, I believe, escaped Molière. Moreover, the public listened to the playwright and understood what it heard so well that the play went through many performances. How else could people have withstood a presentation in which spectator and spectacle are one? The puppets are not on stage as the spectators believe, rather, the spectators themselves are puppets.

Don Juan is the first hero of modernity both numerically and functionally, by the double despair of representation and of will. He qualifies in a third way, undoubtedly more decisive and so profound that we can only guess whether or not Molière was aware of that qualification. Let us suppose that he was: he can thus be classified as a scientific observer of society. Excluding all anachronistic hypotheses, let us restrict our attention to the mystery of literary creation. Let us decide on the basis of the evidence, and remember that we are dealing with a *feast*.

According to Da Ponte, Kierkegaard, Pushkin, Rank, and numerous others, Don Juan is a handsome ladies' man, a fickle voyager in search of an impossible (unique) love, a victim of resurgences of irreducible guilt, a hero of Difference who, in his last incarnation, retires to a Spanish cloister and, beneath the implacable light of the Castilian plateaus, medi-

[1]See my "Don Juan au palais des merveilles: Sur les statues au XVIIe siècle," in *Les Etudes philosophiques* 3 (1966): 385-90.

tates on the saying of Solomon: there is nothing new under the sun. Today Don Juan is nothing more than a metapsychological archetype: this bespeaks Romanticism's deepening of the traditional Don Juan theme but conceals the attending mutilations of the theme accomplished by the Romantics. Molière's character offers few avenues to the analysts of motivation: he is less profound in a Nietzschean sense. His behavior, on the other hand, is richer in extension, and more complex. Once more, Romanticism blinds us, so that outside the seduction scenes we see nothing but scenes of secondary interest—mere padding. In fact the traditional prince is a three-headed devil, a character with three roles: as a ladies' man, he seduces; as a man of ideas, he discourses; as a man of money, he defers his debt. This third man serves to define the first two. He is on stage three times: to give alms to the beggar; with Monsieur Dimanche, the creditor; and in the single post mortem scene.

Sganarelle: "My wages! My wages!" (V, 7).[2] In the end everyone is paid in full, and pleased: the heavens and the law (religion, ethics, and the judicial), daughters and families, parents and husbands, love and the tribe—all are repaid by Tenorio's death, all except the valet. "My wages!" The final word, as it should be, is the moral of the story: contract, word, trust and faith, all broken. A villain and a cheat, the master has not honored his promise. Nor has Sganarelle: he owes his salary to Monsieur Dimanche, whom he has kicked out the door, "making light of such trifles" (IV, 4). The account is unsettled, the balance sheet unbalanced. So much for the moral.

For symmetry's sake, let us refer to the curtain-raiser—the eulogy on tobacco: "it leads souls into virtue and teaches one to become a gentleman (*honnête homme*). Do you not notice, once men have taken some tobacco, how obliging they are with everyone, and how delightedly they give it out, right and left, everywhere they go? They do not even wait to be asked and anticipate the wish of other men; so true is it that tobacco inspires feelings of honor and virtue in all those who take it" (I, 1). From the beginning, the law which will govern the play, a law partially transgressed in the final balance sheet, a law flouted by every contingency, is prescribed on a limited scale. How does one become virtuous, a gentleman? By the offering which precedes the wish, by the gift which anticipates the request, by acceptance and reciprocity. This tobacco, invested with the power of communication, with a binding quality that leads to virtue, is indeed a strange object. How is it that villainy, even for a nobleman, consists in despising tobacco, in refusing to bend to its law, to

---

[2] All quotations from Molière's *Dom Juan* are directly translated from the play. References to acts and scenes are indicated in the text.—Ed.

the obligingness and obligation of gift and exchange?[3] This is a dangerous refusal in which one risks one's head: "whoever lives without tobacco does not deserve to live" (I, 1); whoever will not join the chain of commerce, nor pass along the peace pipe he has received, finds himself condemned to death. So much for the rules of the game, whose execution we know.

I see nothing else to add about the first scene—it contains everything: the outline, the rule, the threat, the outcome. All one has to do is to follow the variations of the structure of exchange revealed by the passage concerning tobacco. Don Juan's three behaviors—toward women, discourse, and money—form three parallel variations on the tobacco theme.

The demonstration begins again. Enter Monsieur Dimanche to collect his debt. "It is only right to pay them with something: and I have a secret which will send them away satisfied without having received a penny," says Don Juan of his moneylenders (IV, 2). The secret is revealed in a combat instantly engaged: "I know what I owe you" (IV, 3), but I am speaking and force Dimanche to be silent, says Don Juan, thus he is already paid with words. But that is not enough, he must be paid with marks of endearment. "I love with all my heart" the pretty Claudine, and little Colin, who makes such a din with his drum, and Brusquet, the dog who growls so loudly (let us make as much noise as possible), and your wife, the worthy woman. "I take a great deal of interest" in the whole tribe. As for you, "are you a friend of mine?" For my part, I am one of yours "and without interest, please believe me." "Embrace me," and the valet will repeat that I like you. Paid with words, paid with love, exit Monsieur Dimanche, knowing he has been swindled, reduced to silence, and carrying an empty purse. The secret? To short-circuit the triple law of exchange. Do not return tobacco for tobacco, that is, goods for goods, words for words, love for love; give instead words for goods[4] and love for money. The creditor can then go fly a kite. But remember: exchange traditionally takes place during a *feast;* primitives know that, as do warriors, fiancés, and horse-traders. "Without more ado, will you dine with me?" No, replies the creditor, the thing is not feasible since the exchange has failed. Who does not see that another feast, another (reciprocal) invitation to dine, will soon settle the score, another score, the same one, in fact? Who does not know that such feasts are only dramatic representations of gifts and remittances, only dramatizations of the law of exchange? Are we at the very birth of comedy?

Everyone knows that there is only one way to break the law and remain

[3]"If I kept this gift for myself, as it is invested with a spirit, some evil, even death, might befall me" (from a legal text of the Maori).
[4]I tell everyone, as I tell you, that I am your debtor.

a gentleman, or, better yet, to become a nobleman. To give without receipt in kind is to give oneself honor and virtue, to display one's power: that is called charity. Who would offer tobacco to someone who has none, without hope of being repaid? Let us seek our answer in the next forest;[5] here we are, lost; the tramp will show us the way (III, 2). He speaks and begs assistance: his advice is thus "interested." On the problem of interest, let us return to the rule of the game. The poor man, like Sganarelle and Monsieur Dimanche, describes and laments that rule, as Don Carlos will soon lament it, but on a point of honor in the latter case (III, 4). The poor man prays on behalf of generous souls that their cup may run over, that heaven may give them "all sorts of goods." The beggar, having received alms, offers sacred words destined to profit his benefactor. Don Juan scoffs: in this profession one ought to make a fortune, to be "quite at ease" and to do "good business." The wretched man, nevertheless, remains needy; he lacks his daily bread. The counterpart of charity, of the gift without counterpart, is the whole of the poor man's conduct. This is the only disrupting gesture where one can short-circuit the law: to give words for goods, but the word is sacred. Don Juan first hesitates at this point of rupture; he asks for something in return: here is a louis, give me a word, and later, here is a louis for the love of mankind. The scene is the inverse of the one with the creditor—the nobleman gives and desires in return the same thing he gave Monsieur Dimanche: words for goods, love for money. He makes his position symmetrical because the law of charity is precisely a rupture of the law of exchange, the only gap permitted in the contract. Don Juan subsequently breaks the very law of rupture and once more finds himself an outlaw. He requests something in return in the only exchange which has no reciprocity; he demands the false reciprocity he customarily gives. But, in a new twist, he rejects the universal law by inverting the very value of the word and the love he requires in exchange for a louis: he wants to substitute the profanation of the sacrilegious word for the sacred word of prayer. "I will give to you, if you swear" (III, 2). For the love of another or the love of God he substitutes the love of mankind.[6] He puts his transgressions directly into practice by plunging, sword in hand, into an uncertain combat where "the match is uneven."

What does one do at a feast if not exchange? Whoever will not come to a banquet refuses the law of the gift and declares war. The play is geared

---

[5] The scene takes place not far from the commander's mausoleum. Alms to the poor are pleasing to the dead (a Bori law).

[6] Later Sganarelle receives the slap in the face destined for Pierrot: "There you are paid for your charity" (II, 3). It is once more the inverse of charity. The slap is what the love of mankind becomes when it's the other fellow who is charitable.

to lead Don Juan to the dinner at which his account will be settled. In the meantime, his debt accumulates, beginning with the debt of money. It is not in the rules to pay with words and marks of endearment: one must pay in kind. The counterproof? Sganarelle, the poltroon, does not dare to speak and cannot sustain a philosophical debate. His vocabulary is not adequate to theoretical disputes with the master. Dressed as a doctor, one acquires science, one wishes to uphold the honor of one's garb. Now the valet's garb is an old doctor's robe picked up at some pawn shop: "it cost me money to get it" (III, 1). Don Juan encourages the exchange, money for words: you have thus acquired privileges, skill, and reason. Discourse is possible and the *Treatise on Man* will be able to counter the atheist's arithmetic. And then there is love. Charlotte tells her Pierrot: leave loving and speaking to me, "I will earn something for you, and you will bring us back butter and cheese" (II, 2)—which Pierrot refuses for even twice the price. It is with blows that Don Juan seeks to conclude the cheese bargain.[7] Money for woman, as a moment ago money for word, and the demonstration is complete.

After your money, your life, in the forest or on the beach. Don Juan saves Carlos from the clutches of thieves, a new opportunity to outline the rules of the game. Those rules still treat owing and possessing: after you have saved my life, the least I owe you is my silence in your presence (III, 3). In exchange for life, one word at least, but for life, exactly life: "allow me to give back now," says Carlos to Don Alonso, "what he has lent me" (III, 4). I "owe him my life," I have an "obligation" which I must "fulfill." To Don Juan: "you see that I take care to return the good I have received from you." Whence the debate which divides Elvira's two brothers, a delicate balance between "insult and kindness" (that it is fitting "to repay" together), between honor and the life which Tenorio has both taken and given. If honor is more than life, the one who dishonors is the debtor; if this is not so, the savior keeps his credit. The decision is deferred twenty-four hours, to make "amends." We are still following the tobacco pattern. A moment ago Don Carlos was bitterly lamenting the tobacco rules as an enslavement of his life, his peace of mind, and his property. The Spanish Cid has grown soft, has lost his "furor."

But, from the standpoint of the law of exchange, Don Juan is once again outside the game. His amorous maritime campaign ended in a tempest (*coup de tabac*) from which he only extricated himself with the help of Pierrot, cold Charlotte's lunatic lover. The peasant knows well

---

[7] In any case, "a marriage costs him nothing to contract" (I, 1), his servant says of him. And Mathurine adds: "It is not good to meddle in other people's business" (II, 5).

that the "important gentleman" owes him his life, wagered, pawned, and won from the big Lucas (II, 1). Pierrot's profit will be at least twice "four smart francs and five sous in duplicate." But his loss is incomparable—he is soon cuckolded and beaten: "that is hardly compensation for having saved you from drowning" (II, 3). In exchange for his life, Don Juan bestows kisses upon Charlotte and blows upon Pierrot. He gives to Don Carlos, who thereby justifies his behavior; he receives from Pierrot and, in return, takes from the peasant again. Our demonstration balances: the villain is outside the law of exchange, in this case because of a beating (*passage à tabac*) he administers.

After giving and receiving, only taking remains. Don Juan has given life to Elvira's brother; he has received it from Charlotte's fiancé; he has taken it from the Commander six months ago, in the very city in which a new beauty entices him. Sganarelle is uneasy there and confides his anxieties to his master. Thus it is learned that Don Juan has received "pardon in this affair," the remission of his crime. According to the valet, the debt is not fully paid: "perhaps this pardon does not extinguish the resentment of relatives and friends . . ." (I, 2). Which is, once again, the rule of the game: life for life, retaliation. The tribunal's word or the king's dictum are not enough to even the account. The hero will have to pay the score with his life, to accept an invitation to the feast at which the statue requests his hand: "Give me your hand," "there it is." At the first giving, at the first remittance, the final rendering and death. Once again, the demonstration closes on itself: law of exchange, refusal of the rule, return to equilibrium. And whoever lives without tobacco does not deserve to live.

The same demonstration begins again in the court of words, when the fair of money and the market of life have closed down. First, faith is sworn, before the exchange, change, and substitution of meaning. You see, Don Juan "talks like a book" (I, 2). How could he have torn Elvira from her religious vows if not with his own vows, with letters, oaths, and protestations? Gusman once more calculates the rule: the ardent oath vanquished the sacred obstacle of the convent. If he deserts Don Carlos' sister, it is incomprehensible, all things considered, that he would have "the heart to break his word" (I, 1). A word for a woman, certainly, but the word is sacred, that is, sacred insofar as the woman is bound by another sacred word. The scene is identical after the shipwreck: Charlotte herself is bound to Pierrot by her sworn faith, "the word that I give you" (II, 2), and Mathurine is bound by "the word that I gave you" (II, 9). But, in fact, the amorous embarkation was also meant to steal a woman from her faith: the goal was to disturb the mutual understanding of a pair of lovers, "to break their attachment" (I, 2). Better yet: "One must do and not talk; and results decide better than words" (II, 5). The word decides, it steals away belief, if it is sacred: "do you want me to swear horrible oaths? May heaven. . . ." "Do not swear," cries Charlotte, echoing, from the water's edge, the beggar in his forest, "Do not swear, I believe you." The second echo, "no, sir, I prefer to die of hunger," is echoed by "I would rather see myself dead than dishonored." The rule is clear: "I act in good faith," but sworn faith is equivalent to life. The tramp, the peasant woman, and the nobleman turn in the endless enchanted circle of word, gold, and love. Outside this circle there is no salvation; whoever breaks it does not deserve to live. As proof, there is the statue and the obligatory exchange of invitations to feast: "yesterday you gave me your word to come to dine with me." "Yes. Where must I go?" "Give me your hand," and so on: this is death.

The law is clear: to fulfill the word that has been spoken. Here, now, is the profession of a faith which does not pride itself on the "false honor of fidelity." I am not bound; no object possesses the binding quality that ties one to virtue. I do not belong to the first object I am taken with. I am breaking the circle of taking and giving, having and owing, offering and receiving. "My engagement is of no use; the love I have for a beautiful woman does not bind my soul and prevent me from doing justice to others" (I, 2). Justice and right can change sides. "I am saving my eyes so they may see the merits of all women, and I render to each the homages and tributes which nature demands of us" (I, 2). The obligation to render tribute is ascribed to nature, not to a sociological, juridical, or sacred law. "I cannot refuse my heart . . . and once a beautiful face has requested it, if I had ten thousand hearts, I would give them all" (I, 2). Once victory is acquired, to speak in the manner of Alexander and other civilizations, "there is nothing more to say" (I, 2). The circle of giving is limited: I cannot resign myself to any limitation. The rupture of the circle or of the contract is brought about by a sham exchange: giving the same thing ten thousand times (*saving* it, that is) in order to acquire (conquer) ten thousand different things. Are one hundred maravedis worth a piaster? In the closed circle of exchange and gift, perpetual motion, strictly defined, is invented. Its mathematical law is as follows: if I receive two without paying out the exchange value, I acquire four; if I take four and do not pay, I acquire eight—the increasing series of injustice (according to Aristotle and his philosophy). I believe, then, that two and two are four, and four and four are eight. Will I thus continue, to *mille e tre*? If I take back what I give, I can acquire indefinitely. The taking back is the beneficial deviation which goes beyond equal rights, which rends the relationship between two persons and creates the possibility of communication between the one and the many. We have left neither tobacco, nor Monsieur Dimanche, nor the savior of the shipwrecked: the disruption of the law's equilibrium is still and always at issue. For the love of ten thousand beauties, for the love of mankind, here we have "the bride-groom of the human race," the unbridled "taker of all hands" (II, 1), who only gives his hand to take it back, except at the fatal feast. A "madman" outside the law of reason, a "dog" outside the law of man, a "devil" outside the law of God, a "Turk" outside the law of Spain, a "heretic" outside the law of Christ. All these rules come down to one: you must give back the hand.

Let us now consider the application of the new rule of profit. Enter Donna Elvira, the forsaken one, abused in word, oath, and faith. Don Juan first answers her philippic with silence and pushes Sganarelle into combat. For a word, not a word is given in return. Donna Elvira then takes his place and proposes that he pay her in words: the scene takes a new twist, and creditor becomes beggar. The abandoned woman offers the rush of false excuses her seducer ought to have spoken: be brazen, lie, say you are going away on business, swear you will return, and so forth. Don Juan, his back to the wall, gives the scene a second twist. True, I broke the contract, he says, I failed to live up to my word; but you must realize I only did it out of conscience for having induced you to break your contract and fail in *your* word: "you have broken the vows which engaged you elsewhere. . . . heaven is extremely jealous in these matters" (I, 3). I am not bound, since you are. You see, my word was not worth yours and our marriage is void for being (divinely) adulterous. In the delicate balance of sacred words (as in the weighing of honor against life a moment ago), your (Elvira's) word prevails. An oath is worth less than a vow; sworn faith is worth less than Christian faith. Your vows are per-petual; mine are only human. A deficit remains which will draw "celestial wrath," "disgrace from above," upon us. From it comes the state of sin-fulness, scruples, fear, and repentance. Thus I must take back my liberty to give you the means to "return to your original bondage." The outsider's finesse consists in hiding one ruptured agreement behind another, sub-stituting one sacramental word for another (the "I will" of renunciation for the "I will" of marriage), and thus transforming the adverse imbalance into a beneficial one: my liberty for your confinement. The situation is the same in the money scenes. Conduct toward sacred words is isomorphic with conduct toward movable goods: the two are strictly parallel varia-tions on the tobacco theme. The goal is to interrupt the egalitarian circulation of anything. Elvira exhibits a righteous anger: "Do not expect me to explode with reproaches and insults" (she would then be giving back still another sacred word); "no, no, my wrath is not the sort to be vented in vain words." Let us break off there; the word game is laughable. Outrage and offense go beyond the ordinary circle of discourse. The imbalance cries out to be avenged.

We pass from the sacred to the truthful word, from breach of contract

to lie, from rupture to imposture. The seducer paid in oaths, the hypocrite pays in appearances. Don Carlos, like Elvira, remains skeptical:
"Do you want me to consider myself satisfied by such a discourse?" (V, 3).
We have seen Sganarelle purchase the costume of a doctor, we have seen
Don Juan propose an exchange of garb to his valet: exchange of garb,
exchange of words, exchange of mortal danger, all this for hard cash. A
new costume: whoever takes "the cloak of religion" takes with "this
respected garment . . . permission to be the most wicked man in the
world." This gives one the advantage of "being held in good credit":
garment for credit, credit for garment; the trick is easy; it always takes
the same twist (V, 2). Don Luis gives Don Juan a warning:[8] in the course
of your career "you have exhausted the merit I acquired in service [to the
sovereign] and my friends' credit." Then he announces a rule: the il-
lustrious deeds of our ancestors "oblige us to do them the same honor"
(IV, 4). Elvira takes a loftier tone, but repeats the theme: "your offenses
have exhausted heaven's mercy." Then she asks to be paid: "I have done
everything for you, and all I ask as recompense is that you correct your
life and prevent your damnation" (IV, 9). In passing, let us note that here
again Don Juan changes his tack and proposes love for discourse: stay, it
is late, and we will find you lodging. In short, we find him converted, but
in an inverse sense. He still returns words for credit—to the forsaken
woman, to her brothers, to his own duped father. His changed ways, or
change of clothes, restore to him those "favors" from which he duly
"intends to profit" until the final reparation, "remission" of his debt
(V, 1). Beneath the mask he can "ensure his affairs": all one must do is
avenge "heaven's interests" (V, 2). Let there be no mistake: the law of
tobacco still reigns. The libertine declared he was not bound (I, 2) by its
binding and obliging quality, but the hypocrite's grimace is a successful
method (*le bon tabac*) for constituting a caste. Thus false piety: "by
grimacing, one can bind together a tight society with men of like mind"
(V, 2). Sign and roll your eyes; you are sheltered, shielded; the cabal will
take up your interests. Thus again, Don Juan is not alone, the solitary
hero outside the common law, the pretext vs. the text. The false exchange
generates the protective social cell.

The reversal here is universal. Don Juan says: I am not the one who is
breaking the promise; it is you who have failed to live up to your vows.
And the extreme conclusion follows: I am not the hypocrite; the whole
society is an imposture. If it is enough to offer tobacco, let us smoke and
continue our caprices. The dog, the Turk, the madman, the heretic, the

---

[8] He includes Don Juan's very *existence* in the cycle of exchange: "I wanted a son . . . , I
asked for one; and this son, whom I have obtained by tiring the heavens with my prayers . . ."
(IV, 4).

devil dubs the society of reasonable men and Spanish Christians a cabal of heretics, of demons, of mad dogs. *The Other designates the Same as Other:* you follow my law and threaten me for not following it. Hypocrisy implies a distance which is the best criterion for making visible, for representing society as it is. What does one do to be a Turk? At this distance, one gives an objective description of morals and customs. No, Don Juan does not become devout; he remains a sociologist, specializing in Ottoman customs and archaic rituals of exchange: once more a Turkish tableau, with its hookahs. The hero of modernity designates contemporary society as a tribe of primitives.

What goes on among them? Well, they exchange women, with words, oaths, and fat dowries. The demonstration would begin again if it were not useless in the *Stone Feast.* Since exchange represents the central theme, everything is clearly legible. Take words, sacred or untrue, take goods, money, butter or cheese, and everything else will be given in the bargain: gallantry results.[9] The tradition concerning the seducer is sufficiently explicit; we may leave him both his discourse and his credit. "Poorly paid for their love," Elvira, Mathurine, and Charlotte would still be justified in demanding their due.

The feast remains, death remains. In the exchange of invitations to dine, in the coming and going of visits, curiously, everyone is in good faith. Don Juan visits the tomb, and the Commander must be pleased, "since [otherwise] it would be a shabby way of responding to the honor I do him" (III, 6). "Paying the courtesy" of a visit, the killer would be surprised if his victim received him ungracefully. One gives; the other must receive; then he, in turn, must give something back in return. One can therefore ask him to dine—to which the statue agrees, as befits him (III, 6). First banquet: "to the Commander's health" (IV, 12)! Second invitation: "I invite you to come to dine with me tomorrow." Don Juan: "yes, I will go," once more as is fitting. Second feast: "yesterday you gave me your word to come to dine with me." "Yes." "Give me your hand." "There it is," and so on (V, 6). He dies. The feast is the elective bond of exchange: you may trample highroads and byroads, but the wedding banquet is served. The nobleman does not cheat the supreme rule, arrives at the privileged place of total prestations, at the final representation of the agonistic variety, where all accounts are settled. There he finds capital punishment in exchange for the Commander's murder. And he cannot cheat because the feast, the festive meal, the banquet is the play itself, not only as title but as living reality. *Dom Juan* is a complete treatise on giving and counter-giving, but, *in the collectivity as it is lived, the structures*

[9]"Without reproach, I will buy you ribbons from all the merchants who pass by . . ." (II, 1).

of exchange are only dramatized, representable and represented, in the course of a festive meal. In order that the treatise be a comedy, *Dom Juan* had to be a feast. Let us eat, drink, to the health of one another, let us exchange tobacco to finish off the meal, while an invisible hand writes upon the wall the unknown words of death.

The demonstration begins again: an incomplete demonstration were it not repeated at leisure. Giving three twists to the law of exchange and gift, the nobleman assumes three personae. The same person, three faces: the bad payer, the mute and liar, the multiple seducer. Nevertheless, the play remains centered on the last subject, the principal model of the structure common to the two others, the tobacco passage being its reduced model. The two other subjects, which expose the principal one, remain marginal, secondary models. Let us once more take up the entire comedy and twist our theoretical operator three times. With the principal model fixed at the circulation of women, we have the *Stone Feast;* one-third turn, and the principal model is fixed on the circulation of goods, so we have *The Miser,* or Master Jacques' feast, furnished with secondary models on the circulation of women—without dowry!—and of words; a one-third turn again, and we discover *George Dandin,* with the principal model fixed on words and secondary models fixed on women and money. One may practice deduction at leisure: clear and simple, it can sound the depths of every detail. By enlarging the spiral, exhaled from tobacco, we cut a wide swath into the work of the classical age's most ingenious sociologist.

Now open *The Gift,*[10] and you will undoubtedly be disappointed. There you will find match and counter-match, alms and banquet, the supreme law which directs the circulation of goods in the same way as that of women and of promises; of feasts, rituals, dances, and ceremonies; of representations, insults, and *jests.* There you will find law and religion, esthetics and economics, magic and death, the fairground and the market-place—in sum, *comedy.* Was it necessary to wander three centuries over the glaucous eye of the Pacific to learn slowly from others what we already knew ourselves, to attend overseas the same archaic spectacles we stage every day on the banks of the Seine, at the Théâtre Français, or at a brasserie across the street? But could we ever have read Molière without Mauss?

Nietzsche said of Dionysus that he was the father of Tragedy and described the explosion of the principle of individuation in the ecstatic delirium of wine. Must it be said of Hermes, the god of commerce, that he is the father of Comedy, by describing the circulation of all things, the

---

[10] Marcel Mauss, *The Gift,* trans. Ian Cunnison (New York: W. W. Norton & Co., 1967).

inter-individual communication in the feast of exchanged tobacco? Is he the god of the crossroads, of thieves and of secrets, this god sculpted on milestones and adorned with such conspicuous virile organs who, like Psychopomp, accompanies Don Juan to Hell?

Laughter is the human phenomenon of communication (reciprocal definition), parallel, in the feast, to all objective communication: it is inextinguishable at the table of the gods.

2

Knowledge in
the Classical Age:
La Fontaine & Descartes

The Wolf and the Lamb

The reason of the stronger is always the best.[1]
We will show this shortly.
A Lamb quenched his thirst
In the current of a pure stream,
A fasting Wolf arrives, looking for adventure,
And whom hunger draws to this place.
"Who makes you so bold as to muddy my drink?"
Said the animal, full of rage:
"You will be punished for your temerity."
"Sire," answers the Lamb, "may it please Your Majesty
Not to become angry;
But rather let Him consider
That I am quenching my thirst
In the stream,
More than twenty steps below Him;
And that, as a result, in no way
Can I muddy His drink."
"You muddy it," responded this cruel beast;
"And I know that you slandered me last year."
"How could I have done so, if I had not yet been born?"
Responded the Lamb; "I am not yet weaned."
"If it is not you, then it is your brother."
"I do not have any." "Then it is one of your clan;
For you hardly spare me,
You, your shepherds, and your dogs.
I have been told: I must avenge myself."

---

[1] As Serres's text will show, "La raison du *plus fort* est toujours la *meilleur*" can also be understood as meaning "The reason of the stronger is always better." — Ed.

> Upon which, deep into the woods
> The Wolf carries him off, and then eats him,
> Without any other form of *procès*.

The notion of structure, recently discovered in the realm of methodology, has an algebraic origin. It designates a set of elements whose number and nature are not specified, a set provided with one or more operations, one or more relations which possess well-defined characteristics. If one specifies the number and nature of the elements of the structure and the nature of the operations, then its model becomes evident. Perhaps the simplest example is that of an *ordered structure*. It designates a set of elements provided with an *ordering relation*. Let there be for example three points *A, B,* and *C* on a line *D,* and a direction defined by the arrow. The ordering relation between these three points, which are elements of the set, can be one of "predecession" or of succession. *A* precedes *B,* which precedes *C. C,* in turn, is the successor of *B,*

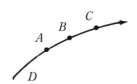

which succeeds *A.* One sees immediately that no point is its own predecessor or successor: the relation is irreflexive. If, on the other hand, *A* precedes *B,* it is impossible for *B* to precede *A*; the relation is antisymmetric. Finally, if *A* precedes *B* and if *B* precedes *C,* then *A* precedes *C:* the relation is transitive. An ordering relation is irreflexive, antisymmetric, and transitive. An ordered structure is a set provided with such a relation. The reader must excuse these prolegomena, which come from basic mathematics.

We are in the countryside, beside a stream; but let us forget all this for a moment—except the fable's last words: the "form of *procès*." This term has at least two meanings: the judicial meaning (trial), and the etymological meaning (process). A process includes a predecession and a succession: it is an order. Question: what is, first of all, the form of the trial, to wit, the form of the process? Here the form is a reason, a ratio, a connection, a relation.

"The reason of the strongest" is definitely an ordering relation. *A* cannot be stronger than itself. *A*'s being stronger than *B* excludes *B*'s being stronger than *A,* and if *A* is stronger than *B,* and *B* is stronger than *C,* it follows that *A* is stronger than *C.* In the set of animals present, being stronger clearly defines an ordered structure. This is the first (we will call it the biological) model. The whole question will soon become one of finding the strongest, he who will have no predecessor in the order, but only successors.

Being "better" is also an ordering relation. *A* cannot be better than itself. *A*'s being better than *B* excludes *B*'s being better than *A*; if *A* is better than *B* and *B* is better than *C*, then *A* is better than *C*. We will call this second model of the ordered structure ethical. The whole question will soon become one of passing from the relative (an ordering relation) to the absolute, of finding the best, he who will have no predecessor in the order, only successors. The movement of the transitive relation is therefore blocked in order to arrive at stability, invariance: *always.* Finally, the use of *is* ("The reason of the strongest *is* always the best") indicates the invariance of the models in the structure, and therefore there is no need for demonstration: it is *always* a matter of the same process.

Let there be "the current of a pure stream." This is a third, topographical model of the same structure. It deals with an irreversible process which can, nevertheless, be determined at any point using an "upstream-downstream" type of relation. I shall no longer verify the axioms, because they are self-evident: no point is upstream of itself, the upstream's upstream is still upstream, and so forth. The wolf "whom hunger draws to this place," and not thirst, is farther up than the lamb, who drinks, in the stream, "more than twenty steps below Him."

In the fourth place, in an irreversible stream, one can define a process of causality. The cause precedes the effect, which succeeds the cause, without any possible reversal, without moving against the current. The third model was sequential; this one is consequential: "Who makes you so bold as to muddy my drink?" Since the cause is upstream from the effect, the lamb replies: "And that, *as a result,* in no way / Can I muddy His drink." One finds here a demonstration. The demonstration by cause and effect is only one particular model of the global structural chain. The lamb demonstrates and La Fontaine shows. Whereas the latter shows the structural invariance using the model's variance, the former demonstrates his point by using only one of the structure's models. Hence the idea, which can help us understand Descartes: the order of reason is only a particular exemplar of order in general. And this result has immense consequences.

One can construct a phenomenon on a spatial-type sequence or on a chain of consequences. Geometry, algebra, and physics constitute the Cartesian construct of the real. As Descartes wrote to R. P. Bourdin, the simplest of these phenomena can be seen in a basket of apples; if one of them is rotten, it diffuses rottenness around it by an irreversible process. In other words, and contrary to certain cosmogonies, the chaotic mixture succeeds separation, and impurity succeeds purity. We have since learned that this belongs to the irreversibility principle of thermodynamics (the law of entropy). The chain of purity or separation followed by mixture is the physical model of the ordered structure. For us, it is isomorphic to the relation of the strongest: maximal energy is always upstream in an irreversible process. It is always a wolf, and not a lamb, who quenches his thirst in the transparent stream of a pure reason.

Now let us choose a political hierarchy, such as that of the classical age. Mark two points on our drawing and name them king and subject. This is a new model of the ordered structure: "'Sire,' answers the Lamb, 'may it please Your Majesty / Not to become angry; / But rather let Him consider / That I am quenching my thirst / In the stream, / More than twenty steps below Him.'" Here there is something new. It is no longer the case of a strong individual who can find a still stronger one, of a "betterable better," an upstream that is downstream from another spot, a cause which can be an effect, or a purifiable energy; it is not, in short, the case of a *greater*, but of a *maximum*. There is nothing above the king. Is this the answer to our previous question?

In seventh place, as Rousseau—and many others—would say, none of these chains and none of these processes can be thought of outside of time. This is a new, temporal model of the ordered structure. On its flow, mark the before and the after, then verify the axioms. "And I know that you slandered me last year." But two events block the continuing movement of the flow: birth and death. "How could I have done so, if I had not yet been born?" If you kill me and then eat me, my time freezes and its order disappears. Relative relation and absolute limits: the wolf, upstream from time, is looking for adventure; he is the master of the future.

Now let us deal with the parental relation. This set is now well known, provided with several ordering relations. Either the ancestor-descendant (parent-child) relation: "I am not yet weaned," or the older child-younger child relation: "If it is not you, then it is your brother." The latter is the elder, since the encounter occurred last year. Or finally the general relation on the irreversible genealogical tree: "Then it is one of your clan." These are the complete models of kinship for the ordered structure.

Finally, let us try a social organization and its various roles. Mark two points on its flow chart and call them (seriously, now) protector and protected. Designated in this way, the relation clearly verifies all the axioms. One thereby obtains the ninth model: "You, your shepherds, and your dogs."

The trial is a process whose global balance sheet can easily be recorded. It consists of an ordered structure with given axioms, a structure that branches out in several models: the social tree, the genealogical tree, the tree of time and history, the political tree, the tree of the production of energy, of entropy, and of pollution, the tree of causes, the hydrographic tree, the tree of the "better," the tree of good, evil, and knowledge, the tree of the distribution of forces—and a tree in general. All these trees together make a forest, into which "The Wolf carries him [the lamb] off, and then eats him."

This is not demonstrated by an order between that which precedes and that which follows, but shown as a forest of models, a forest of symbols. The proof is only one process among others: there exist philosophers from whom a whole forest is hidden by a single tree.

In this way one obtains something like a space, a very general space organized by the ordered structure. All of the fable's model-spaces are deducible from very elementary properties of the ordering relation. Let us take the most general case, the very form of the process. And let us say that this space, organized in this way—a space in which there exist pairs like upstream-downstream, cause-effect, mother-son—is that of a *game-space*. Now the process becomes a trial. What is its form? What are the rules of the game?

Absolute Limit	*Ordering Relation*	*Model*
the strongest	stronger-weaker	biological
the best	better-worse	ethical
source	upstream-downstream	spatial
	cause-effect	rational
	purity-mixture	physical
king	dominator-subject	political
birth-death	before-after	temporal
	ancestor-descendant	genealogical
	protector-protected	social
Maximum	*Greater-Lesser*	*Ordered Structure*

A trial (as elementary jurisdiction) first of all tries to establish a responsibility. Let there be a wrongdoing that a plaintiff claims to have suffered: before evaluating the vengeance (the punishment that the accused must incur), it is necessary to show at least the possibility of injury. The set of possibilities includes physical, moral, temporal, socio-political, and other possibilities. Now, possibility is always the higher point on the tree, whatever that tree might be. If an order is strict, he who occupies the lower position, let us call him the *minorant,* has no control over the *majorant,* who, on the contrary, has complete control over the former. Hence the fable's strategies.

They are all engendered by the wolf's first word: "*Who* makes you so bold as to muddy my drink?" Until now we only knew two terms, which defined an order in the game-space: wolf and lamb. It is necessary to define a third one, namely that which makes the lamb so bold. As a consequence we have the *rule of the game* and the trial's law: the wolf plays, in the order, either the lamb or the third man upstream of himself, the lamb on the contrary plays himself downstream. The term *who* is a reference to the majorant (the upper position's occupant). Now, he who is upstream, he who is greater, is responsible and loses. The minorant wins and eats the other. Whether dealing with drinking, eating, or dying, the *succession of moves* in the game follows the ordering relation: you are the stronger, I am the weaker; you are upstream, I am downstream; you are the cause, I am the effect; you muddy it, I cannot muddy it; you slandered me last year, I had not yet been born; it must be your brother, I do not have any, and so on. The lamb shows, at every move, that he (or the third man) is absent from the upper position where his adversary places him. In short, the wolf "majorizes" or maximizes the lamb, who "minorizes" or minimizes himself. Everything is played upstream from the wolf: however, are the places there occupied or vacant? And how is this going to determine the *results of the game?* Theorem I: the lamb wins. The number of moves is almost infinite. There are as many of them as there are models of the ordered structure and, as a result, the game would never end: it would be necessary to show at every move that the place is vacant. This is what the lamb does. But, in addition, in the ultimate instance, he no longer proves the place's vacancy, but rather its inexistence, and the game is over. Not only is the place vacant, but there is no place. If the wolf is the king, "Sire," and "Majesty," he does not have a majorant. He is in an absolute position, like an absolute monarch. Not only is there no third man, but it is impossible to conceive of one: *quo nihil majus cogitari potest.* Therefore the lamb has won, and the wolf has no majorant. He is himself the maximum. But then there is theorem II: the wolf carries him off, nonetheless, and he does it according to the rule of the game. He succeeds in showing the existence of a third man, upstream from himself, in the lamb's social group. This is because the shepherds and the dogs, protectors of the flock, are, in reality, much stronger than the wolf; they retain, upstream, the constant possibility of doing him harm. "I have been told": *quo nihil majus dici potest.* In the ordering relation, they are clearly majorants. The place preceding the wolf's place is occupied by the shepherd, who is the strongest. The shepherd and his watchdogs are above the "king-wolf." The fable is a perfect operational definition — perfect in that it is free of all psychologism — of hypocrisy. In fact, the term *hypocrisy* comes from the verb to judge, to choose, to decide, and from the prefix underneath. In other words, if you want to win, play the role of the minorant. I imagine that all the *Fables*, by the metamorphosis that they represent, function in a similar fashion.

Structure organizes only the game-space. Without a set provided with an ordering relation, there would be no game. But the structure by itself is not the game. There is a space organized in the form of a tree, and then active and mortal choices associated with each location on the tree, whatever that tree may be. Stable structures and dialectical processes are inseparable.

Besides, let us note the circle: *A* is upstream from *B, A* must place *B* or a third person upstream from himself in order to have the right to eat or kill the adversary. Let us, for the moment, retain the three results: ordered structure, fight to the death, and circularity.

The seventeenth century founded experimental and mathematical physics as well as the calculus of probability. Pascal discovered the equilibrium of liquids; Leibniz developed an acoustics, a game theory, and his logical calculus; Bernoulli dealt with mechanics when he wrote his *Ars Conjectandi.* This simultaneity has a meaning, even though, in the details of the demonstrations and of the works, the relationships are not easily visible. I do not know whether historians have ever described these two births as contemporaneous, or whether they have even questioned their "twin-ness."

If we define nature as the set of objects with which the exact sciences are concerned at a given moment in history, viewed synchronically (which is a restrictive but operational definition), the emergence of physics, in particular, can be thought of only in the global framework of our relations to nature. Now, ever since Francis Bacon's work, these relations have been described, from the heights of his social situation, by the command-obedience couplet. One commands nature only by obeying it. This is probably a political ideology—betrayed by the prosopopeia —which implies practices of ruse and subtlety: in short, a whole strategy. Since nature is stronger than we are, we must bend to its law, and it is through this subterfuge that we dominate it. We are under its orders and turn its forces back against order. This is the circle of ruse and productive hypocrisy: nature is a majorant; we try, ourselves downstream, to majorize ourselves in relation to it. Here one finds again, intact, an ordered structure, a game, its rules (and how best to implement them), the struggle to seize power, and the closed cycle outlined by these moves.

Descartes, after Bacon, picks up the precept: he calls for us to become the masters and possessors of nature. *The impulse to obey has just disappeared.* Baconian physics made science into a duel, a combat, a struggle for domination; it gave it an agonistic model, proposing a form of ruse for it so that the *weak party* would triumph. It transformed science into a game of strategy, with its rules and its moves. But Baconian reason is a weak reason which loses at least the first round, because it first resigns itself to obedience. Descartes rejects this, and, consequently, he suppresses the loss. In the relationship of agonistic forces between ourselves and the exterior world, he seeks the means that will permit us to win at every move. "The reason of the strongest is *always* the best." The best reason *always* permits a winning game. The foundation of modern science is in this word, *always.* Science is a game, an infinite game, in which we always win. Reason is an absolute and constant "optimization."

In a contest, a competitor is not always assured of winning. A player stronger at a given moment because of a given move can later fail when his opponent discovers the means or obtains the power to pass upstream from him. The dichotomy then appears to reverse itself; the weaker has taken the stronger's place. In fact, it is the entire couplet which is displaced in the game-space structured by the ordering relation. This displacement is infinite and does not stop—as long as one stays in the same space—since it is relative. It is the infernal time of hierarchical struggle, the time of human unhappiness. There are two, and only two, strategies that can give a final turn to the sequence of moves. First, one stays with the *dialectical game* and tries to discover a martingale[2] in order to win, whatever the move might be: then the game is over and there is a de-finitive dominant. Old times are over and struggles stop under the in-surmountable power of one of the contestants. With a maximal move, one freezes the game-space in a single pattern of order and hierarchy. It is the end of a slice of history. Second, one attacks *the ordered structure itself*—which is the condition for the game's existence or, rather, without which the game can have neither space nor time—in order to shatter it. This move would mark the beginning of a new history. Philosophers have rarely taken the second path: they have always tried to find the maximum and the minimum points at the edge of the space organized by the couplet of the majorant and the minorant. As soon as it is discovered, one can say: *always.* And it is always the time of the wolf.

Look at Rousseau, for example. He repeats, after many others: the stronger is *never* strong enough *always* to be the master unless he trans-forms his might into right and obedience into duty. As we indicated earlier, this kind of transformation is the shift from one model to the other: another move, same game. The second move is as unstable as the first: jurisprudence and ethics are relative to a cultural space organized by the ordering relation. At times a radical, at others a tiny, change in the ordering relation is sufficient to make an entire group overthrow its morals and its laws. The trial's dialectics remain, based on the majorant's and the minorant's relationships, with the division of the stakes left to the balanced distribution of forces and to the recuperation of ruse. It is therefore necessary to recognize an infinity of moves in the relative field of the "more" and the "less." As in the fable, one must maximize the "more" and minimize the "less." *One must maximize in an absolute fashion,* in such a way that there may not exist, that one may not conceive, a

[2] A martingale is any system by which one tries to make up one's losses in previous bets by doubling or increasing the amount bet. —Ed.

majorant to a maximum and a minorant to a minimum. One must transform force into factual necessity and obedience into an inevitable law.
One may cut off the king's head, kill the dog, or eat the shepherd, yet one
cannot do without Reason's verdicts. And this is why, since Rousseau, *one
no longer hesitates to invoke science in the realm of law, power, and politics. It is
because science has already pointed the way to the winning strategy.* For it must
be remembered that the foundation of science—whether it be the pure
sciences at the Hellenic dawn or the experimental sciences in the classical
age—had taken place in an agonistic field.

I could be accused of forcing the answer. And yet one can show that
abstract mathematics and axiomatics owe their emergence to the Sophists'
discussions and paradoxes, as well as to Plato's dialogue techniques.
Agonistics is there, in the background. And yet the purest positivist
cannot challenge Auguste Comte's analysis, which defines the birth of
geometry (in his eyes a natural science) as a ruse or set of ruses: to be able
to measure inaccessible things, to find indirect means for man to perform
that which he does not have the means to do. Once again, this is a
strategy. And as soon as laws are written, they allow man *always* to have
access to the inaccessible. The stability and constancy of certitudes or
precisions are conceived in the beginning as the end of a prior game.

Another founding word was that of Galileo: nature is written, it is
drafted in a language; everyone agrees that this is a mathematical language. But this writing is not obvious, it is hidden, concealed under the
phenomenal appearance of the material world. One must force open the
secret, find the key to the logogriph, and decode this writing. Now, in
this game of decoding or deciphering, nature defends itself. It is subtle, it
is hidden, it is secret. One must therefore employ subtler strategies in
order to make its defenses fail. Once the key is discovered, the world
surrenders. The isomorphic relation between force and writing, recognized elsewhere,[3] is again brought into play here.

Just as in Plato's work there abound traces of this state of affairs necessary for the founding of the rigorous sciences, so, in the same way, Descartes's work shows such traces at the dawn of exact sciences (conceived,
since the classical age, as the optimal relationship from subject to object).
I have recalled this founding word at the end of which we should have
made ourselves the masters and possessors of nature. And I expressed it
in terms of a game: Baconian obedience having been suppressed, the
project became one of *always* winning. Reason is optimized, it is the
best, it is always invincible. From La Fontaine spring Descartes and the
game, or vice versa—it matters little. The three elements located in the
fable should then be found in the *Metaphysical Meditations:* a space struc-

---

[3]See Jacques Derrida's *De la grammatologie* (Paris: Minuit, 1967). —Ed.

tured by the ordering relation, a circle, a game with its moves, its end, and its winner. Two and only two have been recognized by the commentators; the third, which is the most visible—since it concerns action—remains hidden. I have suggested elsewhere[4] a static type of solution to the problem of the Cartesian circle framed in a historical context. Another solution is possible through the strategy of the game.

First of all, there exists in the text an ordering relation, the famous order of reason, the long chain of the geometricians, such that a link A precedes B, its successor, which proceeds from A, its predecessor, and such that it is impossible that A derive from B. The order of reason is therefore irreflexive, antisymmetric, and transitive, according to the axioms of the relation. Transitivity remains a constant preoccupation with Descartes, who suggests time and again that we reconsider the ordered set in its totality. But, as we have seen in the fable, the demonstrative (or deductive, if one wishes) sequence is only one tree in the forest of model-sequences. One tree alone must not hide the forest from us. Behind, or besides, the premises-consequences couplet, there exist other simple couplets, other models of the ordering relation present in the text: predecessor-successor, upstream-downstream, older-younger, and so forth. Moreover, the demonstrative order, taken from the Greek geometricians, links together relationships or proportions, as is noted throughout Descartes's *Regulae*. The geometric sequence is a series of relationships and analogies. These relationships quantify very different things: relationships of size, height, ruse, and power. Even, occasionally, relationships of sovereignty and slavery, since the first *Meditation* closes with the representation of a slave who, while sleeping, dreams that he is free. From this results an ordered space and no longer just a linear chain whose list of model-relations would be quite long: more powerful/less powerful, better/worse, before/after, more wily/less wily, more or less true/more or less false, and so on, and in which the cause-effect pair is only one particular relation. The set of these models, and not just one of them, makes the ordered structure visible. This is because the word "structure" was taken by commentators in the Latin sense commonly used until the end of the nineteenth century, that is, in the etymological sense of architecture, meaning logical architecture.

If one takes it in the sense defined above, everything changes: the ordered structure is common to several relations. One need only choose a parallel text, such as Leibniz's *Meditationes*, in order to understand the question clearly. These meditations are constructed by pairs, such as light-dark, confused-distinct, aligned so that they constitute a simple

---

[4]*Hermès I: La Communication* (Paris: Minuit, 1968), pp. 113-26. —Ed.

filter. The ordered structure being relative, the pluralist method makes it function iteratively, until it finds one or several remainders. If, in Descartes (or in the Cartesian method), there was only order, and order alone, then Leibniz's text would be Cartesian. Reciprocally, Descartes's text would be Leibnizian, since it posits a maximum and minimum strategy in an ordered space. This switch is exactly what happens. On the ordered structure considered as a game-space, one can, of course, construct a game. And this, again, Leibniz had seen, since he accuses Descartes of staging a whole spectacle, that is, an action in a game. "I would . . . believe myself at fault, if I spent in deliberation the time that remains to me for action."[5] Action: characters or prosopopeias, God, the ego, the evil spirit, defined as opposing elements in a regulated global strategy. In the fable, one saw, quite simply, that if the direction of the moves remained at the level of the formal pair majorant-minorant, the game was endless and without a stable victor. It is therefore necessary to put an end to this once and for all; one of the adversaries must be assured of always winning. That is possible only if one passes from the position of majorant to a maximum without conceivable predecessor, and from the position of minorant to a minimum without any imaginable successor. There is no place above the king, there is no place above the shepherd assisted by his dogs, and there is no place below the lamb. From this comes the global theorem: in the Cartesian *Meditations,* all the moves are maximized.

The syntax confirms this without exception: comparatives of order, superlatives of maxima. Descartes speaks of his age: "*so ripe, that* I could *not hope* for another after it, in which I could be adequate to execute [this enterprise]" (p. 404); of his project: "it made me defer *so long that* I would henceforth believe myself at fault, if I spent in deliberation the time that remains to me . . ." (ibid.). Optimal age, optimal time, such that there no longer remains any better. Descartes again, speaking of doubt: "as much as reason persuades me already that I should no *less carefully* keep myself from believing in things that are *not entirely* certain and indubitable, *any more than* in those that appear to us to be *manifestly* false" (p. 405). Result: the universal quantificator. A constant repetition of all, always, never, absolutely, and so on. Appearances of *always,* the key word, "I shall *always* follow this path" (p. 414).

Quantification, until now, has been rather indefinite. Observe the progression from the first *Meditation* to the second: "*Any* subject for doubt

[5]Descartes, *Oeuvres philosophiques* (Paris: Garnier, 1963), 2: 404. All further page references will be to this volume of the Garnier edition. Given the technical nature of Serres's demonstration, the quotations from Descartes have been translated directly from the original French. —Ed.

that I find will suffice to make me reject *all* [opinions]" (p. 405); "it is *never entirely* prudent to trust those who have deceived us *once*" (ibid.); and "distancing myself from *everything* in which I will be able to imagine the *least* doubt" (p. 414). First we move from the universal (*all*) to the particular (*any*), then, to the reduction of the particular to a single case, (*once*), and finally, to the reduction of unicity to the minimum (*the least*). This is clearly the final move.

God's position and that of the atheists establish the rule: "the *less powerful* the author that they assigned to my origin will be, the *more* probable it is that I am *so* imperfect that I am *always* in error" (p. 410). It will suffice to envisage the extreme case in order to invert the result, to find the *quo nihil cogitari possit,* sovereignly omnipotent, veracious. As far as I know, "perfect" signifies "optimal."

The global description of the procedure follows: "having *so* balanced my [new and old] prejudices that they can *no longer* sway my opinion" (p. 411). With the model of a simple machine, taken up again, later, at Archimedes' point (p. 414) (thus the minimum, to move the earth, the maximum), one obtains the static comparison of relationships. In this space, the optimized move is precisely the Archimedian fixed point. The progression is the same.

Speaking of the evil spirit, Cartesian progression is still the same: first called "*no less* wily and deceiving *than* powerful" (p. 412), the evil spirit is called later in the second *Meditation* "a *very* powerful and *very* wily deceiver, who employs *all* his energy to deceive me *always*" (p. 415). We move again from the comparison of relationships to the maximal relationship such that nothing can exist beyond it. Here is the strategy in relation to this spirit: "I shall prepare my mind *so* well against *all* of this great deceiver's ruses, that, *no matter how* powerful and wily he may be, he will *never* be able to impose *anything* on me" (p. 412). And the final move as Descartes sees it: "let him deceive me *as much as* he wishes, he will *never* manage to turn me into *nothing,* as long as I think that I am *something*" (p. 415). This doubt is called hyperbolic, but no effort is made to understand the hyperbole's function. The word must be analyzed as I have done for the fable's hypocrisy. *Hypocritical ruse and hyperbolic doubt are operators totally devoid of psychologism.*

"My meditation of yesterday has filled my mind with *so many* doubts, that it is *no longer* in my power to forget them . . ." (p. 414); "I am *so* surprised, that I can*not* fix my feet on the bottom nor swim . . ." (ibid.). The existence of the "I," "I am," "I exist" is clearly uncovered by a mini mum-maximum move: it is the minimal remainder of a maximized strategy or ruse. At the end of which, as soon as *everything* that can be in *any way* disputed has been dismissed, I [Descartes] obtain "a *more* certain and *more* evident knowledge than *all* the knowledge I had earlier"

(p. 416). Once again, the universal quantificator is the final move in the quantification of a relationship followed to its limit.

One could continue the demonstration. The syntax is constructed entirely in this way. The process is everywhere quantified, tactics are everywhere maximized, the final move is on the maximum *maximorum*, and even more on the *quo nihil*. . . . Not only is there no one in the places upstream, but there is no longer any upstream locus. To give oneself an adversary and defeat him with the help of an all-powerful and truthful associate, God Himself: this is a game between two players, between three, in which nature disappears—burned, melted, minimized, destroyed. The malleable wax and I become one; thus I always win. God is a point without an upstream, the wax a point without a downstream, and myself in the center, hence the circle; I can no longer lose at this game.

Then everything becomes possible: optics and dioptics, the world and its system, medicine and everything that follows from it. In the game of truth, error has been checkmated; in the game of domination, all is reduced to slavery, including the body. Metaphysics is operatory, it is the strategic set without which physics and the exact sciences are nothing but partial and dispersed tactics. Einstein rediscovered Descartes by turning around a parable: God is subtle, but he does not cheat. To know nature is a game. Not a futile amusement, but a deadly dangerous game. Nature's secret lies in the fact that one sees only the backs of the cards, and that one must play carefully and cautiously, in order to uncover this secret and read the faces of the cards, that is to say, to read them mathematically. Experimentation is a game in which the more one cheats, the less one knows (hence morals and deontology), a game one can lose and win, but in which there exists a guaranteed winning strategy. The development of mathematics, independent of experimentation, is another result: one must try to refine strategies, which are useful against an adversary whose strategies are also extremely refined. "Game," then, is not just a word of science, it is the model of all exact knowledge. Information theory, the daughter of physics and probabilities, has discovered this model once again. But during the classical age, it is a martial game. Like many other philosophers, Descartes pursued his military calling in metaphysics.

It is often said that probability theory and the art of conjecture were born, in a given economic context, from the idea of life annuities, before the large banks and companies thought of insuring against death. This is probable, although not proven by the facts. Leibniz, among others, computed life annuities. Even supposing that one proved it, one would only have affirmed in one case an already established theory which had sometimes proved itself useful. The more significant idea is that of the wager, a wager that is not very specific, since every martial game is a game to the death, a wager on death. If it is a question of dates, you have insurance and annuities; if it is a question of stakes, you have Pascal. Thus it is that the relation between theory and practice, the relation of metaphysics to knowledge, and the relation of the latter to domination come together in the same place, *at the outcome provided by death*.

For Plato and a tradition which lasted throughout the classical age, knowledge is a hunt. To know is to put to death — to kill the lamb, deep in the woods, in order to eat it. Moving from combat with prey outside the species to killing inside the species, knowledge now becomes military, a martial art. It is then more than a game; it is, literally, a strategy. These epistemologies are not innocent: at the critical tribunal they are calling for executions. They are policies promulgated by military strategists. To know is to kill, to rely on death, as in the case of the master and the slave.

Today we live out the major results of these wolfish actions. For the "I," who played the role of the lamb by minimizing his powers and placing the declared powers upstream from himself, this "I" is the wolf. In the ordering relation, in the game-space, the "I" is clearly in the middle, between the victorious sheepdog and the defeated devil or the wax. It has taken the wolf's place, its true place. The reason of the strongest is reason *by itself. Western man is a wolf of science.*

3

Michelet:
The Soup

The Sea is a book of natural history—and of natural science.[1] A book of history, and of science, it is for us today a book of the history of science. A complete theory of observation, as fully worked out as that of Maxwell, for example, lies elegantly concealed beneath anecdote and pathos, together with a general gnoseology, which I shall not discuss, a very elaborate outline of the beginnings of knowledge, and a subtle epistemology of scientific practice, based on an exhaustive utilization of all areas of the encyclopedia. It is as if, for Michelet as for Auguste Comte, natural science were the whole of science.

The Sea constructs a chain of beings which Michelet, in a note, denies having seriously wanted to construct. The chain is metaphorical in a certain sense, and we shall see in what way.

The construction of this chain represents an ontogeny and a phylogeny, each incomplete and displaced. We shall see how this displacement works. What is more, the knowledge I spoke of a moment ago is produced during this genesis, so that the theory of the origins of knowledge is presented as a by-product of the origins of being. By turning back upon itself, nature is the source of self-knowledge, it is itself the origin of the science of nature.

The underlying philosophical thesis of *The Sea*, in sum, is hylozoic. Belonging to a very old tradition, hylozoism[2] was brought back into the scientific universe of Michelet's time and developed into a philosophy through the combination of two schools: Neptunism, which arose in Germany in the nineteenth century, and Heterogeny. What is Nep-

---

[1] Jules Michelet, *La Mer* (Paris: Hachette, 1861). There has been no recent edition of the book, though it should become more accessible when the edition of Michelet's complete works (Jules Michelet, *Oeuvres complètes*, ed. Paul Viallaneix [Paris: Flammarion, 1971-]) is finished. The only English translation dates from the last century: Jules Michelet, *The Sea* (New York: Rudd and Carleton, 1861). —Ed.

[2] Hylozoism was the doctrine according to which matter was thought to be animated. —Ed.

tunism? It is a theory which holds that the sea is the *Ur-Suppe,* the fundamental soup, that is to say the matter from which all other material things originated. On the other hand, Heterogeny, championed at the time of Michelet by Pouchet, supports the theory of spontaneous generation. It maintains that all living beings are derived from matter. As a hylozoist, Michelet applies the two doctrines to each other, the Neptunism of Werner to the Heterogeny of Pouchet. The Neptunian *Ur-Suppe* becomes what we would call today the prebiotic soup. The marine mixture, the primal liquid state, is the original state of life. In Michelet's writings Pouchet carries on from Werner, or, alternatively, Werner is introduced as an essential condition of the Heterogeny of Pouchet. The sea is mother: *la Mer, c'est la mère.* An analytical reading might arrive at this conclusion, but we can reach it by the natural sciences as well.

Here, then, is the soup in the double sense of the *Ur-Suppe* of the geologists and the prebiotic soup, that is, the physiochemical conditions for the origin of living beings. A whole series of animate forms will emerge from this soup: plankton, coral, polyps, mollusks, fish, mammals, cetaceans, the whale. . . . The whale is not the last link in the chain of beings; the last one is the manatee. The whale is still an imperfect being because its mammary glands are situated too low. On the contrary, the manatee, the sea-cow, or, in other words, the siren—not as a mythic animal, but as one that actually exists—which has permanent breasts located high on its body, is the perfect being produced by the soup at the end of the series, an Anadyomene Venus. Thus the following cycle, imperfect if we stop at the whale, but perfect if we end with the sea-cow. A mother emerges from a mother.

The chain of beings is not linear. It is circular, like the time of the eternal return figured on the coral reefs of the South Seas, in which new continents are being produced for a future humanity. In a literal sense, what is described is a circular generation of the eternal feminine. This is the displacement that I mentioned earlier: the chain of beings does not present a linear development, but a series of invariants, genotypic invariants, and the genotype is femininity. If this is, as it turns out, an error, we still have to recognize that in his method Michelet was seeking an invariant genotypic tree, an underlying invariance beneath the phenotypic development of the chain.

This, then, is the acknowledged aim—the development of a circular chain, the disclosure of a structural invariance in genesis. And this, then, is the aim of the laboring earth. The word *labor* is continually displaced from its meaning as *work*—the artisanal labor of the mollusks—to its genetic meaning: the earth is in labor, a labor of metamorphosis, transformation, production, generation.

What are the conditions for the achievement of this aim? What happens in the course of this labor? In answering this question we find ourselves dealing with every area of the encyclopedia. In other words, if we ask the question "What is the prebiotic soup? What is the 'Ur-Suppe'? What does the soup do to produce this cyclical chain, that is to say, the invariants of genesis?" we must answer with the whole of the encyclopedia.

The soup, in Werner's sense as well as in the prebiotic sense, is essentially a mixture. A mixture of what? We shall see a little later. In any case, there can be no mixture without a movement to disperse the solute through the solvent. This movement should be analyzed as such. In addition, there must be a fire to prepare the soup, and a pot to prepare it in, and it has to boil. We must therefore define the pot and the forces of heat at work beneath it—quite simply, as we would do in cooking.

This is not a new metaphor. The Vedic texts long ago recommended the use of a similar recipe for the preparation of the "amrta" of immortality: a pot was needed—this was the sea; it was to be stirred by means of a certain number of utensils—among them, a mountain—and the nature of the mixture was defined. Now the recipe for the soup is the encyclopedia, which, since Hegel at least, is a cycle.

Let us follow the headings of this recipe:

First, Michelet uses geometric concepts. (A specific model of time corresponds to each area of the encyclopedia. Thus, at the end of our analysis, we shall perhaps be able to give a clear and distinct answer to the questions which were raised earlier.)

To return to the geometric models, Michelet observes, and this is not very original, that the equatorial circle is the geometric locus of certain limits, and, in particular, of those limits concerning fire. It is the geometric locus of hot points, of limits concerning water and air—the point of condensation of evaporation from the ocean. The equatorial circle is the geometric locus of the outer edges, the hottest and densest points on the planet. Hence the equator.

This conclusion is given to us twice: first by astronomical observations; secondly by geographical observation.

It turns out, incidentally, that the geometric schemata are naturalistic, as was the case with Auguste Comte and all the positivists.

As for geometric observation, it informs us of a phenomenon which is new in relation to the teachings of astronomy. A circle of active or extinct volcanoes borders the Atlantic Ocean, and a comparable ring surrounds the Pacific. The equatorial circle is orthogonal, in a certain respect, to two other circles, those of the Atlantic and Pacific volcanoes, which Michelet calls the circles of fire. These two circles are centered, roughly speaking, on the equator and intersect it at two points, first at a certain spot in the Caribbean, between Cuba and Florida, and second at Java. These two points are the centers of the world, apexes at either side of it. They could be defined geometrically as *maxima maximorum.*

The first point acts as the center of the world in *The Mountain,* the second in *The Sea,* such that a simple spherical geometry—though fairly elaborate since it has to do with a locus of points *maxima maximorum* and not just with a diagram—hence a simple and a differential geometry, outline the edge of the pot where the soup should be brewing.

The locus defined in the Caribbean near Haiti or Cuba carries an extra value since it is at the intersection of three circles, not of two.

The definition is fundamental to the rest of the gnoseology; the center of the pot in which the soup will get mixed is on the rim of the pot, and the center of the world is on the edge of the circle. This is very important for an understanding of the theory of knowledge.

I said, secondly, that movement was necessary to prepare the soup, to prepare the mixture. A general theory of movement is going to help us to mix and churn the solution. This theory is mechanics. Beneath the anecdote and the pathos, the text mobilizes with great precision certain findings of rational mechanics which were well known at the time.

Two types of movement are necessary to mix the solvent, to make it move. First there must be a horizontal movement. This is ensured by the currents, the streams of the sea, like the Gulf Stream or the Kuro-Shivo, and by the tides, usually produced by astronomical forces.

This would produce only a surface effect were it not associated with a vertical movement, ensured by the surge of the sea, by storms, which Michelet calls spasms, and, in particular, by cyclones, or major hurricanes of circular motion.

Let me go on with this distinction: Michelet tells us that the horizontal movements, generally produced by astral mechanics, as expressed in the achievements of Laplace and his successors, are subject to Chazallon's law. Chazallon's law, published in the almanac of the tides a few years before the publication of *The Sea,* is a revision of Euler's law of the movement of vibrating cords. This latter was expressed in harmonic equations using second-order partial derivatives, and defines sinusoidal movements.

The results I formulated under the first heading concerned a spherical geometry—that is, large circles outlined on the earth's surface; and the definition of points on these circles was a differential definition: curves of *maxima* and points *maxima maximorum.* Geometry gave us a system of circles. Now in the mechanical study of the horizontal movements, we get Euler's law of vibrating cords, that is, a law of sinusoidal form, a coherent whole of component circles—again a circle of circles.

Secondly, vertical movements ensure the mixing of the solvent. Generally produced by the wind system, these movements are subject to what

Michelet calls the law of storms, discovered by Maury. The storms and cyclones, which are themselves spirals, circles of circles, are subject to a circular movement. They move in a levorotatory direction in the Northern Hemisphere and in a dextrorotatory direction in the Southern Hemisphere. And once again, the law of vertical movements articulates something about a circle of circles.

These geometrical and mechanical schemata are naturalistic in character. We must now investigate sciences that deal with the production of movement of this type. Three branches of physics deal with this question, and Michelet put their most recent results to use.

First there is what Auguste Comte calls *barology*, which is the science of weight pressures. It describes the high- and low-pressure areas all along the equator. The winds in each hemisphere circulate in cycles, circles of circles, which both Michelet and Maury remarked, but which Edmund Halley had discovered some decades earlier, to the best of my knowledge, in connection with the tradewinds. In addition, a theory of the cyclone ("*la* cyclone," in Michelet) once again delineates a system of cycles, a circle of circles. In the computations of this kind of barological investigation, the world and the sea are represented by a mechanical model. The world is a static and a dynamic machine.

The second branch of physics which ensures the production of these movements is what Auguste Comte called *electrology*, the theory of electrical phenomena. This science deals with the circulation of electrical flux between terminals, beginning at centers with a fixed difference in potential. Hence, secondly, the world is an electrical engine. First it is a static, then a dynamic machine; now it is an electrical one.

Earlier, I defined the points of Java, or the West Indies, as points *maxima maximorum* on the basis of geometric schemata of spherical and differential geometry. In the context of the sciences which not only describe but produce movement, it is at exactly these same points that the maximum pressure is located, in terms of barology, and the maximum potential, in terms of electricity. Everyone knows that the cyclones are formed in Java and in the West Indies. Hence the following theorem: the points we determined geometrically as *extrema* are *the poles of the two systems of circulation*, that of pressure and that of electricity.

But this is just a conclusion based on the sciences known to Auguste Comte, positivistic sciences that were not particularly new.

Michelet's most original treatment of the material involves thermo-dynamic circulation. Michelet's vocabulary is extremely precise from this point of view: he speaks of a boiler, a source, and a steam engine. Suppose we have to define currents like the Gulf Stream. The problem is to discover how it is possible to represent a movement of circulation in the sea. The movement goes from a very hot source, the point *maxima maximorum* of the West Indies, to a relatively cold source. Michelet's vocabulary is a model of precision here. The cold source is located in Iceland, among the ice floes. But according to Carnot the source is not supposed to be absolutely cold, but only relatively cold. Since Iceland is an ice pack under a volcano, however, the current does flow toward Iceland, and the source is indeed only relatively cold.

When he studies the marine currents of the North Atlantic, Michelet accurately defines what has been known as a Carnot cycle in thermo-dynamics since 1824. The Carnot cycle organizes the oceanic streams and currents.[3] As for the other hemisphere, a similar Carnot cycle extends from Java, considered as a hot source, to the submerged coral reefs of the South Seas, considered as cold sources. The world which was a static machine and an electrical machine a moment ago has become a steam engine. It is the sea, functioning as a steam engine, which performs the stirring of the soup.

Having dealt with geometry, mechanics, and physics, let us consider chemistry, at least rapidly. It studies the concentration of the soup, its concentration of mineral salts. This too is *maximum* at the centers of the world, the points *maxima maximorum* of the West Indies and Java. *The Mountain* deals with the maximal point of condensation, in spices and poisons, on the mountains and coastal flanks of the island of Java.[4] Thus there are points of maximal condensation into mineral salts, spices, and poisons. These points attract and repel. The mineral salts are dispersed throughout the solvent around them, following the circles of circles de-fined by the previous sciences. There are points of condensation and cycles of displacement. The world is now a chemical machine.

Let us pursue our analysis of the sciences: next comes *biology*. I can go quickly from now on because things repeat themselves by variation within the great circle of knowledge of the encyclopedia. The centers we defined earlier in relation to geometry, mechanics, physics, and chemistry naturally become defined as hearts. These centers are hearts and their movement is pulsating. The Carnot cycle was already a pulsating move-ment. The centers are hearts for the vascular circulation of the blood. The soup is no longer just a solution of mineral salts, it is something like

---

[3] In 1824, Sadi Carnot published *Réflexions sur la puissance motrice du feu et sur les machines propres à développer cette puissance* in which he outlined the principles of the functioning of the steam engine in terms of a cycle in four steps: 1) an isothermal expansion as the steam is introduced into the cylinder, 2) an adiabatic expansion, 3) an isothermal compression in the condenser, and 4) a final adiabatic compression in which energy is consumed to heat the steam to its original boiler temperature. The Carnot cycle introduced two fundamental thermodynamic concepts, completeness and reversibility, and thus contributed to the de-velopment of thermodynamics in its formative state. — Ed.

[4] Jules Michelet, *La Montagne* (Paris: Librairie Internationale, 1868). As in the case of *La Mer* (see note 1 above), there is no recent edition of this book. The English translation dates from the last century: Jules Michelet, *The Mountain* (London: T. Nelson and Sons, 1872). — Ed.

the blood of the organism called the Earth. By analogous reasoning, these centers will become breasts, periodic breasts for the nourishing circulation of milk. The soup is milk. The sea is made up of systems of milky ways. Within this chaos it is possible to define the laws of these ways, which astronomy has not yet discovered for the galaxy. The last science has transcended the first. Finally the centers are uteri, rhythmical, for the menstrual cycle, with lunar periods. Hence the cycle: biology closes the circle of astronomy. The world is woman. One might assume a gap between the so-called physical sciences and the sciences of living beings. No such gap is to be found in *The Sea*. The world is a static machine, a compression engine, an electrical engine, a chemical machine, a steam engine; the world is an organism—all without contradiction. The basic philosophy is hylozoism. What is hylozoism if not mechanism coupled with vitalism in a synthesis in which there are no gaps? There are mechanical models of the world which can be considered as elementary models of time, and organicist models. For Michelet the synthesis of mechanism and vitalism is justified by the succession of areas of knowledge within the encyclopedia. Why should the sciences be contradictory among themselves?

To understand the prebiotic soup, therefore, I have only to perform the following simple addition:

1) The centers defined by geometric and differential properties are the poles of the circulation of movements in general.

2) They are the poles of the circulation of fluids in general, through the interaction of high and low pressures.

3) They are the positive and negative poles for the circulation of electric current.

4) They are the hot and cold sources of the Carnot cycle, which functions for all kinds of liquids.

5) They are concentrations for the circulation of saline solutions.

6) They are hearts for the circulation of the blood.

7) They are breasts or uteri for the circulation of milk or for menstrual circulation in which we can recognize, as in a circle, the cycle of the planets and the first factor of the addition.

The sum total of the areas of the encyclopedia can be expressed as follows: *reservoirs exist for the circulation of the soup*. The word "reservoir" is used four or five times in *The Sea*. It first appears in Carnot's theory of the heat engine, and Michelet takes it up to define the *maxima maximorum* poles.

Thus there are reservoirs for the circulation of the soup. What is the soup? It is the sum of all the elements analyzed in relation to the areas of the encyclopedia cited above. It is milk, blood, a solution of mineral salts, an electrical flux, etc., all at the same time.

Referring to the remark I made about analysis at the beginning, one could say that these liquids are overdetermined by Michelet, by his unconscious. This is possible, even probable, if we consider the text analytically. But we can take the word "analytical" in its ordinary sense: given the prebiotic soup, it is analyzed into its constitutive elements. Now these elements are the objects, in turn, of mechanics, thermodynamics, and so forth. The basic liquid, given by the Neptunism of the *Ur-Suppe* or by Pouchet's Heterogeny, is simply the synthesis, the mixture obtained by the horizontal and vertical movements, the synthesis and mixture of liquids already investigated individually by the sciences of the day in accordance with the different areas of the encyclopedia. The observer of the soup may be a voyeur, but he is first of all a scholar imbued with the idea of the encyclopedia. The founder of *psychoanalysis* was also an *analyst* in this very trivial sense. You will find physicalist models in his work distributed as we saw above.

The sea is a mixture, a synthesis, an addition, that we can speak about in three ways:

1) As the sum of concentrations present in the reservoir; the mixture transports the sum of the elements concentrated in the reservoir.

2) It is set in motion by the sum of the circulations issuing from the reservoirs—stirred by the sum of the circulations.

3) The nature of the sea is such that it itself can be analyzed in terms of the sum of the cycles of the encyclopedia. The encyclopedia is a reservoir.

Consequently my method itself enters into the encyclopedia: into a cycle of cycles. It is simply added to the cycles of cycles that I have just defined for each area of the said encyclopedia. Whence the following series of completely stable structural analogies:

1) There is circulation in general, there are cycles, there are spirals—in short there are essentially circles of circles which are defined by laws such as harmonic equations, sinusoidal laws, partial derivative equations, and so forth. The eternal return is a particular case of this universal form.

2) A second series of analogies: there are points *maxima maximorum*, condensations, concentrations, reservoirs. Thus we have two simple notions: circulation and reservoir. These two notions remain structurally stable through all the divisions of the encyclopedia. Indeed, each time I have gone through an area—geometry, mechanics, thermodynamics, biology, etc.—I have found a concrete model involving a circulation and a reservoir. The same scheme is found in the primary cycle of the eternal return or in the last cycle of generation: the mother soup engenders the mother siren. Woman is the genetic reservoir.

At this point the explanatory strategy is found to be completely reversed. I've taken a text and analyzed it in terms of its object. Now what it says, through displacements and variation on the encyclopedia, is the re-iteration of two concepts: *reservoir* and *circulation*—a set of elements present in a given place and the operations by which these elements are distributed throughout a given space. When I say "a set of elements plus operations upon these elements" I am not defining a structure, as I said earlier, I am defining structure itself; for the definition of structure is indeed a set of elements provided with operations.

Now consider the reservoir and the circulation and ask yourself questions like these: where is the reservoir? What is the reservoir? What is in the reservoir? What are its elements and what is their configuration? How does this reservoir function? Is it stable or metaphorical, open or closed? And so forth. . . .

Ask yourself a second series of questions: what is circulation? What are the circulating elements? What is the plan of the transportation system? How do the elements circulate according to this plan? By what law? In a stable manner or transformationally? And so forth. . . .

Here are examples of some answers: the reservoir is capital, the quantity of energy, the constancy of force, the libidinal reservoir, and so forth; what can be applied to the pattern of general circulation or the circle of circles is language, speech, words, vocabulary, values, money, desire. Here are some examples of related questions: What blocks circulation? What stimulates it? Who or what governs or forms the reservoir? And so on. With these questions and these answers, varied and multiplied into several voices, you will reconstruct the entire set of interpretative organons formed in the nineteenth century.

In answering the question: "What is the reservoir? What is the circulation?" you reconstruct the entire set of what you consider to be interpretative organons. And that is why I can no longer entertain the idea that I have explicated a text. For there can no longer be any question of explicating Michelet by any one or other of these interpretative organons, or by the sum total of them, since the most general conditions for the formation of these very organons are explained clearly and distinctly in the book *The Sea* itself. All I can do is apply these same organons to one another. Application is a strategy of conformity; explication is an archaic and vague approximation. The object of explanation explains in turn the set of methods that were to explicate it. Thus the object is to find the law of this diversity of perspectives.

At the beginning of the century, when the chemical and physical scientists worked in the laboratory and manipulated bodies or substances, they constructed their instruments without regard to the particular substance they were working on. They made filters out of a different material from that composing the thing to be filtered. This went on until one day someone realized that the body or substance he was working on, when considered as a crystalline structure, was itself a filter. One did not need a filter to work on the body because the body itself was a filter. It became clear then that the technology of the scientific object was itself the object of science.

I arrive at exactly the same conclusion: the strategy of criticism is located in the object of criticism. All the strategies I need are in the text of Michelet. All I need to do is to answer two simple questions which have been formulated by analyzing the text in terms of the encyclopedia: what is a reservoir? what is circulation? It is not necessary to introduce methods to read this text: the method is *in* the text. The text is its own criticism, its own explication, its own application. This is not a special 'case; it is one that is perfectly generalizable. Why should there be a dichotomy between texts, between the ones that operate and the ones that are operated upon? There are texts, and that is all.

4

$\blacktriangle$
$\blacktriangle$ $\blacktriangle$

Language & Space:
From Oedipus to Zola

I would like to test a hypothesis concerning mythical discourse. I propose it as a non-initiate might present an object for which he has at his
disposal no criterion of authenticity. If my hypothesis finds approval, I
shall have reason to rejoice. If not, I shall rejoice at being guided back in
the right direction. Having stipulated the condition of examination and
supervision, I shall not feel completely out of place in an area about
which it is a bit paradoxical for me to speak. I come here from elsewhere,
from very far away on the encyclopedic, cultural, or university map—as
a foreigner, let us say, who perhaps does not speak the proper language.

Here is the story of my encounter with this hypothesis—the story of
the journey that brings me here. For five years I have been working on
the history of science in the nineteenth century. After some groping
about, I became convinced of the decisive importance, for our predecessors and for us, of the technologies, protocols, and theorems concerning heat—in short, of thermodynamics and related topics. It was
thermodynamics that shook the traditional world and shaped the one in
which we now work. On the other hand, I maintain that the history of
science is not worth an hour's trouble if it does not become as effective as
the sciences themselves. In other words, it offers less interest as an object
or a domain than as a set of operators, a method or strategy working on
formations different from itself. Among these other cultural contents,
one encounters narratives, for example—either literary, historical, or
philosophical. Thus, in the midst of several other undertakings, I attempted to reread the cycle of the *Rougon-Macquart* novels by Emile
Zola.[1] This was an inevitable test since this work presents itself as scientific, and a steam engine circulates therein among hereditary flaws and
murders. The genetic grill, imposed by decision of the author himself,
clarifies the reading of the novels much more than the critical tradition

---

[1] See Michel Serres, *Feux et signaux de brume: Zola* (Paris: Grasset, 1975). —Ed.

grants. Properly generalized, it leads to a thermodynamic grill, more powerful and more efficient still, especially when it is completed by theories concerning processes of transformations, be they chemical or general. However, the filtering of the text by the preceding operators leaves a certain number of irreducible residues.

Now, these residues invariably (I mean for any narrative in the *Rougon-Macquart* cycle) reveal certain series in which the elements of a common set are always combined in whatever order it might be: bridge, well, hotel, labyrinth, prison, and death. The term "combination" does not receive its strict mathematical meaning in this instance, since the criteria of non-omission and non-repetition are not respected: on the contrary, certain vignettes can be repeated and others can disappear. On the other hand, since, in each narrative, games and chance, as well as the pattern of a trajectory circling back upon itself, have a canonical function, I had to conclude that I was in the presence of a *jeu de l'oie*.[2] This game is not reducible to the methods and strategy of the history of science unless one considers that it represents the various stages of an alchemical initiation leading toward the philosopher's stone, and that it is therefore an archaic figure of fire which has lost its original force. The *jeu de l'oie* is local in the sense that one or several games are actually played in each narrative, and it is global for the entire cycle: *Pot-Bouille* is indeed the hotel square, *Germinal* the well square, *Le Rêve,* entirely white, one of the goose's squares, and so forth. At this point we have not gone very far, except perhaps to indicate an exploitation of chance in the genetic protocol or to recognize a pattern in the form of a spiral for the entire cycle that re-emerges indefinitely from itself—hence the name of Pascal, its theoretician. In addition, referring once again to the alchemical tradition, we have discovered that a circulational game is at stake here, that the entire work is a set of circulations within the social body, especially that of the family, of the tree, a circulation that the Preface calls irradiation or a great journey.

Interest is suddenly renewed when one realizes that the aforementioned residual contents, mobilized on the graph of the *jeu de l'oie*, are in fact perfectly recognizable reproductions of common mythical constellations taken from Greco-Latin or Judeo-Christian discourse, or perhaps even from a wider domain, such as the cycle of the festive meal, previously

---

[2] Literally, "goose's game." This game uses a board containing sixty-three squares arranged in a spiral configuration beginning from the outside and moving toward the center (hence the reference in Serres's text to a closed path circling back upon itself). A player throws two dice to advance a token along the squares. When a player lands on certain key squares, he is required to make special moves, for example, on the well square, the bridge square, the hotel square, the prison square, or the goose's square. —Ed.

identified by Georges Dumézil.[3] Example: the character Gervaise in *L'Assommoir* limps. Here is the figure of the hereditary flaw (*tare*), the word *tare* meaning, in the first place, an imbalance. But, in addition, her husband, a roofer, falls from a roof and begins to limp just as she does. Gervaise has fallen to the lower classes, to the Goutte d'Or slum. She is friendly with a blacksmith, Gueule d'Or; she is the mother of Nana, Mouche d'Or, whose career begins when she plays the part of a blond Venus in a Parisian theater. Thus by following the trace of the golden legend, one can reconstitute the whole affair of Vulcan, whose lair is precisely reconstituted on stage. Gervaise limps because of her flaw (*tare*); she is lame because of her fall. Suddenly science falls silent and mythology speaks. And it is mythology that reveals why the lame woman becomes a laundress through an original fault, flaw or fall, filth or crack, that must be washed away or sewn together, that she fails to whiten or to mend: a fault committed at Paradou, in Saccard's winter garden, or in Saint-Mittre field.[4] Henceforth a whole class of lame people is recognizable in the cycle, a class that cannot be explained scientifically except by means of the metaphor of the flaw. Gervaise, then—no, her mythical figure—prepares the festive meal, the cycle of the beverages of immortality perfectly repeated, with the difference that in this case a goose is eaten. And on her wedding day, the procession of wedding guests sets out for the Louvre to behold, as in a theater, the emblems of this festive meal: the *Wedding at Cana*, the transsubstantiation of the water into wine, the *Raft of the Medusa*, the shipwreck, the black marble colossi, the stone statues. On this occasion, the procession becomes lost in the museum, unable to find the way out (the labyrinth), takes shelter from the rain beneath the Pont-Royal (the bridge), observes the walls and roofs of Paris in the depths of a hole (the well), climbs up the Vendôme column by the narrow spiral staircase, stops at the Moulin d'Argent hotel, and, finally, meets the gravedigger, the undertaker clothed entirely in black, who mumbles in his drunken stupor: when you're dead, it's for a long time. A cultivated or barbarous mixture of very old cultural patterns is associated with a circulation the stages of which are the traditional squares of the game. This example that I have chosen for the sake of convenience from the most famous novel,

[3]Georges Dumézil, *Le Festin d'immortalité: Esquisse d'une étude de mythologie comparée indo-européenne* (Paris: Librairie Orientaliste Paul Geuthner, 1924). —Ed.

[4]In Paradou, the edenic garden of Zola's *La Faute de l'abbé Mouret*, Serge Mouret, a Catholic priest who has always lived in the strictest asceticism, experiences physical love with Albine. In Zola's *La Curée*, Saccard's winter garden is a setting for incest between Renée, Saccard's wife, and Maxime, his son. The Saint-Mittre field serves as a meeting place for Sylvère Mouret and Miette in Zola's *La Fortune des Rougon* and is ultimately the site of the cold-blooded murder of Sylvère, which Pierre Rougon permits in order to destroy the republican element in the Rougon family and to profit from the Bonapartist *coup d'état.* —Ed.

L'Assommoir, is only an example, but it is canonical. It is repeated again in the same novel, then is generalized to every novel in the cycle, to become crystallized finally in the general program of the cycle. And thus this global result: once the scientific contents are filtered out, a residue remains in which a circulational game organizes reformulations of mythical material.

We must pose the question of such an association; in other words, how and why, throughout numerous variations of domain and discourse (the myth of Hephaestus, the primal garden and incest, the cycle of the festive meal, the thief, the stone, and death), does there remain an invariant which is the graph of an itinerary? As long as a pattern of invariability through variations is evident, we are left with the fact that the present figure, that of the *jeu de l'oie,* appears weak, very far off the mark with respect to our hope for a hypothesis. Molière and others insist in vain that it is taken from the Greeks: such an assumption is spurious. It is this figure, then, that we must refine.

Let us go back to the game's vignettes or emblems: bridge, well, labyrinth, hotel, prison, and death. For the present we may omit death, which subsequently differs in at least one respect in that it is not an artifact—certainly a very significant difference: death is, but is not, all of that. In short, the series of obstacles in the game's circulation exposes passages, stages, stopovers.

The bridge is a path that connects two banks, or that makes a discontinuity continuous, or that crosses a fracture, or that patches a crack. The space of an itinerary is interrupted by a river; it is not a space of transport. Consequently, there is no longer one space; there are two without common boundaries. They are so different that they require a difficult, or dangerous, operator to connect their boundaries—difficult since at the very least a pontiff is necessary, dangerous since most of the time a devil of some sort stands watch or the enemies of Horatius Cocles stand ready to attack.[5] Communication was interrupted; the bridge re-establishes it vertiginously. The well is a hole in space, a local tear in a spatial variety. It can disconnect a trajectory that passes through, and the traveler falls in, the fall of the vector, but it can also connect spatial varieties that might be piled upon one another: leaves, layers, geological formations. The bridge is paradoxical: it connects the disconnected. The

[5]Horatius Cocles was a legendary Roman soldier who held back the Etruscan army of Porsenna, preventing it from crossing the wooden Sublican bridge before it was demolished. He then jumped into the Tiber and swam to safety. According to some accounts, a wound he received in his leg made him lame (linking him with Gervaise and Vulcan). In addition, the name Cocles is related to Cyclops, "one-eyed" (linking Horatius again to Vulcan and also to Polyphemus, to whom Serres alludes below). -- Ed.

well is more paradoxical still: it disconnects the connected, but it also connects the disconnected. The astronomer falls in (Thales); the truth comes out. The killer dragon lives there, but one draws the water of immortality from there. Mad Aunt Dide throws the key into it, the key to the text, mind you, but the well (*puits*) contains all the seeds; the mine shaft (*puits de la mine*) germinates and it is called *Germinal*.[6] And suddenly, I am speaking with several voices; I can no longer draw the line between narrative, myth, and science. Is this bridge the Königsberg bridge where Euler invented topology, a bridge over the Viorne or the Seine in the *Rougon-Macquart* cycle, or the whole group of bridges revealed in mythical discourses? No, I no longer have the choice, and it is the same bridge. Is this well a hole in Riemannian spatial varieties, a well of potentiality in which, at its lowest ebb, appears the germinating point, as in Thom, or the Plassans well, or Jacob's?[7] No, I no longer have the choice, and it is the same well. In every case, and so much the worse for classification, connection and non-connection are at stake, space is at stake, an itinerary is at stake. And thus the essential thing is no longer this particular figure, this particular symbol, or this particular artifact; the formal invariant is something like a transport, a wandering, a journey across separated spatial varieties. Circumnavigation of Ulysses or of Gilgamesh and topology.

I can begin again and run through the series. I can demonstrate this stable schema with respect to the prison (the enclosed space), or to the hotel (the threshold, relay, or renewal), and, finally, to the labyrinth that is the sum of the emblems: a maze of connection and non-connection, as much closed as it is open, where transport is as much a journey as it is an immobility. All are paradoxical spatial operators indicating that we have given short shrift to space, that we shall never be free of spaces: operators at work in the legendary myths of Crete, in the narratives that we call literature, and in the theory or topology of graphs, games, and networks

---

[6] In Zola's *La Fortune des Rougon*, Aunt Dide (Adélaïde Fouque), the matriarch of the Rougon-Macquart family, throws the key to a door between her property and that of Miette's family into a well located in the wall between the two properties in order to prevent Sylvère and Miette from meeting. Adélaïde had previously used the door to meet her own lover, Macquart, with whom she sired Antoine and Ursule Macquart, thus creating the conflict between the legitimate (Rougon) and illegitimate (Macquart) sides of the family. — Ed.

[7] Born in 1826, the mathematician Georg Riemann was a pioneer in the domains of topology and non-Euclidean geometry, exploring the properties of spaces other than those with three dimensions. The contemporary mathematician René Thom is known for his work on what is commonly called catastrophe theory. See René Thom, *Structural Stability and Morphogenesis: An Outline of a General Theory of Models*, trans. D. H. Fowler (Reading, Mass.: W. A. Benjamin, 1975). For applications of catastrophe theory to linguistics and biology, see René Thom, *Modèles mathématiques de la morphogenèse* (Paris: Union Générale d'Editions, 1974). The Plassans well is the one referred to in note 6 above. For Jacob's well, see Genesis 29:1-28. — Ed.

of transport. Two centuries ago, almost exactly, Kant began his philosophical career by observing a paradoxical property of space. He based an esthetics on an unspoken or unspeakable asymmetry. But his was a twofold mistake: he recognized only one space, whereas one can define a varied, multiple, and increasing number of them; on the other hand, he attempted the foolish project of laying a foundation in the transcendental subject, whereas we can receive everything from language and practical experience.

Hence this temporary result. I have at my disposal operators taken from naive symbols, operators at work upon something unspoken (at least by philosophy), namely, the accidents or catastrophes of space, and at work upon the multiplicity of spatial varieties. What is closed? What is open? What is a connective path? What is a tear? What are the continuous and the discontinuous? What is a threshold, a limit? The elementary program of topology. It is no longer Mother Goose who, stable, recounts all the possible myths or who remains invariable throughout their variations; it is henceforth space or spaces that are the condition of her ancient tales—spaces for which I have the good fortune to possess a new knowledge. And myths are written about them.

Now, in the second *Hermès* I outlined precisely the program of an esthetics, in the wider sense of the term, that would attempt to take into account these multiple proliferations of spaces.[8] My body (I cannot help it) is not plunged into a single, specified space. It works in Euclidean space, but it only works there. It sees in a projective space; it touches, caresses, and feels in a topological space; it suffers in another; hears and communicates in a third; and so forth, as far as one wishes to go. Euclidean space was chosen in our work-oriented cultures because it is the space of work—of the mason, the surveyor, or the architect. Hence the cultural idea of the practical origins of geometry that is a tautology, since the only recognized space is precisely that of work, of transport. My body, therefore, is not plunged into a single space, but into the difficult intersection of this numerous family, into the set of connections and junctions to be established between these varieties. This is not simply given or is not *always already* there, as the saying goes. This intersection, these junctions, always need to be constructed. And in general whoever is unsuccessful in this undertaking is considered sick. His body explodes from the disconnection of spaces. My body lives in as many spaces as the society, the group, or the collectivity have formed: the Euclidean house, the street and its network, the open and closed garden, the church or the enclosed

[8] Michel Serres, *Hermès II: L'Interférence* (Paris: Minuit, 1972), pp. 19-159. Serres is referring to the etymological origin of the word "esthetics" from the Greek *aisthanesthai*, meaning "to perceive." —Ed.

spaces of the sacred, the school and its spatial varieties containing fixed points, and the complex ensemble of flow-charts, those of language, of the factory, of the family, of the political party, and so forth. Consequently, my body is not plunged into one space but into the intersection or the junctions of this multiplicity. Again, whoever fails or refuses to pass like everyone else through the crossroads of these multiple connections—whoever remains in one of these spaces, or, on the contrary, refuses all of them—is treated as ill-adapted or delinquent or disoriented. Such is the case, for example, for whoever remains frozen, hung up, in the family tree, whoever fears leaving a closed paradise between two branches of a river, or whoever wants to tear apart the network which he endures as he would a prison or slavery's iron shackles. This brings us to the beginning. The fact is that in general a culture constructs in and by its history an original intersection between such spatial varieties, a node of very precise and particular connections. This construction, I believe, is that culture's very history. Cultures are differentiated by the form of the set of junctions, its appearance, its place, as well as by its changes of state, its fluctuations. But what they have in common and what constitutes them as such is the operation itself of joining, of connecting. The image of the weaver arises at this point: to link, to tie, to open bridges, pathways, wells, or relays among radically different spaces; to say (*dire*) what takes place between them; to inter-dict (*inter-dire*). The category of *between* is fundamental in topology and for our purposes here: to interdict in the rupture and cracks between varieties completely enclosed upon themselves. "Enclosed" means isolated, closed, separated; it also means untainted, pure, and chaste. Now, that which is not chaste, *incestus,* can be incest. The incest prohibition (*inter-diction*) is, then, literally a local singularity exemplary of this operation in general, of the global project of connecting the disconnected, or the opposite, of opening what is closed, or again the opposite, and so forth. We find ourselves once again in the same domain through this general formal esthetics. Therefore, we must speak about these difficult operations. The identity of a culture is to be read on a map, its identification card: this is the map of its homeomorphisms.

I shall now set forth the announced hypothesis. The most fertile methods today concerning the mythical text in general are regulated by an algebra and, more precisely, by a combinative algebra. There exists to begin with—or, better yet, it is possible to constitute—a set of discrete elements, of units. Out of this reservoir circulate combinative sequences that can be mastered. Hence the theory of musical forms that is certainly the most general available organon, both practical and constructible, for these operations. This algebraic method is, to my mind, a local realization three centuries later of the Leibnizian dream of an alphabet of human thoughts for which its author had forged an *ars combinatoria*—first invention, precisely, of combinative algebra as well as of a logic of the note, of any discrete note. From which Leibniz derived the idea that music was indeed the language closest to the universal language, or to the *mathesis universalis*. This was an idea to which philosophers turned a deaf ear, but which was heard by musicians, since at Johann Sebastian Bach's death, Leibniz's *De Arte Combinatoria* was discovered at the composer's bedside (which, in return, permits us to read several fugues). All this occurred in the midst of the classical age, at a moment when the discourse of rationality was definitively replacing the mythical text. The art has now become a science, a productive and fertile method, the operational realization of a project left in reason's limbo during that period.

Moreover, the same Leibniz, archaic inventor of contemporary algebra and of the theory of structures, was discovering not concurrently but conjointly a discipline that he called *analysis situs* and that we call topology, namely, the sister science of the *ars combinatoria*. We can, therefore, imagine or follow through space and its events a path parallel to the one that was opened in the domain of discrete elements and their combinations. We return to the same point—and this time by way of history.

To work at last. Let us take any discursive chain where space, a space, a singularity of space would appear at a moment, at a link in the series. Then let there be the following decision or choice: either the singularity, for example, is only a discrete unit among others, an -nth term, and we are led down the combinative path, or it is in some way the variable of which the set of the other links constitutes the set of the possible functions. Is this hypothesis interesting? We can really be sure only by putting it to work.

Oedipus wanders and journeys, having set out from the palace of King Polybus to seek counsel from the Delphic oracle. At a crossroads he encounters Laius, his father, and Polyphontes, his father's herald, whom he kills. The crossroads is precisely the sought-for singularity. The roads for Daulis and Thebes meet at Megas; they form the road that rises toward Delphi through the valley. At Megas, the bifurcation. This is a very good point of departure, since in a diagram the example is trivial. There a road passes between two high rocks, as in a crevice or a narrow defile. Crossroads: cross, passage of a road across a ribbon that divides space, passing over a crack. Bridge: connection through the disconnected. To the left, ignorance, blindness, or the unconscious—the unknown and the unsaid. To the right, knowledge, the conscious, the sacred, Delphi and the signifier, the word. Oedipus is driven back from the narrow defile by Laius' team of horses, insulted by Polyphontes. The fact that the murder of the father takes place at this cross, this interrupted, joined edge, this limit or fault, is a catastrophe. Thus the circumstance is the murder and the law is traced upon the ground. To cross the broken threshold of the word. The essential thing is indeed the bifurcation. As soon as the father is involved, once again we come back to the law, a bifurcation traced on the family tree: father, mother, son, here again on the graph is inscribed the triviality of the narrative. To the left the one, to the right the other, and incest, we have already seen, is still another connection upon the disconnected. The text turns inside out like a glove and shows its function: the establishment of separations between spaces and their difficult junction. One can say that Oedipus kills Laius at this place, and miss the place, and thus repress the place of the repressed; or one can say instead that this place is such that Oedipus kills his father there, that it is a point so catastrophic and so confined that he must kill father and mother to go past it. To be the son or to place oneself at the crossroads: two bifurcations and two catastrophes that the myth joins together by its very word. Furthermore, the fact that the son's name is Oedipus repeats the same law. How can one move about in space when one's feet are afflicted? Now, to prevent him from journeying, his parents hang him feet up in the air. Oedipus regains his feet, he sets out for Delphi, the myth regains its feet. This is a discourse that weaves a complex, in the first sense of the term, that connects a network, that traces a graph upon space.

The Sphinx, then, and the same law is repeated. This watchdog of Thebes dies as the result of a solution and lives as a result of solutions of continuity. She keeps close watch on the closed road where Thebans no longer pass, where they are devoured, in pieces. She is a chimera, half-lion and half-woman; half four-legged, also, and half two-legged, and perhaps partly bird. She is a body sewn back together, badly sewn: two parts related by dichotomy, joined in the form of a *chi*, crowned by wings; she is a crossroads, with wings that protrude for one who no longer needs feet. The Sphinx is a bifurcation, and conversely. And the crossroads is a chimera. Thus everything is repeated, enigma and knowledge, on the road to Thebes and the road to Delphi, catastrophe and passage, tear and connection. Oedipus is indeed the last descendant of the Spartoï, of disseminated spaces, of catastrophic separation, of the continuous that must be recovered. Everything is repeated once again when Jocasta recognizes her son by the scar on his feet, a scar in which the lips of a crevice connect. Now, Sophocles gives another version of the recognition scene, and his translation is faithful—Oedipus recognizes himself as a murderer at the moment in the narrative when Jocasta, the mother, mentions the crossroads, the *chi*. It is not I but Sophocles and the son and the mother together who draw the law out of the discourse.

From the beginning of the world protrayed in Plato's *Timaeus*, after reference to the *chōra*, matrix and mother, in which we recognize a topological space, the Same and the Other, separated, are rejoined by the Demiurge in the figure of a *chi*. This figure is formed by the inclination of the ecliptic on the equator; the world is a chimera. The space of the world is described as requiring artful connection.

Now, then, at a certain beginning of a certain story, on the family tree containing ordered paths structured by some ordered relation, incest describes a loop that turns back upon itself toward a previous crossroads and strongly reconnects the spatial complex. I began with a local singularity of space, and I finish with a global law that is invariably written as the connection of what is separated.

From this results the general and simple idea that mythical spaces are chimerical. This is a theorem containing a literal tautology but which uncovers a complicated state. Parts as separate as the Same and the Other are to be joined. Oedipus' itinerary crosses spatial accidents, bifurcations, catastrophes, and loops. Oedipus' discourse (*discours*) is identical to this itinerary (*parcours*). It poses *chi*'s on cracks, crossroads between spatial varieties that do not have common boundaries. This in turn presupposes that before it, in other words, before discourse, there existed a multiplicity of unrelated spaces: chaos.

It would be necessary to demonstrate the generality of the hypothesis. The theme of the Odysseus cycle is not space, this discrete unit rediscovered indefinitely or by repetitions along its discursive sequence. The plurality of disjointed spaces, all different, is the primal chaos, the condition of the series that assembles them. Ulysses' journey, like that of Oedipus, is an itinerary. And it is a discourse, the prefix of which I can now understand. It is not at all the discourse (*discours*) of an itinerary (*parcours*), but, radically, the itinerary (*parcours*) of a discourse (*discours*), the course, *cursus,* route, path that passes through the original disjunction, the bridge laid down across crevices. And the separation is of an impregnable rigor. All the spaces encountered are perfectly defined, without waver or blur. It is impossible to connect them among themselves. They cannot be composed to form a single homogeneous space. They combine such categories as open and closed, exterior and interior, boundary and limit, vicinity and adherence, and so forth, all concepts characteristic of the numerous spaces of topology. Hence comes everything one might desire in the text: inaccessible islands, and countries from which one cannot escape; the beach upon which the catastrophe casts you; the breaking of the waves; the shores from which one is hurled as one approaches. The intrusion of a wooden horse into the heart of the enclosed citadel, where the warriors are at the same time inside the city but outside it by being inside the closed compartment that is inside the closed citadel. The exit of a ram, this bridge, out of an enclosed cavern in which a dangerous fire burns; ram, horse anew, with the difference that the space of touch full of voids is more important here than optical or visual space.[9] Hence the blindness of the Cyclops, in order to demonstrate that a closed system is not the same for the clairvoyant and for one who is reduced to his sense of touch. Likewise, the attractive passage by the Sirens' shore where a vicinity, an adherence, is skirted, open for the deaf and closed for every listener. Original spaces proliferate on the map of the journey, perfectly disseminated, or literally sporadic, each one rigorously determined. The global wandering, the mythical adventure, is, in the end, only the general joining of these spaces, as if the object or target of discourse were only to connect, or as if the junction, the relation, constituted the route by which the first discourse passes. *Mythos*, first *logos;* transport, first relation; junction, condition of transport. Thus we have Penelope at the theoretical position: the queen who weaves and unweaves, the originally feminine figure who, become male, will be Plato's Royal Weaver. As Descartes says in Rule X, a tapestry intermingles threads with infinitely varied nuances.[10] Infinitely: the rational and the irrational. Descartes says this of a barbarous mathematics. Here we are once again. Barbarous or feminine, the logos is present, but still at the level of the hands. They connect. Penelope is the author, the signatory of the discourse; she traces its graph, she draws its itinerary. She makes and undoes this cloth that mimes the progress and delays of the navigator, of Ulysses on board his ship, the shuttle that weaves and interweaves fibers separated by the void, spatial varieties bordered by crevices. She is the embroideress, the lace-maker, by wells and bridges, of this continuous flux interrupted by catastrophes that is called discourse. In the palace of Ithaca, Ulysses, finally in the arms of the queen, finds the finished theory of his own *mythos.* The heroine of *La Débâcle,* on the contrary, finds along her catastrophic route the weaver whose loom has just burned.[11]

I still do not know whether the hypothesis is general. We would have to reread everything, to follow Theseus, for example, after the end of the first two journeys. In Crete the maze is too obvious a confirmation. Moreover, it was my original starting point, or almost, through the

[9]The reader will recall that Ulysses and his men escaped from Polyphemus' cave by clinging to the bellies of the blinded Cyclops' rams. See note 5 above. —Ed.
[10]René Descartes, *Rules for the Direction of the Mind,* in *The Philosophical Works of Descartes,* 2 vols., trans. Elizabeth Haldane and G.R.T. Ross (Cambridge: Cambridge University Press, 1975), 1:31. —Ed.
[11]The reference is to an incident in Zola's *La Débâcle.* In the midst of the Battle of Sedan between the French and the Prussians (1870), Henriette Weiss leaves Sedan to rejoin her husband in the nearby village of Bazeilles. During her dangerous trip through the battle area, she encounters Delaherche, a textile manufacturer who is a friend of her husband's. He informs Henriette that the Prussians have overrun Bazeilles and are sacking the village—thus destroying one of the manufacturing establishments belonging to Delaherche. For the resonances of the word "catastrophic," see note 7 above. —Ed.

analysis of the children's game. But there is also the ring, the ring thrown into the sea that opens Poseidon's domains for the hero: a descent into hell beneath the waters. The ring introduces at least three changes of space: this mythical ring rediscovered in history with Polycarp and in moral allegory with Plato's Gyges. From fortune to misfortune, or from the visible to the invisible. Who does not know henceforth that a torus does not have the same spatial and topological characteristics, the same invariabl s, as a trivial object of ordinary space? It introduces, then, a different space incomparable to and not connected with the one we believe to be our own. Consequently, an entire program takes shape. It would be necessary to draw graphs of itineraries, to define as closely as possible the spaces at stake, to examine nodes, caducei, wheels, arborescences, a whole set òf spatial tools, the technology of this discourse and its special morphologies. They are no longer simply elements; they are like the tables of the law. They are operators expressing the operation of mythical discourse itself, which, from its origin, has as its function the linking of spaces among themselves, the linking, for example, of separate ecological niches, each one defended tooth and nail. No one leaves here and no one enters—except those who speak geometry, the discourse that has communication as its goal. Myth attempts to transform a chaos of separate spatial varieties into a space of communication, to re-link ecological clefts or to link them for the first time: from the mute animal to the proto-speaker. At the theoretical position *in universo* is she who conditions and who prepares the work of the weaver herself, she who produces and who gives the thread: Ariadne.

This can be general. All of Greece about which I am speaking is Dichotomy, Polytomy: Zeno's paradox, the Platonic classificatory trees, the division of segments by relations and proportions in the Euclidean manner, logos and analogy, the sharing of riches on Aristotle's scale, to each his part, his destined part. . . . This unitary discourse through distinctions and partitions, this discourse of the beginnings of mathematics, miraculously established, flows back toward its Pythagorean origin where the speakable, namely, the rational, is the split whole that we call fractions, the set of numbers that are the very things themselves. Here the method, road, path, track propose and set forth medians: the middle term between two terms. The completion of an interval is a problem that has not varied from the dawn of time up to Cantor. Let this bridge be lost and the endless nature of the path or the inaccessibility of the opposite shore be discovered, and we have the crisis, the shipwreck of Hippasus of Metapontum, he who can no longer cross the sea. No one can speak any longer, and we have the irrational or the unspeakable—the incommunicable, to be very precise. In fact, we have the return to the state of things before the establishment of rational discourse, the time when spaces were poorly joined, when transport and itinerary were only myth. The sect is dissolved when faced with the infinitely divisible—until the atomism of Democrites. Hippasus is shipwrecked like Ulysses, both of Metapontum (*meta-pons*, "metabridge"). Pythagoreanism had turned its back upon barbarous topology; it founders once again in myth with the discovery of the topology of real numbers. It had established a space of mediations, of communication, and it dies from losing it. All this was rational, discursive, and speakable, all this was mathematical and logical, but in the closest vicinity to the sources, to the possibility of speaking to one another. The Greek cities were dispersed, reciprocally closed insularities, islands separated like the Sporades, in which every man worthy of the name, in other words, measure of all things, was inside, while on the exterior of this political space animals, barbarians with growling languages, circulated in a chaotic multiplicity of sociopolitical spaces: the world before its formation, the practical world before the emergence of scientific knowledge. This logos was first myth, in order to succeed in creating at least one *koinē*.[12] All the principles of the Greek cities go beyond this arm of the sea, before Troy, in order to found a language of communication—that the gods first make possible. The gods are encountered as the same—here, everywhere—because in their other space they enjoy a single space. It is essential that one no longer know where Dionysus was born, where Oedipus and Theseus died. Anywhere: this is far preferable. Thus, in this discourse, chaos begins again: scattered members, the diasparagmos, the bones of Mother Earth, the first family of Spartoï, dissemination in space, or, rather, dissemination of morphologies themselves. Whereupon the first problem: to find the single space or the set of operators by which these spatial varieties in impractical, inconceivable vicinity will be joined together. To open the route, way, track, path in this incoherent chaos, this tattered cloud, whose dichotomic thicket is reformulated in the common space of transport when it is reconstructed. To find the relation, the logos of analogy, the chain of mediations, the common measure, the asses' bridge; to find the equilibrium or the *clinamen*.[13] Second answers, second words, where

<hr/>

[12] *Koinē* was originally "the Greek language commonly spoken and written by the Greek-speaking population of eastern Mediterranean countries in the Hellenistic and Roman periods." By extension, it can mean "a language of a region, country, or people that has become the common or standard language of a larger area and of other peoples" (Webster's). —Ed.

[13] The *clinamen* is an essential concept in Serres's interpretation of Lucretius's *De Rerum Natura*. It is "the minimum angle to the laminar flow [that] initiates a turbulence" (Serres, "Lucretius: Science and Religion," p. 99 of the present volume). The *clinamen* marks the moment when an atom in laminar flow deviates from its path, collides with another atom, and initiates the formation of things and ultimately of worlds. Serres argues against commentators who maintain that the *clinamen* is a concept introduced arbitrarily by Lucretius to

measure and correct measure presuppose a homogeneous space which is posited as reference and which is the answer to the first question asked: the unitary space of possible transports or of *always* possible transfers. And thus one must find first, find conditionally, a word, a logos, that has already worked to connect the crevices which run across the spatial chaos of disconnected varieties. One must find the Weaver, the proto-worker of space, the prosopopeia of topology and nodes, the Weaver who works locally to join two worlds that are separated, according to the autochton's myth, by a sudden stoppage, the metastrophic caesura amassing deaths and shipwrecks: the catastrophe. He works, according to Plato, in a discourse where rational dichotomy and the myth of the two space-times, common measure and the Weaver, all converge. He untangles, interlaces, twists, assembles, passes above and below, rejoins the rational, the irrational, namely, the speakable and the unspeakable, communication and the incommunicable. He is a worker of the single space, the space of measure and transport, the Euclidean space of every possible displacement without change of state, royally substituted one fine day in place of the proliferating multiplicities of unlinked morphologies. In order to practice dichotomy and its connected paths, one must know that its clefts follow and overlap the ancient mythical narrative in which worlds are torn asunder by a catastrophe—and only the Weaver knows how to link them again or can reunite them. Then and only then geometry is born and myth falls silent. Then the logos or relation unfolds, the chains and networks on the smooth space of transport, which itself alone replaces the discourse (*discours*) of itineraries (*parcours*). Linked homogeneity erases catastrophes, and congruent identity forgets difficult homeomorphisms. Reason, as the saying goes, has triumphed over myth. No, it is Euclidean space that has *repressed* a barbarous topology, it is transport and displacement without obstacles that have suddenly taken the place of the journey, the ancient journey from islands to catastrophes, from passage to fault, from bridge to well, from relay to labyrinth. Myth is effaced in its original function, and the new space is universal, as is reason or the *ratio* that it sustains, only because within it there are no more encounters. As Plato says, one can walk there on two or four legs, follow the diagonal, freely choose the longest or shortest road, route, ode, or period, and so on, as much as one wishes. The earth is measured (geo-metry) by means of just

---

explain the beginning of the world. On the contrary, physics has shown that any laminar flow sooner or later produces a pocket of turbulence which fundamentally alters the original flow. Thus Lucretius' treatise is in suprising ways a true treatise on physics. See "Lucretius: Science and Religion," chapter 9 of the present volume. See also Michel Serres, *La Naissance de la physique dans le texte de Lucrèce: Fleuves et turbulences* (Paris: Minuit, 1977). —Ed.

measure (the King). The multiplicity, the dangerous flock of chaotic morphologies, is subdued. Thus the *Statesman* is written.

Hence the two great vicissitudes of the nineteenth century. Beneath the apparent unity of Euclidean space, mathematics, turning back toward its origins, rediscovers the teeming multiplicity of diverse and original spaces—and topology emerges as a science. We have not finished nor shall we ever again finish dealing with spaces. At the same moment, in an aged Europe asleep beneath the mantle of reason and measure, mythology reappears as an authentic discourse. The coupling of these rediscoveries becomes clear: Euler's bridge and the vessels' bridge across the Hellespont during the storm, Listing's or Maxwell's complex and the Cretan maze.[14] Let us not forget that Leibniz, proto-inventor of the new science, said in time and against his time that one should listen to old wives' tales.

[14] Leonhard Euler (1707-1783), the Swiss mathematician, proved in 1736 that it was impossible to cross the seven bridges of Königsberg in a continuous walk without recrossing any of them. This proof was one of the early contributions to the development of topology. The vessels' bridge refers to an incident recounted in Herodotus' *Histories* (7:34-37). Xerxes' army crossed the narrow strait of the Hellespont into Greece using a bridge constructed of ships lashed together side by side. The first attempt to construct the bridge was a failure when a storm tore the ships apart. The second attempt succeeded. The German mathematician Johann Listing published various works on what was earlier called the geometry of position and what we now call topology. James Clerk Maxwell (1831-1879) used Listing's work (notably *Der Census Räumlicher Complexe*) in his *Treatise on Electricity and Magnetism* in order to devise methods for describing the behavior of lines of force in an electrical field. The Cretan maze refers, of course, to the labyrinth which contained the Minotaur and which was solved by Theseus with the help of Ariadne's thread. — Ed.

5

▲
▲▲

Turner
Translates Carnot

In 1784, George Garrard, who was then twenty-four years old, executed something like an advertising sign showing the warehouse of the brewer Samuel Whitbread. The collection of objects put on display is the *recapitulation* of a perfect world soon to disappear: men, horses, tools, ships. A wooden shed stands on the dock where a three-master with furled sails has just tied up and is being unloaded: flawless timber framework, tie-beams, lintels, and rafters which overhang and cover the scene. This is a world of work and of commerce: to the left, among the chests or the trunks (of gold?), the owner converses with a client; his workers, who are not very numerous, bustle about. Obviously, it is the equipment that is supposed to stand out. Whence the recapitulation. For the study of mechanics, work is a force in motion. What are the origins, the sources, of this force? There are four of them and only four: horses, and here they are, two in profile and one full face, harnessed in all the trappings of the times; men, and here they are, one of them perched on the wagon leans over to lift up a sack; wind, and here are the ships, hawsers tied to the mooring posts, sails at rest, rigging free and in place, ropes, ratlines, sheaves, grommets, scores, chocks, rolling gear for mooring, shackles, pulley-blocks, and gantlines. Nothing is missing from the balance sheet, not even the ton sling and its strop. A real treat for the sailor. Water, finally, and here is the Thames and an immense, dark paddlewheel on the left side of the painting. The producers of force: men, horses, wind, and water. The horse is first; it is valorized, clarified, magnified, magnificent. To apply the force: collars, harnesses, axles, anchorages, masts, shrouds, and more. To transmit it: pulleys and tackle, wheels, gears, and chains. These are simple machines. In front, to the right, one can see an immense scale in its most unbalanced position: one heavily loaded tray on the ground and the counterweight on the raised side of the arm to the left. All the weight is on the side of the owner, and on the other side, the side of the workers, even the tray is missing. To carry things: a wagon for the horse shown in full face, a cask on a sliding strut at the bottom right, and boats. One of the boats with oars, shown in profile, is being rowed by a group of men. To lift: derricks, an archaic crane with a jib, and, once again, pulleys, slings, winches, levers, ropes, and weights. The collection of sources of force and of instruments for leverage, for packing, and for transporting (equipped with their transmission mechanisms) is exhaustive.

At stake here is a tableau, in the sense of "tabulation." The point is to lay out the set of tools and to omit nothing, to tabulate all the products of mechanics, static and dynamic: from the framework to the derricks, from the wheel to the sail. All this makes a world, a world that is drawn, drawable. It is a world in which chains trace motion (the ropes and hawsers) and in which arms and masts trace rest (the truss and the axles). Lines, points, circles—geometry. The cask is a volume, as with Sarrus; the trunk is a parallelepiped; the sling load of Oriental fabrics is unpacked, assessed, unwrapped. This is geometry, the diagram of mechanical forms, the applied geometry of our relation to the world, the geometry of work. The tools are dominated by form, produced by it. Thus line dominates color. The colors are blond, gilded, soft, inward, and somber. Only a scarlet waistcoat stands out at the left: the owner's waistcoat. The drawing is a graph of the tools and of those who use them. Line and geometry dominate color and matter. Garrard says something important here: he says, in and by means of the art of drawing, exactly what Lagrange says by expressly denying himself any possible drawing. *Analytical Mechanics* appeared in 1788, contemporary with Garrard's painting. It contains a Statics, the theory of rest, and a Dynamics, the theory of motion. And the book's introduction, with its pulleys and tackle, describes the tableau of the painter. It *recapitulates,* by its story and in its system, a perfect world that will soon disappear, totally overthrown when fire and its power supplant wind and water, horses and men, as source and origin of force. Lagrange says that the set of objects seen by Garrard at the warehouse of Samuel Whitbread must be a given at the outset: levers, scales, winches, hoisting derricks, pulleys, ropes, weights, tackle. He says that in such a world geometry alone holds sway. Thus, what the painter draws Lagrange deduces abstractly from a single principle, that of virtual velocities—but it is the same world.[1] It is the same objective world and the same understanding of it by means of geometric reasoning. There are

---

[1] Virtual velocity is the velocity "that a body in equilibrium would receive if the equilibrium were upset. In other words, it is the velocity that would actually be imparted to the body in the first instant of its movement. The principle involved here consists of the fact that forces are in equilibrium when they are inversely related to their virtual velocities, which are calculated according to the directions of these forces" (Joseph Louis Lagrange, *Mécanique analytique* [Paris: Mallet-Bachelier, 1853], pp. 17-18). The concept of virtual velocity is a cornerstone of the geometric treatment of statics in classical mechanics. —Ed.

no horses, no men, no water, and no wind for the geometer, but rather forces in general. These forces, however, still refer, in fact, to wind, water, men, and horses. His discourse designates the simple or complex networks traced by the machines. Garrard shows what Lagrange deduces—and at the same moment.

That moment is at the end. One always recapitulates when a certain history comes to a close, perfect and in its death throes. This history is so old, so old that Jupiter (the church steeple) and Mars (Nelson's column?) still tower over the warehouse of Quirinus. In front, in the foreground, is the watchdog. But the forest of masts in the distance, more numerous than these two spires, is also going to fall. What is the Industrial Revolution? A revolution operating on *matter*. It takes place at the very sources of dynamics, at the origins of force. One takes force as it is or one produces it. Descartes and Newton, crowned by Lagrange, chose the first alternative: force is there, given by the biotope, the wind, the sea, and gravity. It is beyond our control except insofar as men and horses are subject to it, but it is not under our dominion when it is a question of heavy bodies, of air, and of water. With it one produces motion, work, by using tools—those mentioned earlier. The mediating function of the tools is inscribed in their form, their lines, their geometry: Garrard's form, Lagrange's formal demonstrations. Then a sudden change is imposed on the raw elements: fire replaces air and water in order to transform the earth. Fire will consume *Analytical Mechanics* and burn down Samuel Whitbread's warehouse. It will destroy the wooden shed, the wooden ships. Fire finishes off the horses, strikes them down. The source, the origin, of force is in this flash of lightning, this ignition. Its energy exceeds form; it transforms. Geometry disintegrates, lines are erased; matter, ablaze, explodes; the former color—soft, light, golden—is now dashed with bright hues. The horses, now dead, pass over the ship's bridge in a cloud of horsepower. The brig-schooner is in dry dock, disarmed: the new ship, which wins the big prize, is called the *Durande*. Here comes Turner.

From Garrard to Turner, the path is very simple. It is the same path that runs from Lagrange to Carnot, from simple machines to steam engines, from mechanics to thermodynamics—by way of the Industrial Revolution. Wind and water were tamed in diagrams. One simply needed to know geometry or to know how to draw. Matter was dominated by form. With fire, everything changes, even water and wind. Look at *The Forge*, painted by Joseph Wright in 1772. Water, the paddlewheel, the hammer, weights, strictly and geometrically drawn, still triumph over the ingot in fusion. But the time approaches when victory changes camps. Turner no longer looks from the outside; *he enters into Wright's ingot,* he enters into the boiler, the furnace, the firebox. He sees matter transformed by fire. This is the new matter of the world at work, where geometry is limited. Everything is overturned. Matter and color triumph over line, geometry, and form. No, Turner is not a pre-impressionist. He is a realist, a proper realist. He makes one see matter in 1844, as Garrard made one see forms and forces in 1784. And he is the first to see it, the very first. No one had really perceived it before, neither scientist nor philosopher, and Carnot had not yet been read. Who understood it? Those who worked with fire and Turner—Turner or the introduction of fiery matter into culture. The first true genius in thermodynamics.

The era of the wooden ship is dead. The *Fighting Téméraire* is tugged to her last berth to be broken up. Contrary to what the history of glorious events recounts, the true battle did not take place at Trafalgar. The old ship of the line did not die from its victory; it was assassinated by its tugboat. Look at the prow, the beam, the sheer—the framework and the geometry; look at the masts and the superstructures of this gray phantom. It is the warehouse of Samuel Whitbread, it is the primary group of Lagrange's objects—the forms, lines, points, straight lines, angles, circles, networks, the mechanics realized from wind, men, and water. The victor who tows it to its torture sits low in the water, is deprived of this lofty form. It is red and black, and spits fire. Behind it, the white, cold sails of the funeral procession are winding sheets. The sun goes down on the black moorings of the final resting place. The new fire is master of the sea and of the wind; it defies the sun. And here is the true Trafalgar, the true battle, the true clash: the immense division of the heavens and the sea into two zones. One of them is red, yellow, and orange, where the hot colors shout, ignited, burning; the other is violet, blue, green, and sea-green, where the cold and icy hues freeze. Within its own matter, the entire world becomes a steam engine between Carnot's two sources: the cold and the hot. Seawater in the boiler tank. Yes, Turner entered *into* the boiler. The 1838 painting is *inside* the tugboat.

Hugo called it the *Durande,* hardly a proper name for this heavy, clumsy galliot with its long black smokestack that traverses Turner's waters. Here it is not named. The geometrically drawn ship with timber and sail has a name, a proper noun. The dirty, ill-defined, servile steamer is only a common noun. It is a sign, a signal, a caption by which one recognizes what must be read, seen, and understood. It carries inside itself a conflagration that it both masters and envelops and from which it draws its force. It carries inside itself fire, air, and water. It is the material microcosm, the model of the world. Look at Turner's *The Burning of the Houses of Parliament* of 1835. At the bottom right, the *Durande* tows a barge almost in place of the signature. And once again the world is its image, its reproduction, in a precise sense. Turner sees the world in terms of water and fire, as Garrard saw it in terms of figures and motion.

Believe me, a ship is always a perfect summary of notions of space and time—of space, of time, of work, as they are at the time—of history. Thus London and the Thames, as well as the steam engine. The conflagration divides the cold canvas in two: half is in the atmosphere and half is reflected in the water. An axis of roaring fire is projected onto a green mass. On the balance sheet: furnace, water, hot and cold, matter in fusion, line abandoned in favor of random matter, without definition, statistically grouped in parcels. On the one hand clouds of ice, on the other clouds of incandescence. Carnot, almost Maxwell, *almost Boltzmann.*[2] Turner understood and revealed the new world, the new matter. *The perception of the stochastic replaces the art of drawing the form.*

Matter is no longer left in the prison of diagram. Fire dissolves it, makes it vibrate, tremble, oscillate, makes it explode into *clouds.* From Garrard to Turner, or from the fibrous network to the hazardous cloud. No one can draw the edge of a cloud, the borderline of the aleatory where particles waver and melt, at least to our eyes. There a new time is being fired in the oven. On these totally new edges, which geometry and the art of drawing have abandoned, a new world will soon discover dissolution, atomic and molecular dissemination. The boiler's fire atomizes matter and gives it over to chance, which has always been its master. Boltzmann will soon understand it, but Turner, in his own domain, understood it before him. Turner enters full force into the swarming cage of Maxwell's demons. Garrard tarried in Poinsot's motion. Turner gives himself over to brownian motion.[3] He passes from the rationalized real, from the abstract or mathematical real, to the burgeoning real that radiates from the furnace where edges collapse. And, again, color-matter triumphs over drawing with geometric edges. There is still another *Durande* in *Staffa, Fingal's Cave* of 1832, another reproduction, an

---

[2] For Carnot, see chapter 3, note 3. James Clerk Maxwell (1831-1879) was a pioneer in the use of statistical methods in treating the stochastic behavior of molecules. Whereas Maxwell used statistical methods as tools suitable for studying particular problems, for Ludwig Boltzmann (1844-1906), statistical analysis and the theory of probability came to be seen more as rules for the logic of the whole world. The behavior of individual particles or units is of no interest; what is important is the statistical law that governs large populations. The statistical mechanics of Boltzmann introduces contingency into the heart of nature. Strict causality in natural events is replaced by probability verified within certain well-defined limits. Maxwell and Boltzmann thus both worked at devising ways of treating the stochastic. —Ed.

[3] In his treatise *Théorie nouvelle de la rotation des corps* (1834), Louis Poinsot worked out an elegant representation of rotary motion by the rolling of the ellipsoid of inertia of a body on a fixed plane; this motion came to be known as Poinsot's motion. Robert Brown (1773-1858) is known for his observation of the continuous motion of minute part les suspended in fluid, which is the result of their bombardment by molecules in like continuous motion. Serres uses these two references to emphasize again the contrast between geometry and the stochastic oscillation of particles. —Ed.

enlarged model of his steam engine. Supposing that I were mistaken, how would you explain the double source of light, so paradoxical at first sight, which divides the cloudy masses in two, with the steam galliot resting between the two? Are there two suns in the Hebrides? Ossian or Mendelssohn would have noticed them. No, it is Carnot who speaks; the Scottish *Durande* says it: doesn't its smoke move from the hot sun to the cold cavern, from one cloudy bundle to another? And how would you explain the microscopic red spot on the quarter of the black ship? The microcosmic *Durande* wears a sun; at twilight the entire world functions on two sources. The cosmos is a steam engine, and inversely. An analogous division of the heavens, a snowstorm in the sunlight, a high, yellow mark towering above some foul murder which occurs during the crossing of the Alps by Hannibal's army. The same division of the scene when the keelmen heave in coals by moonlight. The conflagration reddens, flames, and roars among the topsails, the rigging, the spars, in the corner which is the locus of a greenish-yellow mass. Wooden ships are truly dead. They are burning. Strictly speaking, they are only wrecks. There are two canvases, here at least, where wrecks float in a raging sea. A monster. Read Lucretius and see how the shipwreck, the aplustria scattered in the surf, and the convulsive waves are the obsessive metaphors of dissolution, of mingling, of exhaustion, for a poet who himself had also entered full force into swarming matter. The image, perhaps, of the second principle of thermodynamics. Its archaic, musing, intuited form. At sea, motion is not perpetual; it dissipates, and the sea absorbs its disintegrated details. Yes, one can die from the sea and from the wind; one can die also from the ice floes where the brig is trapped. Two methods exist for freeing oneself: by hauling oneself out using a fixed point, with boathooks, grappling hooks, and heaving at the capstan; clearly, the static technique has failed. One is left with the option of using fire, of burning whale blubber. Fire delivers one from the ice. A new steam engine triumphs here over inertia, over forced immobility. The whole painting is again divided into two cloudy masses: red incandescence and blue-green cold. The ice field is not white; the sun is almost erased. The world disappears; it is man's work that requires the two sources, red fire and green cold. Hope and death.

Fire, the new history, passes like a thunderclap over the green water where a boat rocks.[4] *The Human Beast* and *The Steam House* already existed as early as 1844, well before Jules Verne and Zola.[5] Here, however,

---

[4] The reference is to Turner's *Rain, Steam and Speed: The Great Western Railway*, exhibited in 1844. —Ed.

[5] Railroads are of central importance in both Emile Zola's *The Human Beast* (1890) and Jules Verne's *The Steam House* (1880). —Ed.

there is no relation to man, whether it be one of death or one of optimistic confidence. The fusion of work in the real world. Always the object, always matter. A red, rectilinear axis slants off toward the right and pierces a cold, gray, bluish, sometimes yellowish mass. The material cloud with its aleatory edges becomes a squall, and the water in the tank, driving rain. For a moment the engine dissolves into the world that resembles it; it passes like a scourge of time. Man has constructed a thing-nature. The painter makes one see the entrails of this thing: stochastic bundles, dualism of sources, winking fires, its material entrails, which are the very womb of the world, sun, rain, ice, clouds, and showers. Heaven, sea, earth, and thunder are the interior of a boiler which bakes the material of the world. At random.

Turner changed ships. Whalers themselves light fires among the swans (Melville). Look how he changes studios. As early as 1797 (the date is important) he paints in watercolors, not warehouses à la Garrard, not forges à la Wright, but a foundry.[6] Slowly reascending the chain of material transformations: wood, iron, hammering, fusion. Heading toward the liquid ingot, heading for the furnace. Before the geometrized solid, before the cold form, was the liquid; before the liquid was the gas, the cloud. Hotter and hotter, less and less confined by a boundary. Transition: in 1774, Wright executes in gouache an infernally red *Eruption of Vesuvius* that Turner will soon copy. Volcano, the forges of Vulcan, the foundry of the world (Verne). From human work to cosmic forces the sequence is correct. With Fourier it will be evident that a storm functions like an engine and, with others, that sun and ice are the two sources of the natural motor. But let us return to wood and to ship-builders. In Samuel Whitbread's warehouse the truss is flawless, drawn to perfection. Geometry has left its mark there, as has the static plane of the division of forces. Calm, serene, secure shelter. Yes, a haven. The framework that covers Wright's forge already has gaps, reinforcement rings (iron aids wood that weakens when touched by fire). The ax has left its mark there; the rafters are not in finished form. An enormous tie-beam, twisted braces, a king-post that does not appear to be square. Statics by approximation. The tree more than the beam. As if the blacksmith, arms crossed, with his biceps of steel, were scorning the carpenter of yesteryear, ready to replace him. He knows full well that he will make hulls, masts, ropes, and trusses. Thus we have the rickety roof at Turner's foundry. Everything about the roof is badly squared, the height of disorder. The cut of

---

[6]The reference is to an early watercolor by Turner entitled *An Iron Foundry*, painted in 1797. Unfortunately, the only readily accessible reproduction of the painting is in black and white in John Gage, *Turner: Rain, Steam and Speed* (New York: The Viking Press, 1972), p. 36. —Ed.

tie-beams is never even, the vertical line has been lost, as if the plumb line had melted in front of the furnace. The truss is askew, the jumble of the rafters defies equilibrium. The timber framework is dead. Statics is dead. Mechanics, geometry, the art of drawing vanish before the fire. Three stages of the roof mark the Industrial Revolution, mark the old-fashioned and the new attitude toward old wood, our old pro-tector. Under it, in it, the new matter is born. The nut destroys its shell.

There was no furnace in the inferno of Wright's forge. With Turner the furnace appears as the new model of the world. The ingot is right there in the center, handled by three men, luminous as a hole in the middle of a gray-brown-black mass, flaming in a white stroke of gouache. There are, however, two centers: to the right the opening of the furnace gleams softly, the black radiance, a new sun. One forgets the third, the window in the background. Thus one can have whatever one wants: red and black, the two sources, the wavering of the cloudy silhouettes. Disorder is everywhere, and especially in the back of the shop, where other trails of white gouache accentuate the jumble. Theorem: beneath the forms of matter, stochastic disorder reigns supreme. To smelt is to rediscover chance as fundamental. The furnace is the engine for going back toward chaos. The foundry is where creation starts over at zero. History is recast beginning with primitive matter. But watch out! With Garrard you remember how strict the order of society was. In front was the watchdog, behind, the two church steeples of Jupiter and the martial column. Horses, sailors, and men were forbidden to leave the picture. At the bottom left of Turner's watercolor, a new monster, a new watchdog, is crouched: an enormous, black, terrible piece of artillery. It is a product, the product of the furnace, the cold product of fusion. This is not a new history that starts over at zero; it is the same one. Muzzle of the dog, muzzle of the furnace, muzzle of the cannon—the latter ready to rake the scene with fire, to block the exit of the workshops. The men are for-bidden to leave the picture. The new society resumes a strict order. They believed they were re-creating the world; death recaptured it. Not death swinging from the yardarms and from the gallows of Lagrange, but a lightning death from cannon fire. The scientific Carnot is the son of the military Carnot.[7]

Garrard paints an exhibition, a dense tabulation, plane by plane, from the foreground to the background. Wright exhibits as well. The forge is still a theater, and the painting could have served as an advertising sign. A work scene, the workers seen from behind, nothing is left to chance; a

---

[7] For Sadi Carnot, see chapter 3, note 3. Carnot's father, Lazare Carnot, was a mathema-tician, but he is also known as the great organizer of French military victories during the wars of the French Revolution. —Ed.

family scene, where all are seen full face, except the wife—no, nothing is left to chance. The brawny master is glorified; the watchdog is always there. There is no longer any representation in Turner's foundry. The painting is a furnace, the very furnace itself. It is a disordered black mass centered on the lighted hearths. We pass from geometry to matter or from representation to work. By going back to the sources of matter, the painter has broken the stranglehold of copying in the arts. No more discourses, no more scenes, no more sculptures with clean, cold edges: the object directly. Without theoretical detours. Yes, we enter into incandescence. At random.

The balance sheet is easy to draw up. Tools: locomotive, steamships, furnace, foundry. Fire: conflagration, sun, the trapped ship where whale blubber burns. Ice: Chamonix, glacier, whaler prisoner of the ice field (brash ice and swans). The two sources: the major division of the spectrum into two zones, one with red dominating, the other with blue; the source of heat, the source of cold. The waterfall is a model of energy for Carnot: that of *Reichenbach,* for example.[8] Matter: it is in movement, it forms into aleatory clouds, the stochastic is essential, the border disappears and opens up a new time. The instant is not statically immobilized, fixed like a mast; it is an unforeseen state, hazardous, suspended, drowned, melted in duration, dissolved. Never will it come back again. Like the Indian mail boat at the edge of the Thames, it is irreversible. The balance sheet of the science of fire, of the practical applications of fire, of the world of fire, of matter on fire, is as near to being exhaustive as was that of the world of figures and of motion at Samuel Whitbread's warehouse of mechanics.

Within a half-century, England knew two worlds. And her painters said it better than anyone else. On the continent, the Academy persisted—history and mythology, bloody and cold, ignorant of work and of science. It is true that our neighbors also had the Pre-Raphaelite boy scouts.

Fire. The other, the same. Turner painted only cosmic copulations, so obviously that no one saw them: the love-making of fire and water, materially *drawn* with precision. Turner or the old-style riddles: *cherchez la femme.* When the sun rises, who does not like to navigate between two promontories?

---

[8]The reference is to Turner's *The Upper Falls of Reichenbach,* completed in 1818. —Ed.

II

PHILOSOPHY & SCIENCE

6

Platonic Dialogue

The logicians' extended discussion of the notion of symbol is well known.[1] Without entering into the detail of the arguments that separate the Hilbertian realists, the nominalists following Quine, those who subscribe to the Polish school, and so on, I shall take up a fragment of the issue here, while giving it a new twist.

When I want to communicate with another person, I have at hand a number of old and new methods: languages, systems of writing, means of storing, of transmitting, or of multiplying the message—tapes, telephone, printing press, and so on.[2] It is not important for our present purposes to determine whether they are natural or synthetic. Writing is one of the simplest methods and, at the same time, one of the richest, since I can store, transmit, and multiply information with it. But before entering into these problems, as well as those of style, of the disposition of the narrative, of argumentation, and so on, there is first the physical appearance of the writing, its graphic form: writing is first and foremost a drawing, an ideogram, or a conventional graph. For the moment, let us agree that written communication is only possible between two persons used to the same graphic forms, trained to code and decode a meaning by using the same key.

Suppose, then, we take a written message at its source: it is understood only if the receptor possesses the key to the drawing. This is the condition

---

[1] See Roger Martin, *Logique contemporaine et formalisation* (Paris: P. U. F., 1964), pp. 24–30.

[2] It can be shown easily enough that no method of communication is universal: on the contrary, all methods are regional, in other words, isomorphic to one language. The space of linguistic communication (which, therefore, is the standard model of any space of communication) is not isotropic. An object that is the universal communicator or that is universally communicated does, however, exist: the technical object in general. That is why we find, at the dawn of history, that the first diffusion belongs to it: its space of communication is isotropic. Let there be no misunderstanding: at stake here is a definition of prehistory. History begins with regional language and the space of anisotropic communication. Whence this law of three states: technological isotropy, linguistic anisotropy, linguistic-technical isotropy. The third state should not be long in arriving.

of its reception, and it is essential. But there is another condition at the source of the message that, though it is only circumstantial, still merits analysis. The scribe must execute his drawing as well as possible. What does this mean? First, the graph comprises essential graphic signs, those charged with meaning: the form of the letters (standardized), properly formed clusters of letters and of words (regulated by the rules of morphology and of syntax), and so on. It also comprises inessential, accidental graphic signs, those without meaning whose presence depends on the ability, the clumsiness, the education, the passion, or the illness of he who writes: waverings in the graphic forms, failures in the drawing, spelling errors, and so on. The first condition presupposes an "orthogram" and a calligram. But this is never, or almost never, the case.[3] The calligram preserves form against accident, and if logicians are interested in form, it is also possible to be interested in pathology, in other words, in "cacography." Graphology is the misguided science (or the false science) dealing with the psychological motives of cacography: can we speak purely of the latter, that is to say, speak purely of an impurity?

Pathology of communication is not only a fact of writing. It also exists in spoken languages: stammerings, mispronunciations, regional accents, dysphonias, and cacophonies. Likewise in the technical means of communication: background noise, jamming, static, cut-offs, hyteresis, various interruptions. If static is accidental, background noise is *essential* to communication.

Following scientific tradition, let us call *noise* the set of these phenomena of interference that become obstacles to communication. Thus, cacography is the noise of graphic form or, rather, the latter comprises an essential form *and* a noise that is either essential or occasional. To write badly is to plunge the graphic message into this noise which interferes with reading, which transforms the reader into an epigraphist. In other words, simply to write is to risk jumbling a form. In the same way, to communicate orally is to risk losing meaning in noise. This set of phenomena has appeared so important to certain theoreticians of language[4] that they have not hesitated to transform our current conception of dialogue in reference to it: such communication is a sort of game played by two interlocutors considered as united against the phenomena of interference and confusion, or against individuals with some stake in inter-

---

[3] It is hardly necessary to add that the first benefit of the printing press consists in permitting the reader not to be an epigraphist. A printed text is a calligram (but not always an orthogram). The possibility of an arbitrary multiplication is, of course, the second benefit.

[4] For example, B. Mandelbrojt and Roman Jakobson. See Norbert Wiener, *The Human Use of Human Beings: Cybernetics and Society* (New York: Avon Books, 1967), chaps. 4 and 11.

rupting communication.[5] These interlocutors are in no way opposed, as in the traditional conception of the dialectic game; on the contrary, they are on the same side, tied together by a mutual interest: they battle together against noise. The cacographer and the epigraphist, the cacophonous speaker and the auditor, exchange their reciprocal roles in dialogue, where the source becomes reception, and the reception source (according to a given rhythm). They exchange roles sufficiently often for us to view them as struggling together against a common enemy. *To hold a dialogue is to suppose a third man and to seek to exclude him;* a successful communication is the exclusion of the third man. The most profound dialectical problem is not the problem of the Other, who is only a variety —or a variation—of the Same, it is the problem of the third man. We might call this third man the *demon,* the prosopopeia of noise.[6]

The conception of the dialogue is immediately applicable to some famous philosophemes; it is capable of extracting from them some unexpected meanings. For example, the *Metaphysical Meditations* can be explained according to these principles: the *Meditations* seek out the other with whom one must join in order to expel the third man.[7] For the moment, let us go no further than the Platonic dialogues: the maieutic method, in fact, unites the questioner and the respondent in the task of giving birth. Dialectic makes the two interlocutors play on the same side; they do battle together to produce a truth on which they can agree, that is, to produce a successful communication. In a certain sense, they struggle together against interference, against the demon, against the third man. Obviously, this battle is not always successful. In the aporetic dialogues, victory rests with the powers of noise; in the other dialogues, the battle is fierce—attesting to the power of the third man. Serenity returns little by little when the exorcism is definitively(?) obtained.

It is not within the bounds of this study to develop at any great length the theme of the third man in the Platonic dialogue. That would take us too far afield, and we are, in fact, already very far from our premises—but not nearly as far as it would appear.

Let us return to logic and through it to writing. For the logician, a symbol is a drawing, a graph made on the blackboard with a piece of

---

[5] Similarly, written communication is the battle of the scribe and the reader, joined together by interest and by a project against any obstacles in the way of communication: the message in the bottle.

[6] For an extended discussion of noise and the figures it assumes, see Michel Serres, *Le Parasite* (Paris: Grasset, 1980). — Ed.

[7] This interpretation has as a rough result the notion according to which the Cartesian text outlines the condition of possibility for a physics experiment and is therefore metaphysical in this sense. The Platonic texts had previously laid down the conditions of possibility for mathematical ideation.

chalk.[8] A particular symbol can occur several times in a set of formulas. Mathematicians all agree to recognize a "same" symbol in two or more occurrences of this symbol. Yet by the graphic form itself every occurrence differs from another, whatever it may be: wavering of outline, errors of movement, and so forth. Consequently, the logician reasons not by using the concrete graph drawn on the blackboard, here and now, but rather, as Tarski says, by using the class of objects having the same form.[9] The symbol is thus an abstract being that the graphs in question only evoke. This abstract being is recognized by the homeomorphism, if I dare say so, of the graphs. The recognition of this being presupposes that we distinguish the form of what I have already called cacography. The mathematician does not see any difficulty on this point, and more often than not the discussion appears idle to him.

But at the point where the scientist becomes impatient, the philosopher stops to wonder what would become of this question if mathematics did not exist. He sees all the mathematicians agreeing on this act of recognition of a same form, a form unvarying in the variation of graphic forms that evoke it. Now he knows, as does everyone, that no graph resembles any other and that if we wonder what are the respective portions of form and of cacography in writing, we must flatly admit that noise prevails — certain people will say that it prevails exhaustively. He will, consequently, come to the following conclusion if he takes into account what has been said above: it is one and the same act to recognize an abstract being through the occurrences of its concrete, standardized form and to come to an agreement about this recognition. In other words, the act of eliminating cacography, the attempt to eliminate noise, is at the same time the condition of the apprehension of the abstract form and the condition of the success of communication. If the mathematician becomes impatient, it is because he thinks inside a society that has triumphed over noise so well and for such a long time that he is amazed when the problem is raised anew. He thinks within the world of "we" and within the world of the abstract, two isomorphic and perhaps even identical worlds. The subject of abstract mathematics is the "we" of an ideal republic which is the city of communication maximally purged of noise[10] (which, parenthetically, shows why Plato and Leibniz were not idealists). In general, to formalize is to carry out a process by which one passes from concrete modes of thinking to one or several abstract forms. It means to eliminate noise as well, in an optimal manner. It means to become aware

[8] See Martin, *Logique contemporaine*, pp. 26-27.
[9] See Alfred Tarski, *Introduction to Logic and to the Methodology of Deductive Sciences* (New York: Oxford University Press, 1941), pp. 68 ff. — Ed.
[10] Perhaps the only such city (along with that of music) as Leibniz liked to say.

of the fact that mathematics is the kingdom that admits only the absolutely unavoidable noise, the kingdom of quasi-perfect communication, the *manthánein,* the kingdom of the excluded third man, in which the demon is almost definitively exorcised. If there were no mathematics, it would be necessary to renew the exorcism.

The demonstration begins again. At the dawn of logic, that is to say, at both the historical and the logical beginning of logic, but also at the logical beginning of mathematics, Hilbert and others repeated the Platonic reasoning concerning abstract idealities — which was one of the conditions of the Greek miracle, at the historical dawn of mathematics. But with us the discussion is truncated because it cannot bracket the inevitable fact of the historical existence of mathematics. With Plato, on the contrary, the discussion is full and complete: it makes the recognitoin of the abstract form and the problem of the success of the dialogue coexist. When I say "bed," I am not speaking of such and such a bed, mine, yours, this one or that one; I am evoking the idea of the bed. When I draw a square and a diagonal in the sand, I do not in any way want to speak of this wavering, irregular, and inexact graph; I evoke by it the ideal form of the diagonal and of the square. I eliminate the empirical, I dematerialize reasoning. By doing this, I make a science possible, both for rigor and for truth, but also for the universal, for the *Universal in itself.* By doing this I eliminate that which hides form — cacography, interference, and noise — and I create the possibility of a science in the *Universal for us.* Mathematical form is both a Universal in itself and a Universal for us: and therefore *the first effort to make communication in a dialogue successful is isomorphic to the effort to render a form independent of its empirical realizations.* These realizations are the third man of the form, its interference and its noise, and it is precisely because they intervene ceaselessly that the first dialogues are aporetic. The dialectical method of the dialogue has its origins in the same regions as mathematical method, which, moreover, is also said to be dialectical.

To exclude the empirical is to exclude differentiation, the plurality of others that mask the same. It is the first movement of mathematization, of formalization. In this sense, the reasoning of modern logicians concerning the symbol is analogous to the Platonic discussion of the geometric form drawn in the sand: one must eliminate cacography, the wavering outline, the accident of the mark, the failure of a gesture, the set of conditions that ensure that no graph is strictly of the same form as any other. In the same way, the object perceived is indefinitely discernible: there would have to be a different word for every circle, for every symbol, for every tree, and for every pigeon; and a different word for yesterday, today, and to-morrow; and a different word according to whether he who perceives it is you or I, according to whether one of the two of us is angry, is jaundiced, and so on *ad infinitum*. At the extreme limits of empiricism, meaning is totally plunged into noise, the space of communication is granular,[11] dialogue is condemned to cacophony: the transmission of communication is chronic transformation. Thus, the empirical is strictly essential and accidental *noise*. The first "third man" to exclude is the empiricist, along with his empirical domain. And this demon is the strongest demon, since one has only to open one's eyes and ears to see that he is master of the world.[12] Consequently, in order for dialogue to be possible, one must close one's eyes and cover one's ears to the song and the beauty of the sirens. In a single blow, we eliminate hearing and noise, vision and failed drawing; in a single blow, we conceive the form and we understand each other. And therefore, once again, the Greek miracle, that of mathematics, must be born at the same time—historical time, logical time, and reflexive time—as a philosophy of dialogue and by dialogue.

In Platonism, the link between a dialectical method—in the sense of communication—and a progressive working diagram of abstract idealities in the manner of geometry is not an accident in the history of ideas, nor just an episode in the willful decisions of the philosopher: it is inscribed in the nature of things. To isolate an ideal form is to render it independent of the empirical domain and of noise. Noise is the empirical portion of the message just as the empirical domain is the noise of form. In this sense, the minor Socratic dialogues are pre-mathematical in the same way as is the measurement of a wheat field in the Nile valley.[13]

[11]Whence we see that if we admit the principle of undiscernibles, the monads neither listen to nor understand each other. They are without doors or windows, an implication that Leibniz made coherent. If Zeno is right, the Eleatics are condemned to silence.

[12]And, as has often been seen in any discussion between an empiricist and a rationalist—Locke and Leibniz, for example—*empiricism would always be correct if mathematics did not exist*. Empiricism is the *true* philosophy as soon as mathematics is bracketed. Before the latter imposes itself and in order that it may do so, one must *want* not to listen to Protagoras and Callicles—because they are right. But the more they are right, the less we can hear them: they end up only making noise. The argument put forth against Locke by Leibniz, "You do not know mathematics," is not an *ad hominem* argument; it is the only logical defense possible.

[13]One could object that the cacography of a circle and that of a letter cannot be made the same by reduction. Since the invention of topology, we know that, on the contrary, anexact idealities exist in the same way as exact ones as defined by measurement: so that here we have spoken purely only of the inverse of impurity. One would speak purely of impurity by attempting to pose the problem of cacography in an anexact form. That would already be more difficult, but it would take us out of the limits of this study. Besides, Leibniz assimilates the two forms, graph and graphic form, in a dialogue dating from 1677. See Leibniz, "Dialogue," in *Philosophical Papers and Letters*, ed. Leroy E. Loemker (Dordrect, Holland: D. Reidel Publishing Company, 1970), pp. 182-85.

7

▲
▲ ▲
▲ ▲ ▲

The Origin of Language: Biology, Information Theory, & Thermodynamics

An organism is a system. The notion of system changes through history; it occupies different positions within the encyclopedia. This notion may be logico-mathematical: a coherent set of demonstrable propositions deduced from a small number of postulates. One speaks in this way of a system of axioms or a system of differential equations. For Descartes, Spinoza, or Leibniz, this is the classical ideal of knowledge. The notion of system may also be mechanical: a set which remains stable throughout variations of objects which are either in movement or relatively stationary. Laplace speaks in this sense of the solar system. Within a set of mobile material points distributed in space and governed by a law — Newton's law, for example — it is clear that time is fully reversible. If everything starts moving in the opposite direction, nothing significant in form or state will change. The mathematical or logical system is independent of the time variable; the ordinary mechanical system depends on a time but not on its direction. Hence the displacement, starting with the Industrial Revolution, toward physics and in particular toward the theory of heat, a displacement occurring after Fourier starting with Carnot. In another essay[1] I have called mechanical systems "statues" or *stateurs:* they are based on a fixity or an equilibrium. After Carnot they become motors. They create movement, they go beyond the simple relation of forces, they create them by energy or power. They produce circulation by means of reservoirs and differences of temperature. As soon as one can build them and theorize about them — steam or combustion engines, chemical, electrical, and turbine engines, and so forth — the notion of time changes. The second law of thermodynamics accounts for the impossibility of perpetual motion of the second type; energy dissipates and entropy increases. From this moment on, time is endowed with a direction. It is irreversible

[1]"Don Juan au palais des merveilles: Sur les statues au XVIIe siècle," *Les Etudes philosophiques* 3 (1966):385-90.

and drifts from order to disorder, or from difference to the dissolution or dissemination of a homogeneous mixture from which no energy, no force, and no motion can arise.

Curiously enough, philosophers and psychologists, who never hesitated to adopt as models systems like the first ones, tables of axioms or statues, were often averse, during the nineteenth century, to this new development and to its practical and theoretical results. Almost all of them attempted to find some failing with it: they wished, I believe, that the motor would never stop. With very few exceptions, almost all of them maintain, for example, the existence of an eternal return, despite findings to the contrary in physics. Freud, however, aligns himself with these findings: he manifestly adopts as an initial model a topology like that of Maxwell and Listing,[2] in which lines of force are already called complexes, and an energy theory based on thermodynamics and linked to two fundamental principles: the conservation of energy and the tendency toward death. Freudian time is irreversible.

We are in the presence of three types of systems: the first, logico-mathematical, is independent of time; the second, mechanical, is linked to reversible time; the third, thermodynamic, is linked to irreversible time. However, the three types all have closure in common. They constitute a partitioning of a given universe, either by the so-called closure axiom for the universe of discourse or by the independence of movements and stabilities in relation to all exterior influences (thus Laplace's solar world in relation to the stellar universe) or by thermal insulation. A physical system, in the third sense, is isolated-closed. One must understand by this that no flow of matter, no circulation of heat, light, or energy, crosses the walls that define it and demarcate it in space. Under this condition and this condition only, the two laws of thermodynamics apply and are valid. With the slightest opening, the system is no longer governed by general equations.

Hence the general displacement of philosophical discourse from the nineteenth century to Bergson's posterity. Once couched in terms of differences, reservoirs and circulation, energies, power and relations of force, time and motors, deviations, oppositions and dissolution, suddenly this discourse, as if reverting to the conditions of its own practice, begins speaking in terms of open and closed, of isolation and closures. Today, in many respects, it has not progressed an inch in relation to the global problematic of Bergsonism. It has the same form and function, let us say the same syntax, but it has changed domains. Instead of addressing the direct questions of matter and life, from which, precisely, this language had developed, it brought that language within the domain of the social sciences, language, and texts. Why?

For a very simple reason. Nineteenth-century thermodynamics, restricted or general, classical or statistical, had studied motors and, in general, systems, producers of movement. The energies mobilized by its application and calculated by its theory remained on an entropic scale, by which I mean within the realm of ordinary work and the displacement of objects. Hence one had a discourse which often concluded either with the cosmos in general or with organic life in particular. At the beginning of the twentieth century, communication theory introduced a series of concepts such as information, noise, and redundancy, for which a link to thermodynamics was rather quickly demonstrated. It was shown, for example, that information (emitted, transmitted, or received) was a form of negentropy. Now these energies, manipulated and calculated, were of a different order than energy of the first, or macroscopic, scale—they were very small in relation to this scale. But this change only minimally affected the whole of the theoretical armature already in place: information theory was considered the daughter of thermodynamics; theorizing immediately began about activities as ordinary as reading, writing, the transmission and storing of signals, the optimal technique for avoiding obstacles along their path, and so forth. Of course, the theoreticians of information theory accomplished this with means inherited directly from the physics of energies belonging to the macroscopic scale. Success confirmed their enterprise. Hence, in a parallel manner, the great stability of traditional philosophical categories but their massive application in a different area: discourse, writing, language, societal and psychic phenomena, all acts which one can describe as communication acts. It immediately became obvious, or was taken as such, that a store of information transcribed on any given memory, a painting or a page, should drift by itself from difference to disorder, or that an isolated-closed system about which we know nothing, an unknown of some sort, could be and, in certain cases, had to be a language pocket. By an act of simultaneous translation one can derive with relative ease the philosophical terms in use today. The system under consideration becomes a system of signs.

Right in the middle of the traditional classification of beings, a classification that no longer makes sense since matter, life, and sign are nothing but properties of a system, we find exactly what I want to talk about: the living organism. Most often conceived of according to the models we have already considered, the organism has been seen as a machine (by figures and movements, or by invariance through variations) from the classical age up to the recent notion of homeostasis. Equilibrium and mobility. It is evidently a thermodynamic system, sometimes operating at very high temperatures, and tending toward death according to an unpredictable and irreversible time (that of ontogenesis), but going up the entropic stream by means of phylogenetic invariances and the mutations of selection. It is a hypercomplex system, reducible only with difficulty to known models that we have now mastered. What can we presently say about this system? First, that it is an information and thermodynamic system. Indeed, it receives, stores, exchanges, and gives off both energy and information—in all forms, from the light of the sun to the flow of matter which passes through it (food, oxygen, heat, signals). This system is not in equilibrium, since thermodynamic stability spells death for it, purely and simply. It is in a temporary state of imbalance, and it tends as much as possible to maintain this imbalance. It is hence subject to the irreversible time of the second law, since it is dying. But it struggles against this time. We can improve upon the classical formulation of this problem. Indeed, due to the energy and information torrent which passes through the system without interruption, it is henceforth impossible to conceive of it as an isolated-closed system, except, perhaps, in its genotypical form. It is an open system. It should thus be regulated by a thermodynamics of open systems which has been developing over the past ten years and which provides a complex theory for this state of imbalance. In and by this imbalance, it is relatively stable. But here invariance is unique: neither static nor homeostatic, it is homeorrhetic. It is a river that flows and yet remains stable in the continual collapse of its banks and the irreversible erosion of the mountains around it. One always swims in the same river, one never sits down on the same bank. The fluvial basin is stable in its flux and the passage of its chreodes; as a system open to evaporation, rain, and clouds, it always—but stochastically—brings back the same water. What is slowly destroyed is the solid basin. The fluid is stable; the solid which wears away is unstable—Heraclitus and Parmenides were both right. Hence the notion of homeorrhesis.[3] The living system is homeorrhetic.

This river, almost stable although irreversible, this basin, poised on its own imbalance in a precarious state of quasi-equilibrium in its flow toward death, ferries energy and information, knowledge of entropy and negentropy, of order and disorder. Both a syrrhesis (rather than a system) and a diarrhesis,[4] the organism is hence defined from a global perspective.

---

[3] The word "homeorrhesis" is formed from the Greek words *homos*, meaning "same," and *rhysis*, meaning "flow." Serres replaces the normal term describing the equilibrium of a self-regulating system, "homeostasis," by "homeorrhesis" in order to emphasize the idea of continual movement and exchange as opposed to the less dynamic idea of stasis. — Ed.

[4] The Greek verbs *syrrhein* and *diarrhein* mean "to flow together" and "to flow through." Again the attempt is to capture the dynamic nature of the organism by means of a terminology that avoids suggestions of the static. The word "system" is abandoned because of its origin in the Greek verb *histanai*, "to cause to stand." — Ed.

Not actually *defined* (the word means in effect the opposite of open), but assessed, described, evaluated, and understood. Or, within the context of an even more general circulation which goes from the sun to the black depths of space, the organism is a barrier of braided links that leaks like a wicker basket but can still function as a dam. Better yet, it is the quasi-stable turbulence that a flow produces, the eddy closed upon itself for an instant, which finds its balance in the middle of the current and appears to move upstream, but is in fact undone by the flow and re-formed elsewhere. And experience shows that there is no flux without eddy, no laminar flow which does not become turbulent.[5] Now, and here is the crux of the matter, all times converge in this temporary knot: the drift of entropy or the irreversible thermal flow, wear and aging, the exhaustion of initial redundancy, time which turns back on feedback rings or the quasi-stability of eddies, the conservative invariance of genetic nuclei, the permanence of a form, the erratic blinking of aleatory mutations, the implacable filtering out of all non-viable elements, the local flow upsteam toward negentropic islands—refuse, recycling, memory, increase in complexities. The living organism, ontogenesis and phylogenesis combined, is of all times. This does not at all mean that it is eternal, but rather that it is an original complex, woven out of all the different times that our intellect subjects to analysis or that our habits distinguish or that our spatial environment tolerates. Homeorrhetic means at least that: the rhesis flows, but similarity pushes upstream and resists. All the temporal vectors possessing a directional arrow are here, in this place, arranged in the shape of a star. What is an organism? A sheaf of times. What is a living system? A bouquet of times.

It is indeed surprising that this solution has not been reached more quickly. Perhaps it seemed difficult to intuit a multitemporality. We willingly accept, however, the fact that the things around us do not all share the same temporality: negentropic islands on or in the entropic sea, or distinct universes as Boltzmann described them, pockets of local orders in rising entropy, crystal depositories sunk in ashes—none of these things disturbs us. Living syrrhesis combines sea and islands. In a completely new sense, the organism is synchronous for meanings and directions, for the continuous and discontinuous, for the local and the global; it combines memory, invariance, plan, message, loss, redundancy, and so forth. It is old, mortal, and the transmitter of a new cycle. The organism is fixed on top of a temporal converter—no, *it is a converter of*

---

[5] See *La Naissance de la physique dans le texte de Lucrèce: Fleuves et turbulences* (Paris: Minuit, 1977), and "Lucretius: Science and Religion," chapter 9 of the present volume. —Ed.

time. This is perhaps why it is able to learn about systems differentiated by their individual time: the world, fire, and signs.

Let us shift from the global to the local level, from the whole of the organism to the diverse systems that used to be called respiratory, circulatory, neurovegetal, and so forth, and then to organs, tissues, cells, molecules. . . . The passage could be plotted from homeorrhesis to homeorhesis. In short, from this point of view the complex functions like a set of chemical reactions. The latter occur, in the case of mammals—of which man is one—at high temperatures, indeed, very high, in a homoiothermal environment.[6] There exist approximately a thousand different reactions of this kind. But at a given moment, for the complex in operation (living), their number, although probably finite, is incredibly large, in view of the enormous molecular population. For an idea of its dimensions it must be placed on an astronomical scale. From a thermal and information point of view, these movements and transformations necessarily generate background noise. And this noise is certainly tremendous, for the numbers under consideration are gigantic. What prevents us from hearing it? Why is the sound muffled, the factory insulated?

All of information theory and hence, correlatively, of the theory of noise only makes sense in relation to an observer who happens to be linked to them. Who is the observer here? The simplest answer would be to say that for our own organic system we are the observer or observers in question. Thus we should perceive this noise, the noise of a complex to which a receptor is linked. I use "perceive" in the broad sense that this word had in the classical era. We should hear this deafening clamor just as we hear the roar of the sea at the edge of the beach. It should deafen us, drown us. Leibniz said the following in his language: the cloud of minor perceptions, external and internal, should induce a state of discomfort and dizziness; it should prove intolerable. But, save for exceptional instances, we perceive almost nothing of this intense chaos which nonetheless exists and functions, as experiments have demonstrated conclusively.

---

[6]Homoiothermy is a singular example of homeorrhesis. In a certain sense, the poikilothermal, or cold-blooded, organism is better adapted to the environment. The homoiothermal organism, of more recent date in the history of evolution, is more fragile. It is probably condemned to a niche adjusted for relatively stable temperature intervals. In fact, it produces them as often as possible. Bees had already discovered this process for their hives. Hence the homoiothermal organism is much more dependent than other species on the environment, on its own species, and on the Other or Others. This is especially true when its offspring—and this is the case for a human infant—has not received at birth a perfect set of homoiothermal equipment. The homoiothermal organism generates the need for communication. It is, in energy or thermal needs, analogous to what will be common speech, in terms of signals and information. I imagine that one of the first forms of behavior, like one of the first signals, may be reduced to this: "keep me warm." The homoiothermal organism initiates touch and contact, erotic communication, and language. It is a homeology.

We are submerged to our neck, to our eyes, to our hair, in a furiously raging ocean. We are the voice of this hurricane, this thermal howl, and we do not even know it. It exists but it goes unperceived. The attempt to understand this blindness, this deafness, or, as is often said, this unconsciousness thus seems of value to me. We have eyes in order not to see ourselves, ears in order not to hear ourselves. The observer observes nothing, or almost nothing.

At this point it is necessary to consider the general conditions of organic functioning, the system's globalizing forms. All that we now know about it leads us to describe a series of successive apparatuses called levels of integration — Russian dolls or interlocking objects, according to the image François Jacob proposed.[7] The cybernetic model temporarily allows us to imagine certain links between these levels, from molecular activity to the organization of the cell, tissues, organs, and so forth. In relatively simple cases it would even be possible to write a mathematical model, a system of differential equations representing cellular activity. The conditions at the limits of that activity would describe the state of the boundaries, the limits of the level under consideration, and hence the nature of the proximity of one level to the next, the manner in which one level is submerged in the next. This process of proximity, of implication, of integration merits description. Consider any level of an interlocking system. Locally, as we have seen, it operates like a series of chemical reactions at a certain temperature. Let us forget for the moment their precise equations and the unique elements at work here. Let us consider only the energy conditions at this one level. It mobilizes information and produces background noise. The next level in the interlocking series receives, manipulates, and generally integrates the information-background noise couple that was given off at the preceding level. How does this take place? Several recent studies allow us to elucidate the answer to this question.[8] Indeed, if one writes the equation expressing the quantity of information exchanged between two stations through a given channel and the equation which provides this quantity for the whole unit (including the two stations and the channel), a change of sign occurs for a certain function entering into the computation. In other words, this function, called ambiguity and resulting from noise, changes when the observer changes his point of observation. Its value depends on whether

[7]See François Jacob, *The Logic of Life: A History of Heredity,* trans. Betty E. Spillman (New York: Vintage Books, 1976), p. 302. —Ed.

[8]See Henri Atlan, *L'Organisation biologique et la théorie de l'information* (Paris: Hermann, 1972); "On a Formal Definition of Organization," *Journal of Theoretical Biology* 45 (1974):295-304. (See also Henri Atlan, *Entre le cristal et la fumée: Essai sur l'organisation du vivant* [Paris: Seuil, 1979], pp. 5-130. —Ed.)

he is submerged in the first level or whether he examines the entire unit from the next level. In a certain sense, the next level functions as a rectifier, in particular, as a rectifier of noise. What was once an obstacle to all messages is reversed and added to the information. This discovery is all the more important since it is valid for all levels. It is a law of the series which runs through the system of integration. I now come back to my initial question.

This question only made sense if, at the last level, the most comprehensive of the whole system, the present observer, to whom the noise and information phenomena are linked, had at his disposal or was equipped with a special listening instrument. A point of observation is not sufficient; to observe, one also needs the means to do so. Now the apparatus exists: it is made up of what classical philosophy called internal sensations or what different psychologies have successively described as intropathy, proprioceptivity, or coenesthesia, and whose functionings have to be linked to signals given off or received by the vagosympathetic system. The instrument exists and functions. What does it perceive? Nothing, or almost nothing, it seems, of what we recognize at the purely physical level as background noise and information; nothing which resembles, with perhaps certain exceptions, a signal—a figure against a ground—isolated from a vague and fluctuating cloud, from a multiple halo humming and buzzing at random. It does, however, perceive the signals that we subsume under the two broad categories of pleasure and pain. It receives them and emits them. It is not meaningless to say that it receives signals that we translate immediately into these two words. Thus everything would take place as if pleasure and pain constituted the final state of a general listening, filtered in turn by the set of successive integrations. The final couple, the only one to be perceived, would, in other words, be the last translation, the last rectification of the original physical couple of information-background noise. Of course, no one can call information fortunate and noise painful, for things are arranged in any number of chiasms. Suffering, at least sometimes, is a set of signals which opens up a path of readaptation or strategies for the repair, for the rebalancing, of the homeorrhesis. Here again, a change in sign appears. There must be noise in pleasure and information in pain. But this is probably something we cannot know or evaluate properly.

It is significant that the successive levels of organic integration—we understand the chain of the first levels fairly well thanks to the experimental sciences, and we also understand the final segment because of the direct pathetic tie we maintain constantly with our own body—must always function as languages. On the one hand, at the cellular or molecular level, a proto-language (stereospecific information and thermal noise) is already functioning; on the other hand, at the most highly integrated level, a language is still functioning, but now as individuated signals equipped with something like meaning: calls for desired objects or warnings against dangerous ones. And again, because chiasms and ambiguity complicate matters, we can find a refusal of desire and a call for suffering. Hence the multiple, integrated system, about whose implicative surroundings I often know nothing, may be considered as a series of transformations which effects a move from the noise-information couple to the meaning-obstacles couple and finally to meaning. Each integration functions as a filter, a rectifier. We thus have a hypercomplex apparatus that finally gives a meaning to the Shannon couple—which can only be dealt with as long as it has no meaning.[9] Everything transpires as if the central problem of information theory were resolved, automatically, by living organisms. *They can be described as apparatuses which produce language from noise and information,* each according to its order of complexity: for each system, indeed, for each species, there exists an original set of signals.

For this reason it is simple to generalize several categories or ordinary functions. Repression in the Freudian sense, for example, remained an enunciation based on a mechanical or hydrodynamic model. Henceforth the entire integrative system can take charge of it; its physical model is much more complete and we can speak about it by using a discourse which ultimately can be expressed in mathematical terms. This is because we are dealing with a very general function operating in the proximity of two given levels. On one side, transformations, fixations, a set of energy displacements occur—no metaphor is needed here, for the processes under consideration are simply chemical or thermodynamic. On the other side, the entire complex of these movements is grasped by the observer, that is, by the integrating level as such, by the change in sign of the ambiguity function.

These matters are straightforward. Let us imagine a system with two or several elements. In an initial case, these elements are either completely different or identical with one another, repetitive. The information quantity is thus either a sum or a reduction to the information of a single element. This is the case of disorganization, of inorganization. If the system is organized, the elements are in relation to one another and are therefore different and similar at the same time. Here ambiguity arises. From a point of view within the system, the transmission of information along a given circuit from one element to another subtracts ambiguity because it is a noise, an obstacle to the message. For an observer outside

[9]See Claude Shannon, *The Mathematical Theory of Communication* (Urbana: University of Illinois Press, 1964). —Ed.

the system, ambiguity must be added, for it increases the system's complexity. It functions in this case as information at the level of the unit's organization. In one case, it covers up; in the other case, it expresses. The entire symbolic function is embedded in this process, the entire strategy of free association, Freudian slips, jokes and puns. Now the point is that the theory of changes in sign is valid at the most elementary levels: a cell containing a nucleus, cytoplasm, membranes, and organelles. Henceforth, despite the most radical differences between embedded systems, they will at least share this process of reversal at their boundaries. Repression is only a particular example of this general process, which lays down the law for the chain. It is probably for this reason that we perceive nothing of the deafening background noise given off by the system, except for interesting pieces of information relating to the general functioning of these transformations or to their local breakdown. The senseless din is made meaningful by the series of rectifiers.

At this point the unconscious gives way from below; there are as many unconsciouses in the system as there are integration levels. It is merely a question, in general, of that for which we initially possess no information. It is not a unique black box, but a series of interlocking boxes; and this series is the organism, the body. Each level of information functions as an unconscious for the global level bordering it, as a closed or relatively isolated system in relationship to which the noise-information couple, when it crosses the edge, is reversed and which the subsequent system decodes or deciphers. In each link of the series the question of language is formulated and reformulated by the transformation of the message, the channel, and the noise: by translation. In fact, *residual background noise is progressively eliminated:* what was supposed to interfere begins constructing; obstacles combine to organize; noise becomes dialect. I imagine this occurs from the depths of the molecular chaos, in which information appears in its spatial simplicity and material forms, throughout the signifying and articulated message through the sequence of rectifiers. What remains unknown and unconscious is, at the chain's furthermost limit, the din of energy transformations: this must be so, for the din is by definition stripped of all meaning, like a set of pure signals or aleatory movements. These packages of chance are filtered, level after level, by the subtle transformer constituted by the organism, and they come crashing at our feet, like the surf at the edge of the beach, in the forms of eros and death. In this sense the traditional view of the unconscious would seem to be the final black box, the clearest box for us since it has its own language in the full sense. Beyond it we plunge into the cloud of meaningless signals. Perhaps this box protects us from the deafening gasps of the stochastic; perhaps the box serves to turn them back into symbols. The unconscious is the last black observer of chance. It is an instance of order. It, too, turns destructive randomness into autonomy.

In this way, more generally, categories or common functions of psychoanalysis could be rewritten in terms of the new organon which maintains the advantage of being at the same time a physics of energy and a theory of signals. Formerly, when a given system was analyzed it was a standard —and justifiable—practice to write two distinct accounts of it: the energy account and the information account. For a computer this would be the bits on IBM cards or the like plus the necessary energy for heating the filaments. The two accounts had no proportion in common; they were not even on the same scale. An enormous coefficient separated them (10^{-16}). The same thing is not true for the organism: its extreme complication, the great miniaturization of its elements, and their number bring these two accounts closer and make them comparable. Hence the difference between a machine and a living organism is that, for the former, the information account is negligible in relationship to the energy account, whereas, for the latter, both accounts are on the same scale. Henceforth, the theoretical reconciliation between information theory and thermodynamics favors and advocates the practical reconciliation between those funds of knowledge which exploited signs and those which exploited energy displacements: this was Freud's first dream.[10]

The change in sign for the ambiguity function now resolves an earlier difficulty. It had not been inelegant to conclude that the organism combines three varieties of time, and that its system constitutes a temporal sheaf. No simple matter for intuition, this conclusion remained unexplained. Now it is clear. Let us again consider the rectification of what is transmitted from one level to another. Background noise, the major obstacle to messages, assumes an organizational function. But this noise is the equivalent of thermal disorder. Its time is that of increasing entropy, of that irreversible element which pushes the system toward death at maximum speed. Aging, for example, is a process that we are beginning to understand as a loss of redundancies and the drifting of information into background noise. If the integration levels function correctly as partial rectifiers and transform the noise of disorder into potential organization, then they have reversed the arrow of time. They are rectifiers of time. Entropic irreversibility also changes direction and sign; negentropy goes back upstream. We have discovered the place, the operation, and the theorem where and with which the knots of the bouquet are tied. It is

[10]See Sigmund Freud, *Project for a Scientific Psychology*, in *The Standard Edition of the Complete Psychological Works of Sigmund Freud*, ed. James Strachey (London: Hogarth Press, 1966), 1: 283-343. —Ed.

here and in this manner that time flows back and can change direction. Due to the numerous reversals of the temporal vector, the fluctuating homeorrhesis acquires a fleeting stability. For a moment the temporal sheaf makes a full circle. It forms a turbulence where opposing times converge. Organization per se, as system and homeorrhesis, functions precisely as a converter of time. We now know how to describe this converter, as well as its levels and meanderings, from whence come anamnesis, memory, and everything imaginable.

The body is an extraordinarily complex system that creates language from information and noise, with as many mediations as there are integrating levels, with as many changes in sign for the function which just occupied our attention. I know who the final observer is, the receiver at the chain's end: precisely he who utters language. But I do not know who the initial dispatcher is at the other end. I am confronted indefinitely with a black box, a box of boxes, and so forth. In this way, I may proceed as far as I wish, all the way to cells and molecules, as long, of course, as I change the object under observation. All I know, but of this I am certain, is that they are all structured around the information-background-noise couple, the chance-program couple or the entropy-negentropy couple. And this holds true whether I describe the system in terms of chemistry, physics, thermodynamics, or information theory, and whether I situate myself as the final receptor of an integrated apparatus. By reversing the ambiguity function, things naturally converge. Either I am submerged in signal exchanges or I observe the global set of exchanges. But from now on I understand and can explain what happens when the observer changes his point of view, when the subject becomes object, and the obstacle becomes a piece of information, or when introspection veers off into experience, and psychology flows into physics. Inversely, when the object becomes subject it temporarily increases its autonomy. Everything occurs as if Freud, who started from energy models of thermodynamics, had intuited, by a dynamics of language, the subsequent development of thermodynamics into information theory. The reunions are not exactly unexpected. The realms of the subjective and of the objective are no longer at odds. The observer as object, the subject as the observed, are affected by a division more stable and potent than their antique separation: they are both order *and* disorder. From this moment on, I do not need to know who or what the first dispatcher is: whatever it is, it is an island in an ocean of noise, just like me, no matter where I am. It is the genetic information, the molecules or crystals of the world, the interior, as one used to say, or the exterior—none of this is important any longer. A macro-molecule, or any given crystallized solid, or the system of the world, or ultimately what I call "me"—we are all in the same boat. All dispatchers and all receivers are structured similarly. *It is no longer incom-*

prehensible that the world is comprehensible. The real produces the conditions and the means for its self-knowledge. The "rational" is a tiny island of reality, a rare summit, exceptional, as miraculous as the complex system that produces it, by a slow conquest of the surf's randomness along the coast. All knowledge is bordered by that about which we have no information.

It is no longer necessary to maintain the distinction between introspective knowledge, or "deep" knowledge, and objective knowledge. There is only one type of knowledge and it is always linked to an observer, an observer submerged in a system or in its proximity. And this observer is structured exactly like what he observes. His position changes only the relationship between noise and information, but he himself never effaces these two stable presences. There is no more separation between the subject, on the one hand, and the object, on the other (an instance of clarity and an instance of shadow). This separation makes everything inexplicable and unreal. Instead, each term of the traditional subject-object dichotomy is itself split by something like a geographical divide (in the same way as am I, who speak and write today): noise, disorder, and chaos on one side; complexity, arrangement, and distribution on the other. Nothing distinguishes me ontologically from a crystal, a plant, an animal, or the order of the world; we are drifting together toward the noise and the black depths of the universe, and our diverse systemic complexions are flowing up the entropic stream, toward the solar origin, itself adrift. Knowledge is at most the reversal of drifting, that strange conversion of times, always paid for by additional drift; but this is complexity itself, which was once called being. Virtually stable turbulence within the flow. To be or to know from now on will be translated by: see the islands, rare or fortunate, the work of chance or of necessity.

8

Mathematics & Philosophy: What Thales Saw...

Hieronymus informs us that he [Thales] measured the height of the pyramids by the shadow they cast, taking the observation at the hour when the length of our shadow equals our height.

— Diogenes Laertius

The height of a pyramid is related to the length of its shadow just as the height of any vertical, measurable object is related to the length of its shadow at the same time of day.

— Plutarch

The text attributed to Hieronymus by Diogenes is supposedly one which tells of the Greek miracle, of the emergence of an abstract form and line of reasoning against the ground of an earlier practice or perception. How should we read this tale of an origin which eludes our attempts to classify it as reality or myth? Here are a few of its legends.

The tale dramatizes the theorem of Thales. Two triangles: the first is constituted by the pyramid, its shadow and the first or last ray of light; the second by any object whose height is accessible, its shadow and a ray of light. The triangles are similar since their angles, one of which is 90°, are equal. Hieronymus relates a particular case where the triangles are isoceles, Plutarch the general case where they are not.[1] This depends on the moment of the day: the particular form is observable at a single instant. Both texts are diagrams of Thales's theorem and tell less the story of its origin than the possibility of its application.

Let us assume, then, the existence of the pyramid and its shadow. In this schema the following elements are accessible: the black region which I can measure directly, the peg planted in the earth and its desolate

---

[1] See Tannery's discussion of the tradition that opposes Diogenes and Plutarch, *Géométrie grecque* (1887; reprint ed., New York: Arno Press, 1976), pp. 88-94; see also the texts that Kirk and Raven have gathered for *The Presocratic Philosophers* (Cambridge: At the University Press, 1962). Cf. p. 253, Speusippus: "For 1 is the point, 2 the line, 3 the triangle and 4 the pyramid. All these are primary, the first principles of individual things of the same class."

84

shadow. Inaccessible, however, are the height of the tomb and that of the sun. As Auguste Comte says: "In light of previous experience we must acknowledge the impossibility of determining, by direct measurement, most of the heights and distances we should like to know. It is this general fact which makes the science of mathematics necessary. For in renouncing the hope, in almost every case, of measuring great heights or distances directly, the human mind has had to attempt to determine them indirectly, and it is thus that philosophers were led to invent mathematics."[2] Geometry is a ruse; it takes a detour, an indirect route, to reach that which lies outside immediate experience. In this case the ruse is the model: the construction of the summary, the skeleton of a pyramid in reduced form but of equivalent proportions. In fact, Thales has discovered nothing but the possibility of reduction, the idea of a module, the notion of model. The pyramid itself is inaccessible; he invents a scale, a type of ladder.

Hence, again, Auguste Comte: "It is thus that, for example, Aristarchus of Samos estimated the relative distance of the sun and the moon from the earth by measuring the sides of a triangle constructed to be as similar as possible to the right triangle formed by the three heavenly bodies when the moon is at a right angle to the sun and when, consequently, in order to define the triangle one had only to observe its angle with the earth."[3] Like Thales, Aristarchus constructs the reduced model of an astronomical situation. To measure the inaccessible consists in mimicking it within the realm of the accessible. This is true in many instances, one of which is the example of ships at sea. Glossing the twenty-sixth proposition of the first book of Euclid's *Elements,* Proclus writes: "Eudemus in his history of geometry attributes the theorem itself to Thales, saying that the method by which he is reported to have determined the distance of ships at sea shows that he must have used it."[4] Tannery, in his *Géométrie grecque* (p. 90), reconstructs the measuring technique of the famous *fluminis variatio* used by the Roman agricultural surveyor Marcus Junius Nipsus. In any case, the point is to transpose some unreachable figure into a more immediate realm in the form of a miniaturized schema.

Accessible, inaccessible, what does this mean? Near, distant; tangible, untouchable; possible or impossible transporting. Measurement, surveying, direct or immediate, are operations of application, in the sense that a metrics can be used in an applied science; in the sense that, most

---

[2] Auguste Comte, *Philosophie première: Cours de philosophie positive, leçons 1 à 45,* ed. Michel Serres, François Dagognet, and Allal Sinaceur (Paris: Hermann, 1975), *Troisième leçon,* pp. 67-68.

[3] Ibid., *Onzième leçon,* p. 176.

[4] Proclus, *A Commentary on the First Book of Euclid's Elements,* trans. Glenn R. Morrow (Princeton: Princeton University Press, 1970), p. 275.

often, measurement is the essential element of application; but primarily in the sense of touch. Such and such a unit or such and such a ruler is applied to the object to be measured; it is placed on top of the object, it touches it. And this is done as often as is necessary. Immediate or direct measurement is possible or impossible as long as this placing is possible or is not. Hence, the inaccessible is that which I cannot touch, that toward which I cannot carry the ruler, that of which the unit cannot be applied. Some say that one must use a ruse of reason to go from practice to theory, to imagine a substitute for those lengths my body cannot reach: the pyramids, the sun, the ship on the horizon, the far side of the river. In this sense, mathematics would be the path these ruses take.

This amounts to underestimating the importance of practical activities. For in the final analysis the path in question consists in forsaking the sense of touch for that of sight, measurement by "placing" for measurement by sighting. Here, to theorize is to see, a fact which the Greek language makes clear. Vision is tactile without contact. Descartes knew this, just as he understood better than most what measurement is. The inaccessible is at times accessible to vision. Can one measure visually the distance to the sun, to the moon, to a ship, to the apex of a pyramid? This is the whole story of Thales, who discovered nothing but the precise virtues of the human gaze, just as, somewhat later, Berkeley organized in an erudite manner a spectacle of light beneath his microscope, a rigorous organon of optical representation. Since he cannot use his ruler, he sets up lines of sight or, rather, he lets light project them for him. As far as I know, even for accessible objects, vision alone is my guarantee that the ruler has been placed accurately on the thing. To measure is to align; the eye is the best witness of an accurate covering-over. Thales invents the notion of model, of module, but he also brings the visible to the tangible. To measure is, supposedly, to relate. True, but the relation implies a transporting: of the ruler, of the point of view, of the things lined up, and so on. In the realm of the accessible, the transporting is always possible: in the realm of the inaccessible, vision must take care of displacements: hence the angle of sight, hence the *cast* shadow. Measurement, the problem of relation; sight, the cast shadow; in any case, the essential element is the transporting.

Let us return to the schema, that of Diogenes or Plutarch. It deals with things in motion or at rest. The constant factor is the pyramid, immobile for ten centuries beneath the Egyptian sky. The apparent movement of the sun, the length and the position of the shadow are all variable. Everyday experience tells us that the latter depend on the former. Hence the initial idea: the clock. The pyramid is a *gnomon* and the line of its shadow tells time. Measurement and the gauging of the shadow's variations mark the rhythm of the sun's course. The gnomon, stable and arbitrary, is only an intermediary object; the variances echo one another.

The goal is either civil or astronomical. With a sundial, the measurement of space only measures time. The sundial, whose origin is lost somewhere at the dawn of time,[5] will disappear during the quarrel of the Ancients and the Moderns, a quarrel particularly acerbic in regard to clocks. Hence, in Diogenes and Plutarch, the remains of what was once the problem of time: to wait for the moment of equality between an object's shadow and its height, or to observe the two shadows at the same time of day; to keep the sun and its daily course in mind. This is why I quoted Aristarchus: we begin with astronomy.

Thales's idea (for we must give it a name) consists simply in turning the process around, that is, in considering and then resolving the reverse problem of the gnomon. Instead of letting the pyramid speak of the sun, or the constant determine the scale of the variable, he asks the sun to speak of the pyramid; that is, he asks the object in motion to provide a constant flow of information about the object at rest. This ruse is much more clever than the one we described earlier: the constant is no longer what gauges the regular intervals of the variable; on the contrary, Thales gauges, within the variable realm, the stable unknown of the constant. Or rather, with the gnomon, whoever measured space also measured time. By inverting the terms, Thales stops time in order to measure space. He stops the course of the sun at the precise instant of isoceles triangles; he homogenizes the day to obtain the general case. And so do Joshua and Copernicus. Hence it becomes necessary to freeze time in order to conceive of geometry. Once the gnomon has disappeared, Thales enters into the eternity of the mathematical figure. Plato will follow him. This is the old Bergsonian conclusion.[6]

An initial summary: the proliferation of geneses. How did geometry come to the Greeks? A practical genesis: build a reduced model, have a notion of the module, bring the distant to the immediate. A sensorial genesis: organize a visual representation of that which defies physical contact. A civil or epistemological genesis: take astronomy as a starting point, reverse the question of the gnomon. A genesis that is either conceptual or esthetic: erase time in order to measure and master space. Exchange the functions of the variable and the invariable. The origin of geometry is a confluence of geneses. We must follow the other affluents.

Thales's schema presents an optical diagram which is stable with regard to the apparent movement of the sun, at least in its second version. Vision and its spectacle presuppose the following: a site or a point of

---

[5] Herodotus (*Histories*, 2.109) believes that the Greeks learned the use of the gnomon and the division of the day into twelve parts from the Babylonians.

[6] See Henri Bergson, *Oeuvres*, ed. André Robinet (Paris: Presses Universitaires de France, 1959), pp. 51-92. —Ed.

view, a source of light, and finally the object, either luminous or in shadow. We have said that the essential element is the transporting. For even if measurement can be exact or precise, only the relation is rigorous: the reference of a giant schema to a reduced model. These initial geneses are acts of transporting: reduction, the transition from touching to seeing, and vice versa, the reversal of the gnomonic function, the exchange of the stable and the variant, the substitution of space for time. Hence a new series of questions.

1. Where is the point of view? Anywhere. At the source of light. Application, relation, measurement are made possible by aligning landmarks. One can line up the sun and the top of the tomb, or the apex of the pyramid and the tip of its shadow. This means that the site need not be fixed at one location.

2. Where is the object? It too must be transportable. In fact, it is, either by the shadow that it casts or the model that it imitates.

3. Where is the source of light? It varies, as with the gnomon. It transports the object in the form of a shadow. It is in the object; this is what we will call the miracle.

We are dealing less with the story of how something came about than with the dramatization of a preexisting form, Thales's theorem. The first legend, made up of several geneses, is a mathematical decipherment. One must extract the implicit schema from an anecdote whose "local color" has been used by traditional scholars to show that the Greek sage learned everything from Egyptian priests. The relationship of the circumstantial form to the schema leads one to think less about the invention of the second in the action related by the first than about the covering up of the latter by the former. Or, in case I wish to recall Thales's theorem, the story of the pyramid can serve as a mnemonic device. In a culture with an oral tradition, story takes the place of schema, and theater equals intuition. The diagram of the theorem can only be transmitted in written form, but, in an oral culture, drama is the vehicular form of knowledge. Myth then, the mythical tale, is less a legend of origin than the very form of transmission; it does not bear witness to the emergence of science so much as it communicates an element of science. Here mathematics is the key to history, not the contrary. The schema is the invariant of the tale instead of the tale being the origin of the schema. To know, then, and, in this case, to know Thales's theorem is to remember the Egyptian tale. To teach the theorem is to tell the pseudo-myth of origin. We know that all mythical tales are merely the dramatization of a given content. Only the mathematical decipherment of the text can demonstrate the relationship of the implied schema to the mobilization which turns it into a transmissible tale.

Thales's theorem is itself anecdotal in relation to the invariable concept that it expresses in its own genre: that of similarity. Curiously enough, when the schema is analyzed thoroughly one rediscovers the lived variety of the tale. On the one hand, the theorem is only possible because of the space of similarities; it may only be inscribed on or in that space which is the space of transport. On the other hand, it is perfectly natural to take a trip to the Nile delta; at the foot of the pyramids, what Thales or anybody else perceives cannot be anything other than objects of the same form but of different dimensions. The perception of three pyramids is developed within the space of similarities, and this space is constituted by choice in this place: each pyramid is different and yet the same, like the triangles in Thales's theorem. Hence the story is perfectly faithful to the concept, and similar to the idea of similarity. It is more a question here of technology than of perception: similarity is the secret to the triple edifice, the secret to its construction. The pure knowledge implicit within the design of the pyramids is certainly homothetic. In order to build them one must have (but not necessarily know) Thales and homothesis. The size and the position of the stones are an application of homothesis. Whether this is an application ignorant of this knowledge or an operation executed according to a clearly explicit concept is hard to decide. In any case, the passage in Diogenes is twice deciphered mathematically; further, in each instance the articulation of the various concepts and of the tale is clearly visible. The circle has been completed: Khephren and Mykirionos are reduced models of Cheops.

What is the status of the knowledge implied by a certain technique? A technique is always an application that envelops a theory. The entire question—in this case the question of origin—boils down to an interrogation of the mode or the modality of that enveloping process. If mathematics arose one day from certain techniques it was surely by making explicit this implicit knowledge. That there is a theme of secrecy in the artisans' tradition probably signifies that this secret is a secret for everybody, including the master. There is an instance of clear knowledge that is hidden in the workers' hands and in their relation to the blocks of stone. This knowledge is hidden there, it is locked in, and the key has been thrown away. It is in the shadow of the pyramid. Here is the scene of knowledge, the dramatization of the possible origin, dreamed about, conceptualized. The secret that the builder and the rock-cutter share, secret for him, for Thales, and for us, is the shadow-scene. In the shadow of the pyramids, Thales is in the domain of implicit knowledge; on the other side of the pyramid, the sun must make that knowledge explicit in our absence. Henceforth the entire question of the relationship between the schema and history, of the relationship between implicit knowledge and the artisans' practice, will be posed in terms of shadow and sun, a dramatization in the Platonic mode, in terms of implicit and explicit, of knowledge and practical operations: on the one hand, the sun of knowledge and of sameness; on the other, the shadow of opinion, of empiricism, of objects.

These first two readings reveal convincingly the implicit knowledge that a fabricated object hides within itself. In general, it is easy to determine the nature of theoretical knowledge mixed with actual practice. It is easy as the usual path of science is easy, that is, it is difficult but not impossible, complicated but eventually solvable. The thing which is difficult and ultimately inextricable, which we attempt indefinitely to render explicit without being able to explain it completely, and which is thus forever clouded over, is the modality, the "how" of this implication, which, in an actual application, is clearer. The articulatory mode of luminous knowledge and blind practice is blinder in implication, more luminous in application. The origin of knowledge acquired through everyday practice is on the side of shadow; the origin of a practice acquired through knowledge is on the side of light. One could learn a great deal about the emergence of a theory by diligently asking oneself about its various realizations a posteriori and by reversing the analysis. This theoretical-practical relationship, that of sun and shadow, is also what interests Diogenes.

A shadow adequately designates the folds of hidden knowledge. In the initial technical activity, knowledge is in shadow, and we are also in the dark as acting beings, trying to situate theory in light. We will soon discover that Thales failed in this last attempt. The pyramid has its shadow, and beneath the sun of Egypt everyone has a shadow. What else can I know and do, except measure the relationship between the two shadows (a relationship identical to that between object and subject), except measure the relationship between the secret which is entombed in the stones and the one which lies in the worker? The relationship between these two secrets says, designates, describes the secret of the relationship between man and his wrought object. In the legend, Thales's geometry expresses the relationship between two blindings, that which practice engenders and that which the subject of practice engenders. His geometry says this and measures the problem, but does not resolve it; dramatizes his concept but does not explain it; designates the question admirably without answering it; tells of the relationship between two numbers, the mason's and the edifice's, without deciphering either one. And perhaps one can never do anything but that if one confines oneself to the problem of the logos. The relationship between the two shadows is the problem of designation, the pure naming of the enveloping mode of a piece of knowledge by its technique. The technique of measurement which is still a ruse of application, or, as Auguste Comte says, an indirect path, repeats the implication but does not explain it. Thales extracts a technique from a technique, and from a practice he gets another practice. Of course, architecture and mensuration both envelop the same knowledge, homothesis and the celebrated theorem; still, the application is repeated. The homology of repetition eventually designates the homothesis, but in each instance within the gangue of the applied. The theory expressed by shadows remains in shadow. It was not born in its pristine form that day. There is no longer any original miracle: different techniques give rise to other ones and perpetuate themselves in repetition; measurement and architecture see the theorem differently, that is all. And we remain in the immense shadow of the secret. For, again, one cannot conceive of the origin of technique except as the origin of man himself, *faber* as soon as he emerges, or rather, emerging because he is *faber*. Technique is the origin of man, his perpetuation and his repetition. Hence Thales repeats his very origin, and our own: his mathematics, his metrics of geometry, repeats in another way (and as simply as possible) and designates in another way the modality of our technical relationship to objects, the homology of the fabricator to the fabricated. His mathematics takes its place in the open chain of those utterances and designations, but it does not provide the key to the cipher; it does not excavate the secret articulation of knowledge and practice in which the essential element of a possible origin is located. His mathematics is the relation between two shadows, two secrets, two forms and two ciphers, relation or logos, relationship and utterance to be transmitted, utterance which transmits a relationship. As is commonly said, it measures the problem, takes its dimensions, poses it, weighs it, demonstrates it, relates it, but never resolves it. The logos of shadows is still the shadow of the logos.

Still, what Thales's mathematics recounts, at its very inception, is the de-centering of the subject of clear thought with regard to the body that casts its shadow: the subject is the sun, placed beyond the object, on the other side of the shadow. This was also Copernicus' lesson. What this mathematics articulates is the Platonic decision that a geometry of measurement is but a propaedeutic. What it announces, for the first time, is a philosophy of representation, dominating both the pure diagram and its dramatization beneath the torches of the solstice. From whence one returns to the size of the stones and to the pyramid. The edifice is a volume of volumes, a polyhedron composed of cut-out blocks of stone. Now how is one to study and learn about a volume if not by means of a planar projection? And how can one lay hold of it if not by attacking its surfaces? Thales's geometry says this, and so do architectural technique and the mason's daily practice. In each of the three cases it is a matter of studying a solid in terms of all the bits of information that have been gathered at the relevant levels: the secrets of an object's shaded surfaces and its cast shadow. I know nothing about a volume except what its planar projections tell me. But a projection assumes a point of view and a drawing on a smooth surface, a surface without any shaded area and without any hidden fold. I can know a stone, a solid, even the pyramid, only by its contour described by the sun on the plane of the desert sand. The sun-subject writes a form in the sand, a form that is changing and infinite like the profiles of a Ptolemaic perception, a form that describes a cycle of representation. Each moment of the representation, arrested, fixed in the sand, is nonetheless equipped with a constant: a stable relationship with the same shadow, at the same moment, of another object—with me, for example. Here the geometry of perspectival measurement articulates the invariant in the variations of representation.[7] The cast shadows vary, the secrets are transformed, but they share among them a secret which remains constant and which is the unknown, the pyramid's secret: its inaccessible height. As variable as representation may be, it still designates, suddenly, a portion of the real, a stability proper to the object, its measurement. Which is why, from this position, I can only know about the volume that which is said, written, or described by cast shadows—the bits of information transported onto the sand by a ray of sunlight after its interception by the angles and summit of an opaque prism. This geometry is a perspective (an architecture), it is a physics, an optics: the shadow is a black specter.

The theater of measurement demonstrates the decoding of a secret, the decipherment of a writing, the reading of a drawing. The sand on which the sun leaves its trace is the screen, the wall at the back of the cave. Here is the scene of representation established for Western thought for the next millennium, the historically stable form of contemplation from the summit of the pyramids. Thales's story is perhaps the instauration of the moment of representation, taken up ad infinitum by philosophers, but also and above all by geometers, from Descartes and his representational plane to Desargues and his point of view, from Monge and his descriptive diagram to Gergonne and his legislative transfers:[8] the first word of a perspectival geometry, of an architectural optics of volumes, of an intuitive mathematics immersed in a global organon of representation, the first instance of the Ptolemaic model of knowledge. But from Thales's time to the present day we have forgotten that the shadow was cast, transported by some supporting device, that it itself transported certain information. We have read that first spectral analysis without analyzing its condition. The most important question—which messenger transports

---

[7] The moment of equality (*isomegethes*) is a special case. Hieronymus's lesson, though old, delves further into the application.

[8] René Descartes (1596-1650), Gérard Desargues (1591-1661), Gaspar Monge (1746-1818), and Joseph Gergonne (1771-1859) were all instrumental in the development of descriptive and perspective geometry. —Ed.

(and how?) which message?—was covered over for centuries by the blinding scenography of the shadow-light opposition.

Thales's story is not unanalogous to that of Desargues: the size of the stones, a perspectival geometry, the theory of shadows.[9] Nor, after all, to Plato's stories: the sun of the same, the other and empirical object, the cast shadow of the shaded surface, similarity, the cave of representation. Is it a tale of origin? Yes, and in several ways: the origin of a technology, of an optics, of a philosophy of representation. Of a geometry? Perhaps—if geo-metry is that triangulation which Plato scorned for being pre-mathematical. It is a mnemonic recipe, friend of the cultural memory because of its forceful dramatization and mythification under the sun of Ra, easy to transmit within a homogeneous cultural setting,[10] the ruse of applied mathematics, of an architect and of an expert builder. Even Descartes, followed by Desargues and Monge, remains in the domain of applied geometry as well as that of representation; they perpetuate an engineering geometry that is metric and descriptive. They exhibit the archaic forms of pre-mathematics that run through history. Like Thales, they impede the formation of pure mathematics. And the latter will emerge as soon as this geometry dies—very recently. And Husserl will write *The Origin of Geometry* as the bell tolls its disappearance, as if an immense historical cycle had finally come to an end. Thales's story tells something like the story of the birth of a geometry, the measured division of the earth and the differences in shadow and light written on the earth by solid figures and the sun; it does not tell of the birth of mathematics. As proof, let us cite Plato, who, in order to bring about this miracle, requires something else: the essential reality of idealities. Question: how can the pyramid be born as an ideal form?

To answer this question, let us return to our spectral analysis. Everything transpires as if Plato had relegated Thales's story to the depths of his cave. The flat, even wall is always bright: on it the volume casts a shadow; light creates a shaded area. My knowledge is limited to these two shadows; it is only a shadow of knowledge. But there is a third shadow of which the two others provide only an image, or a projection,

---

[9] One of Desargues's geometrical treatises dealt with methods for cutting stone, and another (which has been lost), sometimes referred to as *Leçons de ténèbres* (*Lessons on Shadows*), dealt with conic sections. —Ed.

[10] The terms currently used, "formation" and "production," are concepts borrowed in part from biology. Have we really progressed in philosophy since the Hellenistic age, when the same problems had different names? The Greeks called it "Thales," whose proper name is close to words meaning "sprout," "young shoot," "to bloom," "to become green," "to grow," and so on; in other words, to take form or to be produced. The mythical age said mythically —by means of a symbolic system all its own—what the metaphysical age says conceptually, by means of its own symbolic system. Perhaps one should decipher the names of the Seven Wise Men, symbolically equal in number to the planets and to the Roman kings. Perhaps one should write about the beginnings of Greek knowledge using Dumézil's method.

and which is the secret buried deep within the volume. Now it is probable that true knowledge of the things of this world lies in the solid's essential shadow, in its opaque and black density, locked forever behind the multiple doors of its edges, besieged only by practice and theory. A wedge can sunder the stones, geometry can divide or duplicate cubes, and the story, indefinitely, will begin again; the solid, whose surfaces cannot be exhausted by analysis, always conserves a kernel of shadow hidden in the shade of its edges. Thales, while reading and noting the volume's traces, deciphers no secret except that of the impossibility of penetrating the volume's arcana, in which knowledge has been entombed forever, and from which the infinite history of analytical progress bursts forth as if from a spring. In this case, his history tells the conclusion of a story, that of the confrontation with solid objects, that of the attack on compact volumes, comprehended like theoretical, objective, unconscious elements, like theoretical, objective, indefinite unknowns. In this case the thing exists *qua* thing, like an unknown and a correlate, like a secret involuted into thousands and thousands of replicas. Two decisions: either I recognize the object by its shadow, which gives rise to geometry or, better yet, to the idealism of representation, or I allow for a kernel of shadow within the object. In the latter case, theory and practice develop this secret infinitely in a perpetually open history, the history of science, which admits that the solid always envelops something that can be rendered explicit. In Plato, the idealism of representation appears repressed in the depths of his cave, and realism is assumed. However, the story begun in the Nile delta will soon be completed by a sudden and incredibly audacious *coup d'état:* the radical negation of interior shadows. The Sun of Thales and Ra, the sun whose rays are shut out for an impeccable definition,[11] is reduced to the meager fire of the prisoners of representation. Thales's theorem, schema of this story, is in the cave's shadow. Outside, the new sun gives off a transcendent light which pierces things and transmits an all-seeing vision. This is how the marvelous miracle is accomplished: the transparency of volumes, the metaphorical naming of the realism of idealities. From the cave to the world outside, the scenography turns into an ichnography: the shadow of solids played on the plane of representation and defined them by boundaries and partitions; now light goes through them and banishes the interior

---

[11] One can dream, but only dream, that geometry could only have been born on a soil and in a climate where things finally appear exact. Beneath a blinding sun that diffuses its metallic light in a transparent and pure atmosphere, the world is outlined like a definition. The sailor's horizon is a circumference without undulating lines; the edges of things are precise; their shadow is rigorously delineated; the blue-black sky is a homogeneous space; and so forth. These conditions, proper to the Greek climate, are necessary, as are so many others—but they are far from being sufficient.

shadow.[12] In place of a planar triangulation of geo-metry there is now a stereometry of empty forms in the epiphany of diaphanousness. The archaic Thales of mensuration gives way to pure geometry, pure because it is cut through by the intuition of transparency and emptiness. Then and only then can the pyramid be born, the pure tetrahedron, first of the five Platonic bodies. By this miracle the sun is *in* the pyramid: the site, the source of light, the object, all in the same place.

Beneath this new sun, solids no longer have a shadow or a secret; light passes through them without being interrupted, just as it glides along a straight line or a plane; the world they constitute is thoroughly knowable. One can understand the importance that Plato and his school constantly attribute to the stereometry of volumes.[13] The open history of infinite explicitations is closed by this power move, by this stroke of lightning that rips away the veils of shadow; this history is reoriented toward the transcendency of forms. There is no more specter, or analysis; the three shadows (the one on the shaded area of the surface, the one cast, and the one buried within) are snatched away by the sun of the Good. And, as if to close the circle in all rigor and for the coherence of global history, the *Timaeus* will constitute the world by means of these five bodies: the first, the simplest, the tetrahedron in fact, will be fire. Plato has the pure pyramid come into existence beneath the fires of the sun, and from this tetrahedron he has fire born again: a double miracle that fulfills the scriptures, the Egyptian legend, and the initiation of intuition by positioning the source of light within the polyhedron. When the pyramid is itself fire (did its name influence its legend?), the sun passes through it. The entire myth of origin, even that of *The Republic,* is thus immersed in a vision of fire and dramatizes a solar rite. The new Thales can no longer see any shadow beneath the furnace that pure form and the solar hearth constitute: original conjunction of mathematical stereometry and the mythical element, blinding atmosphere of the first philosophies of intuition. The kernel of knowledge is continually enveloped by myth, and the myth is ceaselessly generated within the theater of representation. Theory, vision; light, fire.[14] We have here a new genesis with four branches

---

[12]Ichnography is defined as "a horizontal section, as of a building, showing its true dimensions according to a geometric scale; ground plan; map; also, the art of making such plans" (*Webster's*). —Ed.

[13]The message of Book VII of *The Republic* is a message of origin: that the Republic comes into light is not surprising (526d). Stereometry is due, in large part, to Theaetetus.

[14]Liddell and Scott favor the etymology *pyr* ("fire") for the term "pyramid." The *Timaeus* (56b) associates the two terms, and Plato never says "tetrahedron," a term which came into use starting with Pappus. The Pauly-Wissow encyclopedia (5.V. "Pyramids") has nothing definite to say about the origin of this term.

where two tributaries are mixed: science and the history of religions. From astronomy to solar mythology.

Nevertheless, this power move is not exactly a revolution. Plato kills the hen that laid the golden eggs: by cutting through the solids he nullifies history; the eternity of transcendency freezes the diachrony and the genealogy of forms. The future of the square and the diagonal is decided as much on the sand where we describe them through the language that names them as it is decided in the sky of ideas. The realism of transparent idealities is still immersed in a philosophy of representation. Of course, ichnography is substituted for scenography, but the former is a trans-representation from a divine point of view. To go beyond Thales's scene, the shadowless theater is still a theater. The inevitable realism is still an idealism: the geometric form clearly expresses this difficulty. This form is pre-judged to be without shadow or secret, it exists itself and in itself, but it never hides anything that could exceed the definition one has fixed for it. It exists as an ideality, transparent to vision, transparent to noesis. It is a theoretical element known thoroughly, something seen and known without residue. Intuition is blinded by its existence, but intuition passes through it. Its identity guarantees that it is ubiquitously identical, and hence its perception is not interrupted. Vision and knowledge are white specters. Now, precisely when this pure geometry, inherited from Plato, dies, when it is no longer possible to assume intuitive principles, when the theater of representation is closed, the secret, the shadow, and the implication will explode again among these abstract forms before the eyes of dumbfounded mathematicians — explosions that had been announced before all these deaths throughout history. The right angle, the plane, the volume, their intervals and their areas, will be recognized as chaotic, dense, compact — again teeming with folds and dark hiding places. Pure and simple forms are neither that simple nor that pure; they are no longer complete, theoretical knowns, things seen and known without residue, but rather theoretical, objective unknowns infinitely folded into one another, enormous virtualities of noemes, like the stones and the objects of the world, like our stone constructions and our wrought objects. Form hides beneath its form transfinite kernels of knowledge which, one might fear, history will never exhaust; these highly inaccessible instances become our new tasks. Mathematical realism is weighed down and takes on the old density that Plato's sun had dissolved. Pure and abstract idealities create shaded areas; they are full of shadows; they become again as black as the pyramid. Present-day mathematics, although maximally abstract and pure, is developing in a lexicon that derives in part from technology. It is a new way of listening once more to Thales's old Egyptian legend.

The solar myth envelops an implicit knowledge. Oral legend dramatizes an implicit schema and concept. The philosophy of vision, of intuition, and of representation includes and acts out an implicit theory. The technology of construction is the kernel of an implicit science. A triple, quadruple tunic whose surroundings present a new problem: what are the relationships of a technique, of a myth, of a communication, and of a philosophy? Again, the idealities implicit in technology, mobilized in representation, dramatized by myth, and transported by a particular language are filled to the brim with an implicit knowledge. The birth of beauty never stops; Harlequin has never donned his last costume. The myth is perpetuated; representation is spread further and further; archaisms resound through the centuries and are ferried to our feet like alluvia. What Thales saw at the base of the pyramids (the sun, the homothetic edifice, the shaded surface and the cast shadow), what Thales did alongside the pyramids (the partitioning off and the measurement of similar triangles in the parallelism of two gnomons, one of which is our body), are the thousands and thousands of implications that the history of science is slowly developing and that the eternal geometers will see, without always seeing them, and will create, without always knowing it. These implications express nothing less than the obscure articulations of rigorous knowledge and the totality of other human activities, indefinitely abandoned to their obscure fate. If by the birth of geometry one means the appearance of an absolute purity on an ocean filled with these shadows, then let us say, a few years after its death, that it was never born.

The history of mathematical sciences, in its global continuity or its sudden fits and starts, slowly resolves the question of origin without ever exhausting it. It is constantly providing an answer to and freeing itself from this question. The tale of inauguration is that interminable discourse that we have untiringly repeated since our own dawn. What is, in fact, an interminable discourse? That which speaks of an absent object, of an object that absents itself, inaccessibly.

6

▲
▲ ▲

Lucretius:
Science & Religion

Lucretius's *De Rerum Natura* is a treatise on physics. In general, the subsequent commentary of both critics and translators has refused to consider it as such, avoiding the nature of things as they really are, relating the knowledge given in the text to some unknowing prehistoric era, and discoursing instead about morality and religion, about politics and liberty. It cuts Lucretius off from the world; the scholiast abhors the world.

The hymn to Venus is a song to voluptuousness, to the original power, victorious—without having fought—over Mars and over the death instinct, a song to the pleasure of life, to guilt-free knowledge. The knowledge of the world is not guilty but peaceful and creative. It is generative and not destructive. But these words already drift toward morality—toward deeply felt emotions, toward ataraxia and toward the gaze, the theatrical gesture: to see everything serenely, in quiet contemplation; to be at last free from the gods. As if Venus were not a god. As if *De Rerum Natura* did not begin in prayer. A believer, an atheist? It is a clear-cut decision: there is only transcendence. Let the figures on the mountain carouse endlessly. We shall come back later to these peaks which are untouched by marine waterspouts. Transcendence is all there is, and it must be allowed its own peculiarity. But it is a matter of immanence. *Venus sive natura. Mavors sive natura.* It is a question of physics and not of feelings, of nature and not of cruel hallucinations. Immanence: laws criss-cross the world, which is unreservedly the locus of reasons. But before poetry, one must choose between two laws: the law of Eros or the law of Thanatos; springtime or the plague; birds or cadavers; and the wounds of love or rotting arms and legs. *Venus, verna, volucres, volnere amoris:* these are the lines that I want. To choose, then, between two sorts of physics, and the first hymn is the axiom of this choice. Venus, that is to say, nature; or Mars, that is to say, nature. And the two remain true, violence and the plague plummeting down the steepest slope, falling, without recourse, according to law. Thus, if I want to tell Memmius the laws of Nature, I first have to decide what its identity is, what its name is.[1] This decision, however, is so important historically and so serious culturally that perhaps nothing greater can be imagined. It so happens—and I am powerless in this matter, for I am the slave of science—that Western science has consistently *not* chosen Lucretius. And by that choice, it has opted for war and plagues, for brawls, blood, and bodies burnt at the stake. Western science, from Heraclitus to Hiroshima, has only known martial nature. What has been modestly called Lucretius's pessimism, seen in the drifting of his text from Aphrodite to the plague in Athens, is the recognition that he has lost his bet, and that his physics has been lost as well. Thus science, or what we call science, forbids us to read this lost science. The laws of Venus-Mother Nature cannot be deciphered by the children of Mars—these children who die and will continue to die at the stake before they ever understand that locally, within the walls of Athens for example, but also globally, at some indefinite time and place, the aforementioned decomposition brings back a large, teeming, atomic populace sliding down some thalweg, and thereby, by this declination, reconstitutes a world. The poem's text is nature itself, that of Venus. The text loops back upon itself at the end of the martial events, but not in a perfect circle. The spot in which the atoms fall is not necessarily plague-ridden Athens; the time of the *clinamen* is not necessarily simultaneous with leaving the dead to bury the dead.[2] Space and time are thrown here and there. There is no circle. But, stochastically, turbulences appear in space and time. And the whole text creates turbulence. Everywhere. Venus, *circumfusa*, is diffused all around the reclining body of Mars, who has been thrown down to the nadir he had searched for. She bothers him and disturbs his law. The creative science of change and of circumstance is substituted for the physics of the fall, of repetition, and of rigorous trains of events. Neither a straight line nor a circle: a spiral (*volute*).

Return to the declination, to the text that has finally been translated into its differential parts. The minimal angle to laminar flow initiates a turbulence. And from these pockets of turbulence here and there in indefinite times and places, there is one world among many, that of things and of men.

Without the declination, there are only the laws of fate, that is to say, the chains of order. The new is born of the old; the new is only the repetition of the old. But the angle interrupts the stoic chain, breaks the *foedera fati*, the endless series of causes and reasons. It disturbs, in fact, the laws of nature. And from it, the arrival of life, of everything that breathes; and the leaping of horses.

---

[1] Gaius Memmius was a Roman praetor and patron of poets to whom Lucretius addressed his *De Rerum Natura.* —Ed.

[2] See chapter 4, note 13. —Ed.

The order of reasons is repetitive, and the train of thought that comes from it, infinitely iterative, is but a science of death. A science of dead things and a strategy of the kill. The order of reasons is martial. The world is in order, according to this mathematical physics in which the Stoics are met by Plato up the line and by Descartes further down, and where order reigns supreme over piles of cadavers. The laws are the same everywhere; they are thanatocratic. There is nothing to be learned, to be discovered, to be invented, in this repetitive world, which falls in the parallel lines of identity. Nothing new under the sun of identity. It is information-free, complete redundance. The chains of cause and effect, the fall of atoms, and the indefinite repetition of letters are the three necessary figures of science's nullity. You might very well think that the bloodied rulers were thrilled to find this world and to seize upon its laws of determination—their own, in fact—the very same ones as they had: the laws of extermination. Determination, identity, repetition, information-free, not a drop of knowledge: extermination, not even the shadow of a life, death at the end of entropy. Then Mars rules the world, cutting up the bodies into atomized pieces, letting them fall. This is the *foedus fati,* what physics understands as a law; things are that way. It is also the legal statute in the sense of dominant legislation: they wish things to be that way. Mars chose this sort of physics, the science of the fall and of silence. And here again is the plague. It is always the same sequence of events: an epidemic becomes pandemic in proportions, if not to say a pandemonium; violence never stops, streaming the length of the thalweg; the atoms fall endlessly; reasons repeat indefinitely. Buboes, weapons, miasmas, causes: it is always the same law, in which the effect repeats the cause in exactly the same way. Nothing is new under the sun of identity and nothing is kept under the same old sun. Nothing new and nothing born, there is no nature. There is death forever. Nature is put to death or it is not allowed to be born. And the science of all this is nothing, can be summed up as nothing. Stable, unchanging, redundant, it recopies the same writing in the same atoms-letters. The law is the plague; the reason is the fall; the repeated cause is death; the repetitive is redundance. And identity is death. Everything falls to zero, a complete lack of information, the nothingness of knowledge, non-existence. *The Same is Non-Being.*

The angle of inclination cures the plague, breaks the chain of violence, interrupts the reign of the same, invents the new reason and the new law, *foedera naturae,* gives birth to nature as it really is. The minimal angle of turbulence produces the first spirals here and there. It is literally revolution. Or it is the first evolution toward something else other than the same. Turbulence perturbs the chain, troubling the flow of the identical as Venus had troubled Mars.

The first vortices. *Turbantibus aequora ventis:* pockets of turbulence scattered in flowing fluid, be it air or salt water, breaking up the parallelism of its repetitive waves. The sweet vortices of the physics of Venus. How can your heart not rejoice as the flood waters abate (*décliner*) and the primordial waters begin to form, since in the same lofty position you escape from Mars and from his armies that are readied in perfect battle formation? In these lofty heights that have been strengthened by the wisdom of the sages, one must choose between these two sorts of physics. The physics of the military troops in their rank and file formation of parallel lines, chains, and sequences. Here are the federated ones bound to fate, sheets of atoms bearing arms, exactly arranged, *instructa*, in a well-ordered fashion, in columns. This is the learned science of the teachers, the structure of divisions, the Heraclitean physics of war, rivalry, power, competition, which miserably repeats to death the blind shadows of its redundant law. Arrange yourselves in ranks; you will learn about order, about the structure of order, about the chain of reasons, the knowledge of ranks, of blood. Or else the physics of vortices, of sweetness, and of smiling voluptuousness. On the high seas, people work among these vortices: they are tossed about in the roll that, until recently, was called "turbination." They are perturbed. The *uexari*, however, is only cruel to a few landlubbers who have never been at sea. The sea-swept movement of intertwined lovers, or the voluptuous movements of the roll of the high seas. Listen to the line that swirls its spirals: *suaue, uentis, uexari, uoluptas.* It's the revolution of voluptuousness, the physics of Venus chosen over that of Mars.

A new return to declination. The difficulty of establishing or reading the theoretical text is added to the usual misinterpretations of translating it. Why, here and now, will (*volonté*) and voluptuousness (*volupté*)? Despite all their discussions, grammarians don't really know where to put the consonants: *volu(n)tas, volu(p)tas.* This doubt is a meaningful one. Once again, the demonstration begins. But from the beginning, we are forewarned. Maritime turbulence, looked at in bad weather from the shore, only stirs up fluids: winds and waters, *turbantibus aequora ventis.* And in the theoretical text, the reference to individual bodies again is only related to fluids: *imbris uti guttae*, like drops of rain, *per aquas atque aera rarum*, through the water or the rare medium of air; and again, *corpus aquae naturaque tenuis aeris.* It is certainly a question of weight, of gravity, but never of solids. It is the fall of heavy bodies, but not in the same sense that we have thought of these words as if instinctively since the dawn of the classical era. And from this comes the increased probability of the proposed solution: the schema is a hydraulic one. In the same way that the scattered examples throughout all the books are chosen from the animal kingdom, the models here are chosen from what we call fluid mechanics. In nature, living beings are born from flows. And these flows are laminar, their laminae parallel to one another; the declination is the tiniest angle necessary and sufficient to produce turbulence. From this comes the text that follows: what are these *foedera fati,* these laws of fate that are broken by declination? The subsequent lines define them: they are sequences, where cause repeats cause *ad infinitum.* From this, the bundle, the sheaf, the infinite cylinder of parallel consequences. Trains of reason rain down in torrents. No longer, as in the model, are they atoms; they are neither concrete nor quasi-concrete, but laws or equations. The fall is the plan of their necessity. However, the declination interrupts the model as well as the theory, perturbing them, introducing turbulence. And since the model and theory are necessitarian, what can we call this declination except liberty? But beware: it is only a question of *animantibus.* Life has a degree of freedom relative to mechanical constraints. The Latin *libera* remains concrete relative to weights, shackles, chains, and burdens. The laws of necessity, however, remain those of fall and equilibrium. And its follows, then, that life deviates from equilibrium. How can this be explained *materially?* By visible and tangible phenomena that can be produced in experiments on flows; by analogy with the concrete model. Turbulence deviates from equilibrium. And the beginning of the vortex is the minimal angle of declination. The fact that life disturbs the order of the world means literally that at first, life is turbulence. What you see from the top of the cliff, in its sweetness, is the first-born being arising out of the waters, Aphrodite, who has just been born in the swirl of liquid spirals, Nature being born in smiling voluptuousness.

This is not contrary to the law, nor delirious, nor absurd, nor illogical. Nor is it as opposed as people have said to the teachings of Epicurus, which are strewn with vortices and turbulent clouds, as in the letter to Pythocles, or in one of the lost treatises which was in fact named "Of the Angle in the Atom."[3] It is a physics, and, in a given flow, the *clinamen* is experienced, required by experimentation. But it is a kind of physics under a law different from the preceding ones. The *foedera naturae* are in no way *foedera fati.* Today we would say that the paradigm has changed. Science remains science and laws remain laws, but what changes is the global contract, the general scheme of things that scientists agree to call "physics." The fact that the declination has been mocked, that it seemed to be a distortion or a strain on the system, a fiction, as Cicero says, and that we have remained blind to such a simple phenomenon is really quite

[3] See Epicurus, *Letter to Pythocles,* in *The Philosophy of Epicurus,* trans. George K. Strodach (Chicago: Northwestern University Press, 1963), pp. 157-73. Concerning the lost treatise, see Diogenes Laertius, *Lives of the Eminent Philosophers,* trans. R. D. Hicks, 2 vols. (New York: G. P. Putnam's Sons, 1925), 2:557. —Ed.

normal, considering that we looked at it by using another paradigm. If you consider the history of fluid mechanics, even the most recent, you will see how much trouble physicists have had in escaping from theory to get back to the things themselves. Flow did not follow the theorems of general mechanics that had been around since the eighteenth century. Until the beginning of this century, no one could bring himself to describe flow in all its concrete complexity. It is as difficult to become a phenomenologist again as it is to break the contracts of fate. Epicurus and Lucretius change the paradigm. And Marx, who, while seeing subjectivity in the atom just as if it were a question of a Leibnizian monad, and seeing the arbiter in the *clinamen* as if he were rewriting the *Theodicy,* is doubly right to call Themistocles to mind.[4] Athens is near destruction; let us leave the city and wage a sea battle. I shall explain what I mean, but I shall eliminate the strategy, since Mars is now at rest. The new knowledge is mindful of stochastic phenomena: *incerto tempore incestisque locis* does not mean the absence of space and time and therefore the transition of the soul out of the tangible realm; it simply means random dispersion. Since Democritus, the new knowledge is aware of infinitesimal questions. It gets inspiration from hydrodynamic models and turns its attention toward the formation of living systems. It is more physical, less mathematical (since the probabilist organon is missing) than Platonic knowledge, more phenomenological and less measured. But, most important, Athena is in the ocean. The chosen model is a fluid one. It is no longer a crystal, nor the five regular polyhedrons that are the solids of the *Timaeus;* it is flow. The nature of Mars, of martial physics, is one of hard, rigid, and rigorous bodies; the physics and nature of Venus are formed in flows. The residual hardness of the atom is beyond the threshold of perception; what counts in experiments and in phenomena is large numbers, the crowd of elements, the unmeasurable cataract, the river. And henceforth we are able to understand this, since our newly developing physics tells somewhat the same story too, by flows, random events, systems, disequilibria. We misunderstood Lucretius because we were the children of Plato and the Stoics, because the fundamental facts of Epicurean nature remained marginal in traditional science, which was really not very Archimedean. From that point on, we ruled them out of the game in the history of science. Moreover, we put their nature outside nature, placing them in the soul and the subject. On the contrary, however, these facts are the foundation of materialism. Atoms are not souls; the soul itself is atomic. From this comes something which I hope

---

[4] Karl Marx, *Différence de la philosophie de la nature chez Démocrite et Épicure,* trans. J. Pommier (Paris: Ducros, 1970), p. 171.

will make people laugh for a long time to come: all non-physical interpretations of the *clinamen* remain essentially idealist, as it were, or, more precisely, spiritualist, along the classic lines of philosophies of the mind, of ideologies of power and of military science. Classical science deserves classical philosophy. Find a good dictionary and verify for yourself that "classis" in Latin means "army."

But we have arrived at the contract—at the change Lucretius made in the contract. Why should the laws of nature or the necessity of fate be named *foedus* or *foedera*? *Foedera naturae* or *foedera fati:* pacts, alliances, conventions. Are we able to understand a political or strategic terminology, like the presence of the divine figures of Venus and Mars, in a treatise of objective science that is supposed to release us from the hold of the gods, and that is directed toward a type of wisdom in which political ambition and the dealings in the forum will no longer play a part? Our vocabulary is itself mired in just such an ambiguity: the order is of the world and of the street; the law is of the code and of the laboratory; the rule is operative and civil; the class is logical, social, and scholastic, etc.

Every war finally ends by a treaty of alliance, a *foedus,* unless it continues to the point of total annihilation or to the pandemonium of the plague. In the beginning of the fifth book, the struggle with nature is set out in the labors of Hercules, the first singular case of every war in general. Here the laborer and the soldier are one and the same. The field of Quirinus is occupied by Mars. The land of the producer is ravaged by the legionnaire, who disguises himself as a laborer. This theft, for it is a theft or an embezzlement, is part of a stubborn tradition. In the last century, Michelet always used Herakles as both model and god; he is the fighter who seems to be the worker-hero. In point of fact, the real producer has too much to do to exhaust his energies in non-productive aggression. Lucretius denounces unlawful occupation perpetrated, as usual, in the name of terror. Who today is afraid of the Nimean lion or of the Hydra of Lerna? If there are monsters here or there, go elsewhere, and that's the end to that. Once the battle is over, Hercules is useless—theatrical, in fact. Epicurus put down his weapons. He speaks, gives the laws, dictates the *foedus.* The new alliance with nature. With Epicurus, the Heraclitean period, in which war is the mother of all and in which physics remained in Ares's realm, comes to an end. Thus Lucretius criticizes Heraclitus with severity but treats Empedocles with consideration: this other Sicilian had guessed the coming of the contract, in his introduction of Friendship or Love. Faced with Hatred or Discord, a joyful Aphrodite had already arisen. Epicurus and Lucretius have put down their weapons and driven Mars out of physics. Can we understand that, outside of mythology and its old-fashioned naïvetés? Yes, and in spades.

At the dawn of modern science, Bacon decreed that one cannot rule

Nature except by obeying her. Descartes said that one has to become her master and possessor.[5] The contractual alliance has been broken and the battle starts again, with nature as the adversary; hydra, boar, or lion. Against nature, one plays without cheating, abiding by the laws of the hunt until checkmate. Epicurus has just failed, as well as the Aphrodite of Lucretius. It is the well-armed Syracusan who takes the lead. The method is no longer a contract but a strategy, a tactic and not a pact, a fight to death and not a coitus. Hercules returns in Bacon's work to go beyond the pillars of Hercules. And Archimedes, in Descartes's, moves the earth.[6] And thus the figures of antiquity, such as Herakles, Mars, and Venus, are prosopopoeiae, since they can be reduced to principles and conditions.

In the establishment of objective knowledge, as in its historical beginning, there is a set of decisions or preliminary choices that often remain unnoticed. Here is one of them: either there is a contractual agreement or there is a military strategy; either there is the *foedus* which calls an end to combat or there is the tactical game of command and mastery. Who leads science and who decides what it shall be? The answer to the question, which appears to be mythological or religious, might be Mars or Venus, Hercules or Quirinus. Modern thinkers substitute other questions: what? or how? By contract or by strategy. Yet behind the abstract principles of method, our contemporaries rediscover the question: who? and the language of antiquity; behind metaphysics, they discover the groups in power. Who? the producing class or the dominating class? And thus the military and its generals. Lucretius speaks of eponymous heroes; Descartes and Bacon speak in abstract principles, but these principles sparkle with metaphors; we speak as historians. The question, however, remains the same in all three languages, bearing on the very conditions of possibility of science. What can be said about nature: is she an enemy or a slave, an adversary or a partner in a contract that Lucretius would have made with Venus? The question is neither naive nor frivolous, but consequential. Will knowledge follow the downhill slope of destruction, violence, and the plague or, inversely, that of peace and rejoicing? Life or death, that is the question. And there again, our knowledge hears the voice of Lucretius.

It is a condition and a postulate. It will be said that perhaps these

[5] See "Knowledge in the Classical Age: La Fontaine and Descartes," chapter 2 of the present volume. —Ed.

[6] See Francis Bacon, *Of the Proficience and Advancement of Learning Divine and Human*, in *Great Books of the Western World*, ed. Robert Maynard Hutchins, 54 vols. (Chicago: Encyclopedia Britannica, Inc., 1952), 30:29. See René Descartes, *Meditations on First Philosophy*, in *The Philosophical Works of Descartes*, trans. Elizabeth Haldane and G. R. T. Ross, 2 vols. (Cambridge: Cambridge University Press, 1975), 1:149. —Ed.

choices precede science, orienting it, or, better yet, that those who have changed the course of science profit from them. But anyway, the content, norms, and results of science remain invariable in relation to these postulates. The theorems and protocols are free in relation to these decisions. This is one of the weightiest problems that we have had to bear. It is difficult to think of a rigorous and exact science that might have been conditioned by Venus and not by Mars, for peace and not for destruction, by a contract and not by a strategy, by workers and not by generals, since Western science has always followed the weight of power. In other words: science is conditioned by postulates or by decisions that are generally social, cultural, or historical in nature, which form it and orient it; nevertheless, science is universal, and independent of the type of pre-established contract. Two and two make four; heavy bodies fall, according to the law of gravity; entropy increases in a closed system, regardless of the latitude and whatever the ruling class. I cannot think of a mountain, a border, or a date which makes the agreement of scientists and everyone else relative on these points. Science is conditioned but unconditional. No one has ever escaped this dilemma.

It is, however, rather easy to distinguish the first conditions which give rise to what is conditioned while leaving the content of what is conditioned independent. They are said to be conditioning and not determining. These first conditions are, moreover, sufficient. A small room, a table and a chair, three notebooks, two pencils, and the average salary needed to make all these things possible, and, thus, the whole society, with its history and its divisions, all form a set of conditions for me to write a book. But this book can come to exist or not, and if so, it can be a collection of equations or of poems, copied or inventive, exact or erroneous, red-hot or warmed over. In short, in this case and a thousand like it, *you can always proceed from the product to its conditions, but never from the conditions to the product.* This rather simple principle has led some or all of contemporary philosophy into a process of retrospection. Even its lucid discourse is unflagging as long as it goes backward, with perfect hindsight, toward the multiple conditionings; but it is powerless once it has to go forward from the condition to the thing itself. And for that reason it occupies a position of non-productivity, not for any poverty inherent in the theory, but because of an interminable and indeterminable theory.

Let us now suppose conditions that do not determine the contents of what they condition. The initial contract of scientific practice is certainly of this sort: mathematical operations, the law of gravity, and so forth, are independent of the conditions of the initial contract. But they determine, rather strongly, what I would call the map of the thing conditioned; its placement, the position of its various members, the centering of its space, the classification of its component parts, and the schema of their relations—in short, the global form and its relief at local points. Science is always the same, but its topography changes depending on the initial contracts. It is always the same clay, but the shape changes. For all I know, one might make a sword or a ploughshare from the same piece of iron. The physics of Lucretius—I have just shown this through these models—is in fact the same as that of Archimedes, but the postulation of Venus and the exclusion of Mars transform it.[7] Hydrostatics in the first is related to the constitution of living beings; in the latter, it is related to the theory of ship-building. Fluid mechanics can be a basis for biology or for a technology of the inert. The model does not vary; the relief changes. The parts and regions are upset. In a more general fashion, the postulate does not determine the sort of discourse or protocol, but rather the sort of classification. But the guiding light in science is, more often than you think, the arrangement of the parts. Science has made the necessary arrangements, as it were. We forget all too often that exploitation is originally a spatial term, from "explicit," related in turn to "explicate": the network of folds (*plis*) on a manifold. Classification, not only that of sciences, is always already there. It shows where to begin, where to go, the best route to take, and the region with the most interchanges. This is true for knowledge in general, for the encyclopedia: why put one discipline first, or in the middle; why start with a certain proposition or a certain experiment? What shapes a generation is less what it knows than the learning process that led it to this knowledge. Invention, discovery, rediscoveries, or what you will, all follow from a certain type of training. The pedagogue is a guide, the word itself says so; education is conducted by a *duce,* the word again attests to the fact; and the method is a path. And the global plan of this complex and the local connections of its graph are determined by a preliminary choice. Then the condition determines the outcome. If knowledge is used for death and destruction, it is because Mars or the military, Bacon's commander, or Descartes's master and possessor stood guard in the beginning. This is true as well outside of science: there are few untrammeled spaces: the paths have already been blazed and the classifications posited. Well before forces come into contact with each other, well before confrontation is produced, finds its equilibrium, or wavers, some nameless predecessor has chosen the battlefield and the firing lines that will decide the outcome. Strategy is not only a form of dynamics or energetics but first of all a topology. The presence of Mars or of Venus determines the shape of the realm of knowledge. Science has always been led by its flow charts. And from that point on,

---

[7] See Michel Serres, *La Naissance de la physique dans le texte de Lucrèce: Fleuves et turbulences* (Paris: Minuit, 1977), pp. 22-27. —Ed.

the master pays no attention to the contents. But all that is no longer important.

Foedus is thus the pact after the war, the peace treaty. The two enemies had been locked in combat with one another, and now the armistice has been signed. Up to now, it has been a question of science, and we did not understand the part played by decision. Postulate and decision, products of culture. Still more? *Foedus* is generally a contract, a social contract, for example. The social contract, however, can easily be rendered in the form of an armistice, once the all-out war is over. It is the plague and the end of the plague. The plague is a figure of violence in general, a multiple chain with an explosive power to propagate itself, and something which threatens a city or group with extermination: Athens, in Lucretius's work, or the realm of the Lion. From this comes the fable which tells how the judicial process was invented after a jackass had been killed as an emissary victim.[8] This violent communication, where the group's problems are at maximum—for its very existence comes into play here—stops with the use of force: the sacrifice of the one who will bear all the sins of the group. Justice is rendered, which means that justice appears, forming and formulating itself as an institution. And hence, the whole poem loops back upon itself without closing, just like a spiral. The plague at Athens has started: everyone whips himself bloody before the funeral pyres. The process only ends when all the fighters have died. To check the crisis, to interrupt it, that is to say, to topple the body of Mars, forcing him to bend over backwards, there has to be a convention, a pact, a *foedus,* a judicial institution, or something like it. This contract can only be reached through a sacrificial murder. But whose? Mars can only be stopped at the altar of Iphianassa. The elite of Greek warriors stain the stone of the virgin Trivia with the blood of Iphigenia. This is the ordinary, trivial, and traditional solution, offered by every religion and every brand of politics. Iphigenia, that is to say, the genealogy of sovereign power. Lucretius makes it a point to give her name in Greek. She dies, and the ribbons of her untied headband dangle down, all the same; there is an abolition of differences. Her throat slit by her father's sword, she is a virgin who had not yet bled; non-violent and innocent, she causes the agitation of the wind-swept high seas. For the storm, too, is the plague. There are two figures of violence: flood and pandemonium. Murder increases along the chain, the two figures growing or escalating, as it were. Without the ritual killing of the virgin, the war would have

8See La Fontaine, "Les Animaux malades de la peste," in *Fables,* ed. Antoine Adam (Paris: Garnier-Flammarion, 1966), pp. 180-81. —Ed.

taken place among the Greek warriors themselves before they could ever have gotten to Troy. The waters are finally in movement and the miasmas reappear. Here then is the contract, the blood contract, a contract of the oldest tradition, maybe even a predestined one: the *foedera fati*.

From that point on, what has to be stopped is the major threat, but its archaic safeguard as well. The plague, of course, and the storm (Lord, while you sleep we sink), the fatal propagation of murder, but also—especially—the solution offered by the sacred to this collective problem: human sacrifice. Iphigenia must be saved. Science, here played against religion, is not the laic played against the church, this fraternal rivalry that we studied in school. How silly an idea. The problem at hand consists in stemming a series of murders without another assassination. For that solution is only temporary until a new crisis, a new squall, or a new epidemic erupts and the whole process is repeated. Nothing is new under the bloodied sun of history. The plague reappears in an Athens bestrewn with cadavers. The scapegoats too must be saved by putting a stop to the series of sacrifices. From this comes the reversal: he who speaks and thereby gives rise to a new history does not place the sins of the world on the shoulders of another; of his own volition, he takes upon himself the thunderous roars of the heavens, the fire that has been set at the world's gates, the wrath of Jupiter. Spontaneously, he accepts the dangerous position that is determined by his knowledge of the laws of the universe and of human mechanisms. Faced with these horrible menaces, he goes forward unarmed. Epicurus, therefore, once again takes us away forever from the storms, putting us in a quiet spot away from the water. Yes, Memmius, Epicurus is a god, and he has a perfect right to the title of god; there is no contradiction here. Neither Cicero nor his successors understood anything of this matter. To take on oneself alone the fires of the heavens and not to foist unleashed violence on the first passerby, the virgin Iphigenia, to go forward unarmed, straight ahead, lucidly deciphering what is happening, is to proceed in a fashion opposed to the world's religions and contrary to the terrifying constitution of the sacred. But this conduct can only be practiced if one knows the laws of constitution and if one is a master of justice. Epicurus is a god outside of all the gods, the new god of another history who has examined all the archaic traditions and turned against them. He abolishes the sacred by fulfilling it. The atheistic Epicureans were not wrong to venerate the founder of this science as a god. And through his courageous gesture, heroic above the call of heroism, Epicurus lets Venus be born above the troubled waters. That is to say, the *foedus*, love, and friendship; the contract of nature, *foedera naturae*. It is finally definitive, and the gods are no longer in the world, since an end to the ancient repetition of the sacrificial crisis has intervened, a cessation which is the basis of Epicurean wisdom.[9]

Freed, then, from this violence, henceforth independent of sacred space and time that no longer have any relation to us, with our feet firmly planted on high ground, protected from the sea, strengthened by the wisdom of the sages against the machinations of Mars, we are now able to let things come into being as objects, outside the mechanisms that regulate our deregulated violence. The sacred had formed a field of knowledge of the intersubjective and of polemical relationships. Nature thereby veiled itself in the dynamic laws of the group. Once the sacred is placed outside of the world in faraway locations which are of no interest to us, Nature is born, objectively, bearing her own laws. *The solution founds science,* the science of Venus without violence and without guilt, where thunder is no longer the anger of Zeus and where the level of the waters remains stable. In the new contract, the exact word can be spoken.

Might this be a general solution? Does science regularly appear in history in the wake of figures like Epicurus?

Foedus is the pact made after the war. The laws of nature, pronounced by the sciences, remain conditioned and then determined in their global arrangement by such a preliminary contract: the choice between Venus and Mars, for example. *Foedus* is, moreover, the convention that puts an end to all-out war. During a first period of history, exterminating violence freezes, coagulates, stops during the sacrificial murder: Iphigenia. But a new crisis makes it start up again, and the plague begins anew. One must start over. The sacred is formed by this catastrophic and repetitive dynamic. The hero Epicurus willingly takes the place of the virgin; unarmed, he disarms the process, gives rise to a new history, an objective science. One is finally able to see how Venus replaces Mars. *Foedus* is, once and for all, a political constitution.

Is calling the *foedera naturae* what we call the laws of nature a projection of such a constitution on the world? Is it a ruse, a ruse of reason, to give the status of a natural necessity to arbitrary power, that is to say, to the dominance, here and now, of certain people? It cannot be denied that such cheating has often occurred. All powers seek to be legitimate since, abusive by nature, they always lack legitimacy. To establish dominance through science is really an ordinary strategy and, moreover, rather a simple one, since the sciences themselves are usually based on dominance. All that is necessary is to move around a circle; it is so evident that it can

---

[9]This is, I believe, the solution that René Girard would have given to the whole question, a solution parallel to my own. (See René Girard, *Violence and the Sacred* [Baltimore: The Johns Hopkins University Press, 1977] and René Girard, *Des Choses cachées depuis la fondation du monde* [Paris: Grasset, 1978]. —Ed.)

hardly be called a ruse or a trick. The Greeks, including Plato and others, did not miss the opportunity to do so, and they have been imitated rather well since their time, right up to the present.

However, two matters still remain: one is very general, pertaining to "Greekness"; the other is specific to the Epicureans and to Lucretius. No one is better endowed by nature for trickery than a Greek, who is always a bit of the child of Ulysses and Metis; elsewhere I have shown how a simple effect of perspective allowed for the belief in democracy even though the unchanging archaic hierarchy persisted all the while: an effect of optics and of geometry, a scientifically projected illusion. However, these perfect masters of the arts of trickery invented dichotomy, separation, and partition at the same time. They founded classicism as the theory of the specificity of various realms: Olympus was for the gods, the world for the atoms, and the axe came between the two. I admit, I even underline, the fact that this word "classicism," or another like it, is multivalent, referring at once to myth, to the sacred, to power, and to physics. But in point of fact if we today have the weak and awkward fancy to read the word as polysemic and out of sync, it is because of the Greeks. It is due to the divisions and clarifications that they brought to the fore. No one but the Greeks knew how to divide or to classify. For the first time, they made a discrete kind of cartography: the constitution and meteors, mathematics and myth, medicine and theory of exchange, and whatever else one wishes. Greekness is "polytomy," the clear awareness of any metabasis to another genre. Greekness is dichotomy, the theory of segments in the representation of distinct worlds. Without that, is it conceivable that atoms would have been invented? From this point on, the question can be decided. Certainly the Greeks tricked, rused, cheated, connived, and defrauded, almost as much as we have, and that is saying a lot; like us, they tried to pass off a sow's ear as a silk purse, to pass off just about anything as science. But if all they had ever done, in every situation, was a bit of underhanded sleight-of-hand, would they have invented geometry? No, that is impossible. If there is a separate field in which no one can keep cards up his sleeve without being resoundingly defeated, it is certainly mathematics. Let no one enter here if he is an illusionist. Inversely, all philosophy, all discourse, all texts which avoid this field keep some elbow room to cheat *ad infinitum* and to seem to everyone never to be mistaken. The criterion of truth is used at the risk of error. The only path to invention is complete consent to be mistaken in front of others. Everything else is only power. And the physics of the atomists, as I have shown, does not avoid the mathematical model.[10]

---

[10] See Serres, *La Naissance de la physique*, pp. 17-125. — Ed.

I am not saying that it is sure, just that it is probable, that from this point on the fraudulent projection of a political schema as is onto the world does not occur here. Polytomy—dichotomy—is the chosen field of the atomist thinkers, from their elements to their transcendental theology. And their wisdom expressly tends to keep them away from trying to garner power. Just like their scientific praxis: the method using clusters of multiple explanations clears the way for them to agree to error and closes off the path to taking power. And, on the contrary, for the first time the world is autonomous, not bound to a commandment but self-directed. On the contrary, for the first time the ruse is removed from the free play of things. And it is really the first physics, in the way Einstein understood it, that is to say, one that is subtle but that does not cheat.

The reversal occurs immediately. Far from being a political convention projected onto nature, it is on the contrary that natural constitution which finally takes every other federation into account. Either I am greatly mistaken or that is materialism. On the contrary, to decide how to read the state of things starting from the state of public relations, that is idealism again. The individual subject may be replaced by a collective "we" with its habits and history, but the function of idealism will not vary one jot. Things remain changeable forms for a pole armed with force and consciousness. This is simply generalized idealism: from the individual to the group, from the represented forms to the whole of practicable transformations, from the fleeting moment to historical time. Through the corpus of these concrete extensions, idealism is kept and transmitted to us. Materialism is always hidden behind it. The state of things becomes the reason of the state instead of that of the transcendental ego. This is the very fight of Lucretius against Mars, and against power. The natural constitution is, after all, nothing but the atomic constitution. Men, no less than things, are composed of atoms, both in their soul and their consciousness. The collective is thus composed of things that are themselves compound. Henceforth, what does the *foedus* mean?

One must get back to things themselves. Almost at the beginning of the first book, Lucretius distinguishes the *coniuncta* from the *euenta*, according to a standard division of Epicurean physics. What is conjoined to a body is that which is destroyed if this thing is separated from it. Thus it is the conjunction as such. The examples given clarify the definition. What is conjoined to the stone is weight; to fire, heat; to water, liquidity. Thus, all bodies are tangible and the void is not tangible. It is a question of what Leibniz in the seventeenth century would have called a well-founded phenomenon, whose internal relations and specific external relations are stable. For the fundamental states of matter, atoms, and the void, tactility is the condition that makes the experiment possible. In order to conceive of these residual bodies (themselves borderline cases) as a borderline case, and to conceive of the conditions for the existence of others, all one must do is to extrapolate from the tactile. These are the two founding conditions of physics. From that point on, physics is the theoretical science of the void and of the atoms—on the one hand, what could be called fundamental physics—and on the other hand, the experimental science of the phenomena that are grounded or founded on them. Experimental physics is triple: it is concerned with weights, fluidity, and heat. Our model has been confirmed. In traditional language, the studies of weight, of heat, and of fluid mechanics are the three major disciplines of the natural sciences. We rediscover them constantly in the text and they are all we find. The fall of atoms and of bodies not at equilibrium, the formation of flows, turbulent fluxions, fire. They are charged with the birth of everything and everyone. What is a living thing? A thing in equilibrium and in disequilibrium, a flow, a vortex, heat—perhaps like any other object. The definition is Lucretius's—as it is our own. Atomist physics is our own.

Again then, what is the *foedus*? Atoms are organized here in well-established phenomena. Their reunion is a convention, a coition, *coitus*, and a conjunction, *coniuncta*. Without this conjugation or meeting, the gatherings become undone and the phenomena have no basis; physics, in its three fields, disappears. Physics remains the fundamental theory of the void and of atoms, as if it were the science before the birth of things, but it is destroyed as the science of nature. Bodies are made of atoms and void, and the study of bodies consists in finding out how they are made. Their substance is particular to them and their nature is relational. The essential thing, then, for an exact discourse *de rerum natura* is relation or interrelation—the simplex, as combinatory topology says; bonds, as chemistry says; interaction, as modern physics says. This set of relations without which nothing can come into being or exist is made up—from the factual point of view—of *coniuncta*, which are the stable networks of composition. And in theory, it is enunciated by the *foedus*. In a certain sense, the proto-model of fundamental physics has no laws. Given an infinite void in which atomic clouds move about, a space in which sets and groups move, as soon as a phenomenon appears or a body is formed a law can be stated. The laws of nature come from conjugation; there is no nature but that of compounds. In the same way, there are the laws of putting together letters-atoms to produce a text. The alphabetical proto-cloud is without law and the letters are scattered at random, always there as a set in space, as language; but as soon as a text or speech appears, the laws of good formulation, combination, and conjugation also appear. These laws, however, are only federation. The law repeats the fact itself: while things are in the process of being formed, the laws enunciate the federated. A thing or a state of things, like fluid mechanics and the theories of equilibrium and heat, can take these laws into account, and are conjugated *de facto* and federated *de jure*. But there is neither difference nor distance. How can the laws of *foedera* be expressed if not in a language or in a text in which composition is *reproduced*? The *foedera naturae*, the laws of nature, are the *foedera coniunctorum*, the laws of conjugation, but they are only possible by dint of this conjugation: *coniuncta foederum*, the composition of the laws. There is no distance from the fact to the laws; the space between things and languages is reduced to zero. In both cases—but there is really only one case—every formation is a linking; everything is only relation. Aside from relation, there are only clouds in the void, be they made of letters or of atoms. Language is born with the birth of things and by the very same process. Things appear as the bearers of their own language. *Coniuncta* and *foedera* are the same word: stable gatherings of elements, of whatever sort.

And from this comes something essential. At the same time that atomism produces physics and constitutes it as a fundamental theory of the elements and a triple discipline that is faithful to testable phenomena, it answers the radical question constantly asked but never answered: how is it possible that our laws, hypotheses, and models agree with the real world? Lucretius makes it understandable that the world is understandable. My text, my word, my body, the collective with its agreements and struggles, bodies that fall, flow, burn, or resound just as I do, all these are only a network of primordial elements in communication with each other.

Again we ask, what is physics? It is the science of relations, of general links between atoms of different kinds. Conformities, conventions, congeries, coitions. And from this comes the prosopopoeia of the overture: the goddess who alone is sufficient to govern nature. Venus states the *foedus*, the contract, as an *ego coniungo vos*. Venus assembles the atoms, like the compounds. She is not transcendent like the other gods, but immanent in this world, the being of relation. She is identical to the relation. *Venus sive natura sive coniuncta sive foedera*. She inspires inclination; she *is* inclination. Declination is also a differential of voluptuousness, the first trouble before a linking. Only Aphrodite governs: who was ever able to govern without the angle of the rudder (*gouvernail*)? Look at lightning in Heraclitus's work: it is said to be the governor of all things. But how could that be without the inclination of the rudder blade or the inclined zig-zag with which it marks the sky? It is the furrow of the world, inscribed and traced in the clouds, the mark of the rudder solicited in an oblique fashion, the seal struck by the government, by its one and only law. Here again: nature is formed by linkings; these relations, crisscrossing in a network, necessarily begin with a differential angle. And Venus inclining is the declination itself.

Lucretius carefully distinguishes the conjunctions which make the stable objects from *euenta*—events or accidents. He marks the separation between physics and history, exactly what had to be shown. On one hand, there are weight, heat, and liquidity, conjoined to the bodies which themselves are conjunctions. These are the primary qualities of conjunction itself, the qualities of Venus, who weighs, who flows, who is hot. These are the ways in which a relation is established. These various necessary links ensure the stability of natural things, that is to say, the possibility of experience. Our determinism says exactly the same thing. It is a guarantee of repetition. This has been reproduced, and it will reproduce itself again. And so it goes with *coniuncta:* so tied up with things that one remains assured of always finding them. The stability of their tissue, of the conjunctive network. Events, however, are cut out of another cloth. They come and go. Look at the words themselves: *aduentu, euenta,* they form an unstable flow from their advent to their eventual dispersal (*de l'avent à l'évent*). The atoms flow downstream from upstream, and do not form a *convention.* Events are adventitious, neither uniting nor joining in a coitus, but becoming immediately undone by *abitu.* They spread out and spill over, *funditus,* from top to bottom and back again. Unstable, they flow around the resistant and conjoined centers of objects. They cross, irrevocably, carried along by the flow.

Here is the complement of the model. Given a flow of atoms, by the declination, the first tangent to the given curve, and afterward, by the vortex, a relatively stable thing is constituted. It stays in disequilibrium, ready to break, then to die and disappear but nonetheless resistant by its established conjunctions, between the torrential flow from the upstream currents and the river flowing downstream to the sea. It is a stationary turbulence. At the heart of this nucleus, the *coniuncta* crystallize in a network. The thing thereby has weight and, as a liquid, it heats up. Physics studies these stabilities. All around these volutes, which together are the very nature of things, the unending flow continues to shower atoms. They occur, finding these voluminous knots here and there, conjugate vaguely with the profiles of the objects, and then quickly move toward the exit, disheveled and undone, resuming their parallel path. Barely a disturbance or ripple on the water's surface. Without objects of matter and space, without quasi-stationary formations, this movement would not be thus, nor would it be perceived. It is a poorly grounded phenomenon, totally bereft of conjunctions. It occurs, crosses, expires, or disperses: it is an event.

Time itself would be nothing without objects situated in space, without their respective movements, their formation, their disintegration. My readers will forgive me this, but the clock that Lucretius placed right in the middle of nature cannot mark Newtonian time; as the clock is the totality of things, between their birth and death, it marks a Bergsonian, that is, thermodynamic, time—an irreversible and irrevocable time, marked like the endless flow of atoms, flowing, running, crumbling (*coulant, courant, croulant*) toward their downfall and death. Things have weight: they fall, seeking their peaceful rest. Fluid, they flow; hot, they cool off. Downfall, death, dispersal: breaks, dichotomies, atoms. Atomic flow is residual: the background of being, white noise. This world set adrift never to return is bestrewn, here and there, at indefinite times and in indefinite places, with pockets, where vortices are born in pseudo-returns. Clocks appear with these objects, spiraling, shifting clocks which from their moment of birth begin to mark the time of death. The Lucretian world is globally entropic, but negatively entropic in certain swirling pockets. Conjunction is negative entropy; the complex thus formed counts the quantity of information set adrift. The event which barely occurs and almost immediately disintegrates minimally resists the irreversible flow, carrying little information. Newtonian time, which is reversible, marks resistance to the irrevocable. It is absent from this sort of physics, and that is why our forefathers were unable to imagine that Lucretian physics ever existed, with the possible exception of Bergson, who thrived on it. Irreversible time is the master here: the physics of things resists it in spots, but in the flow of the drift; history follows, producing barely a ripple in the flow. History flows around physics.

Hence Lucretius's examples. In the same way that conjunctions were heavy, liquid, and hot, and thereby produced the classifications of physics, events are all of a sociopolitical order. Slavery and freedom are placed on either side of the couple poverty-wealth, as if the central pair were the nucleus of the surrounding pair. The condition of the slave and that of the free man are placed alongside material and spatial objects: a dearth of bread, a wealth of money. *Symptômata*, says Epicurus, of events; *symbebēkota*, he says, of conjunctions. Slavery and freedom are symptoms of wealth and poverty, themselves symptoms of better-connected material things. History is a symptom of nature. Time is the symptom of symptoms. Let us take the war now, be it the current one or the Trojan War. Mars is only an accident of stable Venus, a temporary relief outside the assembled convention. Mars passes by, badly connected. Vulcan would have to capture him in his net, as Homer says, meaning a *penis captivus*. Otherwise, Mars is only in transit, passing through. Final example, agreement. Here is the *foedus*, the political *foedus*, pronounced after the war, and following every war. Far from projecting the constitution of political order on the state of things, unconsciously, as they say, Lucretius distinguishes very clearly the conjunctival, contractual, stable links among atoms themselves from the circumstantial and unstable historical contract which would be nothing without the existence of the former and which quickly disappears around them. Politics and history are only the phenomenal symptoms of the basic, fundamental combination.

Lucretius translates *symptômata* by *euenta*. Once again the Greek word has to do with falling. Things fall and meet each other along the way. There are bodies, be they solid, liquid, living, or whatever. Atoms are a basic example: collision and chance. Cournot says exactly the same thing when he talks about the intersection of independent series.[11] Falling disappears from his definition, always to reappear metaphorically: the shingle falling on the back of the passerby, like the tortoise on Aeschylus's head, and so forth. However, it also disappears in the translation of Lucretius. As far as I know, that is still favorable to the model: less a fall than a transition. It occurs, while in Greek it falls. Things arrive and occur and only crumble or disintegrate for a unique figurative case. Moreover, the prefix is erased, though it is kept in the word *coniuncta*, for *symbebēkota*. Thus the small amount of linkage between events, as if the encounter produced no, or few, relations. Venus is absent from history and politics. Lucretius adopts, instead of this *con-*, a prefix of emission. This is very important, for it is at the exit that we see that it was only a question of politics and history; nothing remains but ruins, and the scattered pieces are once again in parallel free fall, while the world continues to turn in a more or less stable way. The symptom was a phantom. And it was only a symptom, in the modern sense of the word, of natural objects. And as far as I know, that is really materialism.

The peace of the Garden, its tranquil serenity, is called "ataraxia." But the soul is formed of atoms, like the body, like the world. Ataraxia, a moral state, is thus a physical state, one without divergence or distance. But the latter model shows in infinite space a chance multiplicity of vortices of which one of the sets is nature, this nature, and of which the set of all the sets is the plurality of worlds. For Lucretius, and for us as well, the universe is the global vortex of local vortices. And so it goes in his poem. Ataraxia is the absence of trouble. Nature is rivers and whirlwinds. The life of the wise man is free from turbulence, yet his life is the closest to nature. In the name of Epicureans, Seneca gives this bit of advice: *ad legem naturae revertamur*. Return to the natural law, to the *foedus. Revertamur*, morals and vortex again.

What nature teaches us is the streaming of the endless flow, the atomic cascade and its turbulences—waterspouts and whirlwinds, the celestial

---

[11] The nineteenth-century mathematician, economist, and philosopher, Antoine Cournot, argued that there are two sorts of causal chains: *interdependent* ones and *independent* ones. The intersection of independent causal chains gives rise to chance occurrences. See Antoine Cournot, *An Essay on the Foundations of Our Knowledge* (New York: The Liberal Arts Press, 1956), pp. 39-53. — Ed.

wheel endlessly spinning, the conic spiral that generates things. The soul, like the body, like bodies, is made up of hot atoms, airborne and windswept, unnamed; that is to say, it is made up of the principles of heat, of fluidity in general, and of weight; it is the seat of turbulences. It burns, it is disturbed, it loses its balance, like the sea, like a volcano, like thunder. The same space and the same substance produce the same phenomena according to the same laws. Disturbances that we give names to out of our fear of the gods, or of the anguish of death. The soul is tied in knots, just like the world. And like the world, it is unstable, in a state of disequilibrium.

Physics and psychology account for these scattered knots where disturbances occur. Within the three physical disciplines, the fundamental theory is connected to atomic laminar flow, the void, and basic principles. Within cultural psychology, marked with anguish and anxiety by the gôds and by history, burdened with the relative and adventitious events of strife and combat, morals are linked to a primary state of things. Ataraxia returns to the initial turbulences before there was a disturbance in the straight line of the flow. The wise man *is* the basic world. He rediscovers material being, the base of being itself, where no ripple has yet troubled the surface of the waters.

Once more, we have to mark irreversible time on the clocks. It ticks away, irreversibly, marking degradation. The things that were formed in the hollows of the vortices lose their atoms little by little in the downstream flow. It is the time of wear and tear, the statues of the gods worn out by the kisses of the faithful. The world is mortal. This is thermodynamic time: time of heat, weight, and flow, the disciplines of the *trivium.* It is the drift toward the plague and toward dissolution. We call this the second principle of thermodynamics, known to the Greeks at least since Heraclitus. History, or the idea of history, is only the translation or transposition of this material principle. It is not only the copy or reproduction of a mythical paradise lost. If, from the beginning until today, the earth has become tired and no longer creates any new species, if men are less solid and more fragile, it is because the devouring downstream flow has stolen a share of their atoms. More and more, they are the hollow men, offered up to the erosion of irreversible time. Atomist physicists take up an old tradition, but they place it in the realm of the demonstrable and experimentally provable. From this point on, history has two components: irrevocable wear and tear and the human labor which tends to compensate for erosion. The farmer adapts to the aging of the earth: through his labor, he wrests from the earth what it used to give freely. Progressive civilization is merely a response to the wear and tear of time. Civilization goes upstream in the entropic river. Hence labor, of course, but also language and writing. Culture and agriculture have always been on the same vector.

Given all that, the physics of the Atomists also has an equivalent of what we call the first principle. The universe is regulated on a constancy, an *isonomía*. We are not yet at the invariability of forces or energy, but everything occurs as if this were the case. To the degradation of one thing corresponds the birth of another somewhere else; to the death of a world from plagues and funeral pyres, the appearance somewhere, anywhere, of a new world. The thesis of the plurality of existing worlds is thereby made necessary. The struggling, dying world gives up its atoms in a cataract to the basic flow; it is untied and undone analytically; elsewhere, in an indefinite place and time, a declination is the herald of a new vortex. It is therefore necessary to have a multiplicity in infinite space for a constancy to be established in the field of eroded disappearance, of irreversibility, and of chance. Invariability is global. Physics presents a system, but not a hierarchical, deductive, or closely woven one like that in the series of the Stoics; it is a physics of set theory whose general equilibrium is a balance sheet that takes the stochastic into account. Locally, this meta-stability is seen for the time being on the threshold marked by the rising of the waters; the theory announces it by unchangeable laws; praxis ensures it by the success of the provisions. Here again is a *foedus:* the pact is constancy and the contract, insurance. Lucretius goes still further, and, without a doubt, more deeply, into the matter. He guarantees the stability of the flow itself in its movement and direction, so it attains homeorrhesis. Whatever the changing combinations of atoms, whatever the obstacles in front of them, be they monsters or androgynes, the aleatory vortices end up by producing a coherent, well-founded (that is to say, conjoined) world. Further on, the conjunction is undone in the streaming of mortality. Still further on, in that which is foreseeable globally but unforeseeable locally, the declination reappears. The *clinamen* is a principal element of homeorrhesis, assuring the stability of the chreodes, being a differential of a chreode. In order to be no longer only static, in order for the system to be no longer only a statue, in order for stability itself to attain movement, what else is necessary at the beginning besides an inclination? I am not saying that it is sufficient, but necessary. The river must have a fall line for it to remain stable in its variable bed. Declination is a powerful discovery of physics and mechanics. It breaks with the common antithesis of rest and movement of Parmenides and Heraclitus, much better than Plato had done it. In evidence and in simplicity, in that which can be touched and tested. With the declination, what is stable is movement along the path of its flow, both in its general direction and in its point-by-point passage. It is declination which ensures the deepest and most exact invariability, although tradition, up to modern times, has only seen it as paradoxes. For it is the condition of a great synthesis between static and dynamic. Hence, the following recapitulation: the old unitary Being is multiplicity; there are atoms. The stable Being at rest is movement: atomic flow, streaming, cascades. The global fluidity of local solids. Here is irreversible time. The tiniest possible angle, the angle of contingence, marks a direction, which needs no other referent than the intrinsic one of the flow: and we have a thalweg. A stability is recognized, exists, is thinkable and tangible in and through fluvial flow; it is homeorrhesis. Through conjunction a reunification is possible. The physics of things has made the round of ancient physics, leaving the head gods atop their mountain. In the same way that the analysis of being produced atoms, the analysis of vectorial directions of space produces the *clinamen*. Movement and rest are joined in turbulence, constancy and variation, life and death. There was perhaps nothing in all of Antiquity more accurately seen and stated.

Everything is abraded by irreversible atomic erosion. The increasing work of humanity seeks to check this irrevocable movement. It is progress; it is not progress: history advances on the surface but backs up below, climbing back up a flow which goes down more quickly than it can advance. Catching up is forestalled; the plague will return. The *euenta* slide over the *coniuncta;* history skids over matter. The first global vortex. Humanity builds weak cohesions on top of material centers with strong cohesion in the process of coming undone. Athens, preeminent city of culture, grapes and figs, discourse and science, has to end, despite all this work, in a scattered pile of atomized bodies. The ashes of the funeral pyres are given over to the cataract. The irrevocable fate of laborious transformations. This history is doomed from the beginning. Hence, one should expect nothing from struggles, competition, agitation, activity, or growth, for they are all just a little brownian motion on the surface, superficial disturbances hiding the incurable erosion of matter, of things, and of the world.

Everything is constant, but in the aleatory and the directional. Venus watches over rebirth, a whim of her springtime desire: the first occurrence of meetings and of collisions. Here and there, yesterday and tomorrow, for the perpetuation of the species. Athens is lost; this city is erased from history; that universe is crumbling; a turbulence starts again, twinkling somewhere in the infinite void, formed in the wink of an eye or clinker-built. It is born with its own time; elsewhere there are smoking ruins: Troy. The second global vortex, but exploded globally. The dead and the constitutions are distributed and dispersed in a spatiotemporal infinity.

Thus, the wise man comes back to natural pacts, beginning at the beginning. Well versed in the temporality of degradation, he knows that the vortices will come undone. Not only the pointless agitation of turbulent men, simple ripples on the water's surface, but also—and especially —things and the world produced from turbulence. All these disturbances return to the original streaming. Born of dust, to dust they return. And it is the same with the soul, my soul, a thing among things. Not only here and now, troubled with anguish and anxiety, with fear and suffering, but born some night from a chance occurrence, a meeting, a collision, an inclination, a disturbance. This morning my soul is tumultuous, convulsive, and tempestuous, but from its birth and in its very being, it is only a troublemaker, a product of a storm in the atomic cloud, of an oblique lightning bolt. It is a taraxia, just like my body, and like things themselves. I know it; the laws of physics tell me so. And I make my revolution. The physics of the vortex is revolutionary. It goes back to the first disturbance, toward the original *clinamen*. And from there to the streaming, to the constancies of movements, to general invariabilities, whatever the random variations, to the primordial paths of matter itself, pricked here and there, marked with convulsions. Thus, ataraxia is a physical state, the fundamental state of matter; on this base, worlds are formed, disturbed by circumstances. Morality is physics. Wisdom completes its revolution, going back up the helix toward this first state of things; ataraxia is the absence of vortices. The soul of the wise man is extended to the global universe. The wise man is the universe. He is, when pacified, the pact itself.

Greek wisdom reaches one of its most important points here, where man is in the world and of the world, in matter and of matter. He is not a stranger in the world but a friend, at home in the world, a fellow voyager, an equal. He has a contract of Venus with things. Many other wisdoms and many other sciences are founded, antithetically, on breaking this contract. Man is a stranger in the world, alienated from the dawn, from the sky, from things. He hates them and fights against them. His environment is a dangerous enemy who must be fought and who must be kept in servitude. Martial neuroses from Plato to Descartes, from Bacon to us. The hatred of objects at the root of knowledge, the horror of the world at the heart of the theoretical. The universe of Epicurus and Lucretius is a reconciled one in which the science of things and the science of man go hand in hand, in identity. I am a disturbance, a vortex in turbulent nature. I am an ataraxia in a universe in which the heart of being is undisturbed. The wrinkles on my brow are the same as the ripples on the water. And my appeasement is universal.

The crisis temporarily subsides after a sacrificial murder. Iphigenia is put to death, the wind rises up, the Trojan War will take place, a new crisis of violence. Here the war takes place in Athens, atrocious brawls among the funeral pyres. The plague, like the unleashed ocean, like the swelling waters of the river, is a figure of violence. In the sixth book, there is no sacrifice to interrupt the new crisis. No Iphigenia in a plague-ridden Athens, the priest has fled. Instead of one unimportant funeral pyre, there are a hundred, all afire, one at each crossroads. Have we gained anything in the exchange? In other words, if you suppress violence, it reappears. Remove its local setting, that is to say, the solution of religious sacrifice, and immediately the global space of the city is plague-ridden with violence. An important question which Lucretius did not avoid, and which perhaps he could not answer and which pushed him to his limits.

Violence is the only problem so poorly resolved that our own culture is, without a doubt, the continuation, through other means, of barbarianism.

Violence is a major component of the relations among men. It is there, running free, perhaps fatal for us; maybe it is our destiny and our greatest risk, our greatest disequilibrium. Lucretius is well aware of sacrificial purging, and, recognizing the sacrificial solution, sets it aside. He is also aware of the legal solution, which is merely the interpretation of the previous solution by the rationalization of the guilty parties.

The most revolutionary event in the history of mankind and, perhaps, in the evolution of hominids in general was less, it seems to me, the attainment of abstracts or generalities in and through language than it was a turning away from the set of relations that we have within the family, the group, and so on, and that only concern us and them, toward an agreement, maybe a confused one, but a sudden and specific one, about something exterior to this set. Before this event, there was only the network of relations in which we had been plunged without any other resort. And suddenly, a thing, something, appears outside the network. The messages exchanged no longer say: I, you, he, we, they, and so on, but *this, here. Ecce.* Here is the thing itself.

As far as we know, the animals that are the most closely related to us, namely, the mammals, communicate among themselves by repeating in a stereotyped fashion the network of their relations. The animal signals or makes known to another animal: I dominate you and I give to you, I am dominated by you, therefore I receive from you. What? That is not important or it is implied within the relation. You are large and strong, I beg from you. Lucretius speaks in this manner of *our relation to the gods.* Hence, the necessitating condition that forces animals to regulate the set of problems born of these relations within the network itself. There are only contracts, and such is their fate.

The human message, however, even if it often repeats the network of relations among men until it becomes a stereotype, in addition sometimes says something about the thing. If it does not, the message is immediately brought back to the schemas of the political animal, in other words, to the animal alone. Humanization consists of the following message: here is some bread, whoever I am, whoever you are. *Hoc est,* that is, in the neuter. Neuter for the gender, neutral for war. Paradoxically, there are men or human groups only after the appearance of the object as such. The object as an object, more or less independent from us and more or less invariable in the variation of our relations, separates man from mammals. *The political animal, the one who subordinates every object to relations among subjects, is only a mammal among others, a wolf, for example, a wolf among wolves. In pure politics, the dictum of Hobbes, that man is a wolf to other men, is not a metaphor but the exact index of a regression to the state which precedes the emergence of the object.*

The origin of the theater, comedy and tragedy, where it is only a question of human relations and where there is never an object as such, is as old as the origin of political relations: it is submerged in animality. Politics and theater are merely mammalian.

The discovery of the object as such and, in a global fashion, of the exterior world, if it is not yet the first scientific invention, remains the preliminary condition to any sort of investigation of this type. Moreover, it makes an opening and something like a chance to escape from the network of our relations, and, therefore, to free us from the problems posed by this network, in particular, the problem of violence. What pertains to the object will perhaps be neutral terrain. The prehistory of physics, and of non-violence, given at the same time. The prehistory of hominids. Is an object conceivable outside of relations of force?

Listen now to the lessons of Epicureanism, which boil down to the following: reduce to a minimum the network of relations in which you are submerged. Live in the garden, a small space, with a few friends. No family, if it is possible, and, in any case, no politics. But especially this. Here is the object, objects, the world, nature, physics. Aphrodite-pleasure is born of the world and the waters. Mars is in the forum and in the armed crowd. Reduce your relations to a minimum and bring your objects to the fore; reduce the intersubjective to a minimum and the objective to a maximum. With your back turned on politics, study physics. Peace through neutrality. Such knowledge brings happiness, or at least the end of our worst pains. Forget the sacred; that means: forget the violence which founds it and forget the religious which links men to each other. Consider the object, objects, nature. Yes, Memmius, he who said here, *ecce, hoc est,* that one, is a god, a god among men, for he changed human nature.

Nevertheless, the plague returns, destroying Athens and bringing violence and death. Why? *Let us return to the object.* There are only two objects that constitute everything: atoms and the void. The void, *inane,* has its root in the Greek verb *inein,* which means to purge, to expel, or, in the passive, to be chased by a purge. The void is a part of chaos but is also a catharsis. Iphigenia is sacrificed, a purge or catharsis for the petty kings in Greece, but at the end of the sacred dynamics there is the Trojan War and extermination. A passage to the object to be freed from Mars. But the first object is the purge; *it is only the physical concept of catharsis.* The second object, the atom. The sacred solution begins with a division and separation of space. The temple is a dichotomized space; the word itself tells us so. Inside is the religious, outside is the profane. A two-valued logic, a two-valued geometry, a two-valued ontology, inside, outside; sacred, profane; matter, void. *The word temple is of the same family as atom.* The atom is the last or the first temple, and the void is the last or the first purge. The two objects are, in the balance, the physical concepts of catharsis and temple. We return to the network of relations. For having erased the sacrifice of Iphigenia in the temple of Trivia, the local religious event inundates the globe. Atoms in the void, little temples in the great purge. Nature is still another sacrificial substitute. Violence is still—and always—in physics. Thus the atoms-germs sack Athens and the last survivors kill each other. Q.E.D. It is not politics or sociology that is projected on nature, but the sacred. Beneath the sacred, there is violence. Beneath the object, relations reappear.

The question, for us, stays the same: violence is not only in the use of science but still hides in the unknown of its concepts. Athens generalized, the world after Hiroshima, can still die from the atoms. Where lies the madness of the irrational in our rational?

10

The Origin
of Geometry

Renan had the best reasons in the world for calling the advent of mathematics in Greece a miracle. The construction of geometric idealities or the establishment of the first proofs were, after all, very improbable events. If we could form some idea of what took place around Thales and Pythagoras, we would advance a bit in philosophy. The beginnings of modern science in the Renaissance are much less difficult to understand; this was, all things considered, only a reprise. Bearing witness to this Greek miracle, we have at our disposal two groups of texts. First, the mathematical corpus itself, as it exists in the *Elements* of Euclid, or elsewhere, treatises made up of fragments. On the other hand, doxography, the scattered histories in the manner of Diogenes Laertius, Plutarch, or Athenaeus, several remarks of Aristotle, or the notes of commentators such as Proclus or Simplicius. It is an understatement to say that we are dealing here with two groups of texts; we are in fact dealing with *two languages*. Now, to ask the question of the Greek beginning of geometry is precisely to ask how one passed from one language to another, from one type of writing to another, from the language reputed to be natural and its alphabetic notation to the rigorous and systematic language of numbers, measures, axioms, and formal arguments. What we have left of all this history presents nothing but two languages as such, narratives or legends and proofs or figures, words and formulas. Thus it is as if we were confronted by two parallel lines which, as is well known, never meet. The origin constantly recedes, inaccessible, irretrievable. The problem is open.

I have tried to resolve this question three times. First, by immersing it in the technology of communications. When two speakers have a dialogue or a dispute, the channel that connects them must be drawn by a diagram with four poles, a complete square equipped with its two diagonals. However loud or irreconcilable their quarrel, however calm or tranquil their agreement, they are linked, in fact, twice: they need, first of all, a certain intersection of their repertoires, without which they would remain strangers; they then band together against the noise which blocks the communication channel. These two conditions are necessary to the dialogue, though not sufficient. Consequently, the two speakers have a common interest in excluding a third man and including a fourth, both of whom are prosopopoeias of the powers of noise or of the instance of intersection.[1] Now this schema functions in exactly this manner in Plato's *Dialogues*, as can easily be shown, through the play of people and their naming, *their resemblances and differences*, their mimetic preoccupations and the dynamics of their violence. Now then, and above all, the mathematical sites, from the *Meno* through the *Timaeus*, by way of the *Statesman* and others, are all reducible geometrically to this diagram. Whence the origin appears, we pass from one language to another, the language said to be natural presupposes a dialectical schema, and this schema, drawn or written in the sand, as such, is the first of the geometric idealities. Mathematics presents itself as a successful dialogue or a communication which rigorously dominates its repertoire and is maximally purged of noise. Of course, it is not that simple. The irrational and the unspeakable lie in the details; listening always requires collating; there is always a leftover or a residue, indefinitely. But then, the schema remains open, and history possible. The philosophy of Plato, in its presentation and its models, is therefore inaugural, or better yet, it seizes the inaugural moment.

To be retained from this first attempt at an explanation are the expulsions and the purge. Why the parricide of old father Parmenides, who had to formulate, for the first time, the principle of contradiction? To be noted here again is how two speakers, irreconcilable adversaries, find themselves forced to turn together against the same third man for the dialogue to remain possible, for the elementary link of human relation-

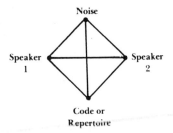

Noise

Speaker 1

Speaker 2

Code or Repertoire

The line from Speaker 1 to Speaker 2 represents the channel of communication that joins the two speakers together. The line from Noise to the Code or Repertoire represents the indissoluble link between noise and the code. Noise always threatens to overwhelm the code and to disrupt communication. Successful communication, then, requires the exclusion of a third term (noise) and the inclusion of a fourth (code). See "Platonic Dialogue," chapter 6 of the present volume. See also Michel Serres, *Le Parasite* (Paris: Grasset, 1980). —Ed.

ships to be possible, for geometry to become possible. Be quiet, don't make any noise, put your head back in the sand, go away or die. Strange diagonal which was thought to be so pure, and which is agonal and which remains an agony.

The second attempt contemplates Thales at the foot of the Pyramids, in the light of the sun. It involves several geneses, one of which is ritual.[2] But I had not taken into account the fact that the Pyramids are also tombs, that beneath the theorem of Thales, a corpse was buried, hidden. The space in which the geometer intervenes is the space of similarities: he is there, evident, next to three tombs of the *same* form and of *another* dimension—the tombs are *imitating* one another. And it is the pure space of geometry, that of the group of *similarities* which appeared with Thales. The result is that the theorem and its immersion in Egyptian legend says, without saying it, that there lies beneath the *mimetic operator,* constructed concretely and represented theoretically, a hidden royal corpse. I had seen the sacred above, in the sun of Ra and in the Platonic epiphany, where the sun that had come in the ideality of stereometric volume finally assured its diaphaneity; I had not seen it below, hidden beneath the tombstone, in the incestuous cadaver. But let us stay in Egypt for a while.

The third attempt consists in noting the double writing of geometry.[3] Using figures, schemas, and diagrams. Using letters, words, and sentences of the system, organized by their own semantics and syntax. Leibniz had already observed this double system of writing, consecrated by Descartes and by the Pythagoreans, a double system which represents itself and expresses itself one by the other. He sometimes liked, as did many others, to privilege the intuition, clairvoyant or blind, required by the first [diagrams] over the deductions produced by the second [words]. There are, as is well known, or as usual, two schools of thought on the subject. It happens that they trade their power throughout the course of history. It also happens that the schema contains more information than several lines of writing, that these lines of writing lay out indefinitely what we draw from the schema, as from a well or a cornucopia. Ancient algebra writes, drawing out line by line what the figure of ancient geometry dictates to it, what that figure contains in one stroke. The process never stopped; we are still talking about the square or about the diagonal. We cannot even be certain that history is not precisely that.

Now, many histories report that the Greeks crossed the sea to educate

[2]See "Mathematics and Philosophy: What Thales Saw . . . ," chapter 8 of the present volume. —Ed.

[3]This third explanation appears as "Origine de la géométrie, 4" in Michel Serres, *Hermès V: Le Passage du Nord-Ouest* (Paris: Minuit, 1980), pp. 175-84. —Ed.

themselves in Egypt. Democritus says it; it is said of Thales; Plato writes it in the *Timaeus*. There were even, as usual, two schools at odds over the question. One held the Greeks to be the teachers of geometry; the other, the Egyptian priests. This dispute caused them to lose sight of the essential: that the Egyptians wrote in ideograms and the Greeks used an alphabet. Communication between the two cultures can be thought of in terms of the relation between these two scriptive systems (*signalétiques*). Now, this relation is precisely the same as the one in geometry which separates and unites figures and diagrams on the one hand, algebraic writing on the other. Are the square, the triangle, the circle, and the other figures all that remains of hieroglyphics in Greece? As far as I know, they are ideograms. Whence the solution: the historical relation of Greece to Egypt is thinkable in terms of the relation of an alphabet to a set of ideograms, and since geometry could not exist without writing, mathematics being written rather than spoken, this relation is brought back into geometry as an operation using a double system of writing. There we have an easy passage between the natural language and the new language, a passage which can be carried out on the multiple condition that we take into consideration two different languages, two different writing systems and their common ties. And this resolves in turn the historical question: the brutal stoppage of geometry in Egypt, its freezing, its crystallization into fixed ideograms, and the irrepressible development, in Greece as well as in our culture, of the new language, that inexhaustible discourse of mathematics and rigor which is the very history of that culture. The inaugural relation of the geometric ideogram to the alphabet, words, and sentences opens onto a limitless path.

This third solution blots out a portion of the texts. The old Egyptian priest, in the *Timaeus*, compares the knowledge of the Greeks when they were children to the time-worn science of his own culture.[4] He evokes, in order to compare them, floods, fires, celestial fire, catastrophes. Absent from the solution are the priest, history, either mythical or real, in space and time, the violence of the elements which hides the origin and which, as the *Timaeus* clearly says, always hides that origin. Except, precisely, from the priest, who knows the secret of this violence. The sun of Ra is replaced by Phaethon, and mystical contemplation by the catastrophe of deviation.

We must start over—go back to those parallel lines that never meet. On the one hand, histories, legends, and doxographies, composed in natural language. On the other, a whole corpus, written in mathematical signs and symbols by geometers, by arithmeticians. We are therefore not con-

___
[4] Plato, *Timaeus*, 22b ff.

cerned with merely linking two sets of texts; we must try to glue two languages back together again. The question always arose in the space of the relation between experience and the abstract, the senses and purity. Try to figure out the status of the pure, which is impure when history changes. No. Can you imagine (that there exists) a Rosetta Stone with some legends written on one side, with a theorem written on the other side? Here no language is unknown or undecipherable, no side of the stone causes problems; what is in question is the edge common to the two sides, their common border; what is in question is the stone itself.

Legends. Somebody or other who conceived some new solution sacrificed an ox, a bull. The famous problem of the duplication of the cube arises regarding the stone of an altar at Delos. Thales, at the Pyramids, is on the threshold of the sacred. We are not yet, perhaps, at the origins. But, surely, what separates the Greeks from their possible predecessors, Egyptians or Babylonians, is the establishment of a proof. Now, the first proof we know of is the apagogic proof on the irrationality of $\sqrt{2}$.[5]

And so, legends, once again. Euclid's *Elements,* Book X, first scholium. It was a Pythagorean who proved, for the first time, the so-called irrationality [of numbers]. Perhaps his name was Hippasus of Metapontum. Perhaps the sect had sworn an oath to divulge nothing. Well, Hippasus of Metapontum spoke. Perhaps he was expelled. In any case, it seems certain that he died in a shipwreck. The anonymous scholiast continues: "The authors of this legend wanted to speak through allegory. Everything that is irrational and deprived of form must remain hidden, that is what they were trying to say. That if any soul wishes to penetrate this secret region and leave it open, then it will be engulfed in the sea of becoming, it will drown in its restless currents."

Legends and allegories and, now, history. For we read a significant event on three levels. We read it in the scholia, commentaries, narratives. We read it in philosophical texts. We read it in the theorems of geometry. The event is the *crisis,* the famous crisis of irrational numbers. Owing to this crisis, mathematics, at a point exceedingly close to its origin, came very close to dying. In the aftermath of this crisis, Platonism had to be recast. The crisis touched the logos. If logos means proportion, measured relation, the irrational or alogon is the impossibility of measuring. If logos means discourse, the alogon prohibits speaking. Thus exactitude crumbles, reason is mute.

Hippasus of Metapontum, or another, dies of this crisis, that is the legend and its allegorical cover in the scholium of the *Elements.* Par-

---

[5] An apagogic proof is one that proceeds by disproving the proposition which contradicts the one to be established, in other words, that proceeds by *reductio ad absurdum.* —Ed.

menides, the father, dies of this crisis—this is the philosophical sacrifice perpetrated by Plato. But, once again, history: Plato portrays Theaetetus dying upon returning from the the battle of Corinth (369), Theaetetus, the founder, precisely, of the theory of irrational numbers as it is re-capitulated in Book X of Euclid. The crisis read three times renders the reading of a triple death: the legendary death of Hippasus, the philo-sophical parricide of Parmenides, the historical death of Theaetetus. One crisis, three texts, one victim, three narratives. Now, on the other side of the stone, on the other face and in another language, we have the crisis and the possible death of mathematics in itself.

Given then a proof to explicate as one would a text. And, first of all, the proof, doubtless the oldest in history, the one which Aristotle will call *reduction to the absurd*. Given a square whose side $AB = b$, whose diagonal $AC = a$:

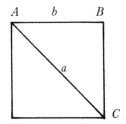

We wish to measure AC in terms of AB. If this is possible, it is because the two lengths are mutually commensurable. We can then write $AC/AB = a/b$. It is assumed that a/b is reduced to its simplest form, so that the integers a and b are mutually prime. Now, by the Pythagorean theorem: $a^2 = 2b^2$. Therefore a^2 is even, therefore a is even. And if a and b are mutually prime, *b is an odd number.*

If a is even, we may posit: $a = 2c$. Consequently, $a^2 = 4c^2$. Consequently $2b^2 = 4c^2$, that is, $b^2 = 2c^2$. Thus, *b is an even number.*

The situation is intolerable, the number *b is at the same time even and odd*, which, of course, is impossible. Therefore it is impossible to measure the diagonal in terms of the side. They are mutually incommensurable. I repeat, if logos is the proportional, here a/b or $1/\sqrt{2}$, the alogon is the incommensurable. If logos is discourse or speech, you can no longer say anything about the diagonal and $\sqrt{2}$ is irrational. It is impossible to decide whether b is even or odd.

Let us draw up the list of the notions used here. 1) What does it mean for two lengths to be mutually commensurable? It means that they have common aliquot parts. There exists, or one could make, a ruler, divided into units, in relation to which these two lengths may, in turn, be divided into parts. In other words, they are *other* when they are alone together, face to face, but they are *same*, or just about, in relation to a third term, the unit of measurement taken as reference. The situation is interesting, and it is well known: *two irreducibly different entities are reduced to similarity through an exterior point of view.* It is fortunate (or necessary) here that the term *measure* has, traditionally, at least two meanings, the geometric or metrological one and the meaning of non-disproportion, of serenity, of nonviolence, of peace. These two meanings derive from a similar situation, an identical operation. Socrates objects to the violent crisis of Callicles with the famous remark: you are ignorant of geometry. The Royal Weaver of the *Statesman* is the bearer of a supreme science: superior metrology, of which we will have occasion to speak again. 2) What does it mean for two numbers to be mutually prime? It means that they are radically different, that they have no common factor besides one. We thereby ascertain the first situation, their total otherness, unless we take the unit of measurement into account. 3) What is the Pythagorean theorem? It is the fundamental theorem of measurement in the space of *similarities.* For it is invariant by variation of the coefficients of the squares, by variation of the forms constructed on the hypotenuse and the two sides of the triangle. And the space of similarities is that space where things can be of the *same* form and of *another* size. It is the space of models and of imitations. The theorem of Pythagoras founds measurement on the representative space of imitation. Pythagoras sacrifices an ox there, repeats once again the legendary text. 4) What, now, is evenness? And what is oddness? The English terms reduce to a word the long Greek discourses: *even* means equal, united, flat, *same; odd* means bizarre, unmatched, extra, left over, unequal, in short, *other.* To characterize a number by the absurdity that it is at the same time even and odd is to say that it is at the same time *same* and *other.*

Conceptually, the apagogic theorem or proof does *nothing but* play variations on the notion of same and other, using measurement and commensurability, using the fact of two numbers being mutually prime, using the Pythagorean theorem, using evenness and oddness.

It is a rigorous proof, and the first in history, based on *mimesis.* It says something very simple: *supposing mimesis, it is reducible to the absurd.* Thus the crisis of irrational numbers overturns Pythagorean arithmetic and early Platonism.

Hippasus revealed this, he dies of it—end of the first act.

It must be said today that this was said more than two millennia ago. Why go on playing a game that has been decided? For it is as plain as a thousand suns that if the diagonal or $\sqrt{2}$ are incommensurable or irrational, they can still be constructed on the square, that the mode of their geometric existence is not different from that of the side. Even the young slave of the *Meno,* who is ignorant, will know how, will be able, to construct it. In the same way, children know how to spin tops which the

Republic analyzes as being stable and mobile at the same time. How is it then that reason can take facts that the most ignorant children know how to establish and construct, and can demonstate them to be irrational? There must be a reason for this irrationality itself.

In other words, we are demonstrating the absurdity of the irrational. We reduce it to the contradictory or to the undecidable. Yet, it exists; we cannot do anything about it. The top spins, even if we demonstrate that, for impregnable reasons, it is, undecidably, both mobile and fixed. That's the way it is. *Therefore,* all of the theory which precedes and founds the proof must be reviewed, transformed. It is not reason that governs, it is the obstacle. What becomes absurd is not what we have proven to be absurd, it is the theory on which the proof depends. Here we have the very ordinary movement of science: once it reaches a dead-end of this kind, it immediately transforms its presuppositions.

Translation: *mimesis* is reducible to contradiction or to the undecidable. Yet it exists; we cannot do anything about it. It spins. It works, as they say. That's the way it is. It can always be shown that we can neither speak nor walk, or that Achilles will never catch up with the tortoise. Yet, we do speak, we do walk, the fleet-footed Achilles does pass the tortoise. That's the way it is. *Therefore,* all of the theory which precedes must be transformed. What becomes absurd is not what we have proven to be absurd, it is the theory as a whole on which the proof depends.

Whence the (hi)story which follows. Theodorus continues along the legendary path of Hippasus. He multiplies the proofs of irrationality. He goes up to $\sqrt{17}$. There are a lot of these absurdities, there are as many of them as you want. We even know that there are many more of them than there are of rational relations. Whereupon Theaetetus takes up the archaic Pythagoreanism again and gives a general theory which grounds, in a new reason, the facts of irrationality. Book X of the *Elements* can now be written. The crisis ends, mathematics recovers an order, Theaetetus dies, here ends this story, a technical one in the language of the system, a historical one in the everyday language that relates the battle of Corinth. Plato recasts his philosophy, father Parmenides is sacrificed during the parricide on the altar of the principle of contradiction; for surely the *Same* must be *Other,* after a fashion. Thus, Royalty is founded. The Royal Weaver combines in an ordered web rational proportions and the irrationals; gone is the crisis of the reversal, gone is the technology of the dichotomy, founded on the square, on the iteration of the diagonal. Society, finally, is in order. This dialogue is fatally entitled, not *Geometry,* but the *Statesman.*

The Rosetta Stone is constructed. Suppose it is to be read on all of its sides. In the language of legend, in that of history, that of mathematics, that of philosophy. The message that it delivers passes from language to language. The crisis is at stake. This crisis is sacrificial. A series of deaths accompanies its translations into the languages considered. Following these sacrifices, order reappears: in mathematics, in philosophy, in history, in political society. The schema of René Girard allows us not only to show the isomorphism of these languages, but also, and especially, their link, how they fit together.[6] For it is not enough to narrate, the operators of this movement must be made to appear. Now these operators, all constructed on the pair Same-Other, are seen, deployed in their rigor, throughout the very first geometric proof. Just as the square equipped with its diagonal appeared, in my first solution, as the thematized object of the complete intersubjective relation, formation of the ideality as such, so the rigorous proof appears as such, manipulating all the operators of *mimesis*, namely, the internal dynamics of the schema proposed by Girard. The origin of geometry is immersed in sacrificial history and the two parallel lines are henceforth in connection. Legend, myth, history, philosophy, and pure science have common borders over which a unitary schema builds bridges.

Metapontum and geometer, he was the Pontifex, the Royal Weaver. His violent death in the storm, the death of Theaetetus in the violence of combat, the death of father Parmenides, all these deaths are murders. The irrational is mimetic. The stone which we have read was the stone of the altar at Delos. And geometry begins in violence and in the sacred.[7]

---

[6] The reference is to René Girard's theory of the emissary victim. See chapter 9, note 9 in the present volume. — Ed.

[7] It is just as remarkable that the physics of Epicurus, as Lucretius develops it in *De Rerum Natura*, is framed by the sacrifice of Iphigenia and the plague of Athens. These two events, legendary or historical, can be read using the grid of physics. But, inversely, all this physics can be read using the same schema, since the term *inane* means "purge" and "expulsion." I have shown this in detail in *La Naissance de la physique dans le texte de Lucrèce: Fleuves et turbulences* (Paris: Minuit, 1977). (See also "Lucretius: Science and Religion," chapter 9 of the present volume. — Ed.)

POSTFACE: Dynamics
from Leibniz to Lucretius
by Ilya Prigogine
& Isabelle Stengers

A Question of Style

One often speaks of "classical" science. The modifier is sometimes invested with a precise meaning. Most often, it serves as a means to an end in a strategy of opposition. We fear that for the faithful, "classical" evokes the idea of a "before": before the rupture, before the "No" that founds our science. Or even before science itself: in that case, the act of demarcation rejects a preceding "pseudo-science," naive, riddled with presuppositions, and too close to "common sense."

But the term classical has one very important attribute: it designates a style, and therefore a culture. Modifying science, it helps to show science's links to a set of economic, artistic, philosophical, technical, and social practices. It helps to overcome the appearance of autonomy given science by its organization and its system of apprenticeship within academic institutions. We owe to Michel Serres the renewed reflection on the effects of style in science. To reflect on the question of style is not only to do the work of a historian (even though Serres is before all else a specialist in Leibniz and in the relations between science and culture in the seventeenth century, and thus it will not be astonishing to find Leibniz on every page of this essay). To reflect on the question of style is also to explore the resources of different contemporary problematics. It is noteworthy that, in opposition to theories, styles profit from a sort of stability. The history of their complex relations with the disciplines they inspire and the fields of research they make fertile gives to whoever can seize them a connecting link to an understanding of the stakes in science, the innovations brought to light, and the permanence of certain questions and of certain regulatory fictions. To study styles, not merely the history of theories, is to see to what extent the sciences are marked today by some of the temptations that were present at their various beginnings.[1]

---

[1] The Demon of Laplace, who haunts our essay, comes to mind first, or the temptation of

The *Système de Leibniz*[2] begins by positing the major problematic of Serres's work: what is at stake in the hypothesis of the great classical rationalist who supposes that the passage from local to global is always possible? As we shall see, the question of the integrable world authorizes dreams of determinism. What we shall call here the classical style in physics is expressed in Laplace's dream of a world made of determinist and calculable trajectories. Laplace's demon observes the instantaneous state of the world and integrates its trajectory. He thus has access to both the past and the future in the minutest detail. This dream of omniscience translates Leibniz's baroque monadology using the unidimensional platitude characteristic of the nineteenth century.

Nine years later, in *La Naissance de la physique dans le texte de Lucrèce*, Serres takes up, fulfills, and modifies the project sketched out in *Le Système de Leibniz:* the confrontation of the rationalism of differential and integral calculus (Leibniz) with the rationalism of ancient atomism. Regarding the matter that will occupy us henceforth, we observe that, as a good Epicurean, Lucretius answers "no" to the following question: "Is the passage from local to global always possible?"[3]

The text that follows will explore only one of the registers brought into play by Serres's work, which ranges from esthetics to the analysis of myths and from literary criticism to ethical questions. The work of Serres is Leibnizian enough to make our choice not exclusive, and thus we hope that our discussion will leave to others the possibility of opening channels of communication toward his other themes. We have chosen one question that modern physics itself asks with insistence: that of the local and the global. In so doing, we wished to demonstrate the pertinence for contemporary problematics of the questions Serres analyzes in the works of the past.

To begin with, let us set aside several objections which are used to attempt to separate, in the domain of science, what is legitimate (hypothesis, theory, measurement, what Bachelard called the scientist's

---

Thales in the desert, where the possibilities of indefinite transport are arrayed before his eyes, authorized by the space of similitudes (see chapters 8 and 10 of the present volume). More generally, one thinks of the construction of the ideal republic of mathematicians, "the city of communication maximally purged of noise" (see chapter 6 of the present volume). For Serres, yielding to these temptations has the ultimate effect of creating a situation in which the industrialized world is frequently condemned to considering the concrete universe as its representation. Thus a practical idealism comes into being, immune to the contradictions regularly inflicted on it by the unmasterable elements of the world (see Michel Serres, *Hermès IV: La Distribution* [Paris: Minuit, 1977], p. 156).

[2] Michel Serres, *Le Système de Leibniz et ses modèles mathématiques* (Paris: Presses Universitaires de France, 1968), 2 vols.

[3] Michel Serres, *La Naissance de la physique dans le texte de Lucrèce: Fleuves et turbulences* (Paris: Minuit, 1977), p. 253.

diurnal activity) from dream, ideology—from the night. This distinction between the pure and the impure crippled Leibniz's reputation as a physicist. Though his role in mathematics is recognized, in physics he figures more often than not as the inopportune and obstinate adversary of Newton, the person whose ambition to create communicative paths between physics and metaphysics led down the road to perdition.

Thus Leibniz's rigor was judged severely. It is commonly agreed that, though he was the creator of the term "dynamics," he nevertheless "missed" the mathematical physics created by Newton at that very moment. This is explained by the fact that for him philosophical rigor came before the needs of an inductive and necessarily approximate science. He refused to give up the idea of the rational nature of the real, measured not by the yardstick of man, who observes and generalizes, but by that of God, who, calculating, created the world. Thus Leibniz was unequivocally a "pre-Newtonian."[4] This is a condemnation, moreover, that is sufficiently justified by his rejection of the principles of inertia and of interaction at a distance—in short, of Newtonian physics. In the face of this condemnation, we can make three remarks.

In the first place, one might well ask, solely based on the facts, whether it is not the history of physics that has "missed" Leibniz. The discovery of his role and influence will undoubtedly offer a few surprises when the history of Continental physics is better known: Bernoulli, Euler, and D'Alembert were neither Newtonians nor pre-Newtonians.[5] Second, the role played by God in Leibnizian physics does not allow the opposition of this physics to Newton's in the same way that metaphysical speculation might be opposed to positive scientific praxis. Think of the controversies between Leibniz and Clarke, Newton's proxy,[6] or of Newton's own considerations on the production of forces of attraction by the active principles that show the action of God on the world:[7] these will suffice here as

[4] Let us mention, for example, Yvon Belaval, in *Leibniz critique de Descartes*, Collection Tel (Paris: Gallimard, 1976), pp. 502-3, according to whom Leibniz, in the name of rigor, disregarded the precision that could only be achieved by measurement. This disregard had consequential results: "Leibniz does not measure. And thus, how could he admit a force other than impulsion? Only measurement could have made him admit the idea of a force of attraction whose nature was unknown but which was demanded by calculation."

[5] Clifford Truesdell has brought to light the extent to which this history is poorly known. See "A Program toward Rediscovering the Rational Mechanics of the Age of Reason," *Archives for the History of Exact Science* 1 (1960):1-36, as well as the works of the historians Thomas Hankins, Yahuda Elkana, and W. Scott.

[6] See, for example, Alexandre Koyré, *Du monde clos à l'univers infini* (Paris: Gallimard, 1973).

[7] It is useful to consult the study of P. H. Heimann and J. E. McGuire, "Newtonian and Lockean Powers: Concepts of Matter in Eighteenth-Century Thought," *Historical Studies in the Physical Sciences* 3 (1971):233-306. The recent study of Newton's alchemical writings has brought to light how little the concept of force was "imposed" by measurement. See B.J.T.

examples. Certainly Laplace (the "second Newton") was not wrong to say to Napoleon that his system had no need for the hypothesis of God: this remark merely expressed the fact that God, in the role assigned to him by Newton, did not resist the progress of dynamics. Last, it cannot be denied that, if not since Newton, then at least since Laplace, we have accepted the systems of interactions at a distance as part of our physical world.[8] But one must distinguish between such a conception and the development of "mathematical physics," that is to say, the creation of the formalism that is today called dynamics. We have said, and we wish to show, that the *language* of dynamics has, in a certain sense, changed from a Newtonian to a Leibnizian one. The world of trajectories determined by forces can henceforth be thought of as being identical to the Leibnizian system of the world in which every point locally expresses the global law.

Forces and Energy

To introduce this thesis we propose some little-known satiric verses of James Clerk Maxwell, which are doubly interesting because they celebrate both what we call the "Leibnizian" transformation of dynamics and someone who was among the first to explore the possibilities and powers of a role that was then new within the scientific community, that of "textbook writer":

> But see! Tait writes in lucid symbols clear
>   One small equation;
> And Force becomes of Energy a mere
>   Space-variation.
>
> Force, then, is Force, but Mark you! not a thing,
>   Only a Vector;
> Thy barbèd arrows now have lost their sting,
>   Impotent spectre!
> Thy reign, O Force! is over. Now no more
>   Heed we thine action;
> Repulsion leaves us where we were before,
>   So does attraction.

Dobbs, *The Foundations of Newton's Alchemy* (Cambridge: Cambridge University Press, 1975), and R. S. Westfall, "Newton and the Hermetic Tradition," in *Science, Medicine, and Society in the Renaissance,* ed. Allen G. Debus, 2 vols. (London: Heinemann, 1972), 2:183-98.

[8] Any two masses, whatever the distance separating them, are linked by a gravitational force that is inversely proportional to the square of the distance between them. The eighteenth-century rationalists were extremely distrustful of this force, regarding it as a very suspicious occult property.

Both Action and Reaction now are gone.
  Just ere they vanished,
Stress joined their hands in peace, and made them one;
  Then they were banished.
The universe is free from pole to pole,
  Free from all forces.
Rejoice! ye stars—like blessed gods ye roll
  On in your courses.[9]

The stars and, following their example, all physical bodies travel through the universe like free and self-determined gods, each following its own law. Newtonian physics posits a body assumed to be isolated, endowed with a rectilinear and uniform inertial movement, and calculates the modifications of this movement as determined by the action of forces. For Leibniz, the forces are not "given" and are in no way the real causes of the modification of a movement but rather are local properties within a dynamic system: at every point, they characterize a momentary state belonging to a series regulated by a law.[10]

In the same way, since Lagrange[11] and especially since Hamilton, mathematical physics has abandoned Newtonian representation. Instead of calculating the action of each force on each point, it first of all proposes the system in its canonic form, and constructs a function (the Hamiltonian in particular, a representation of energy—see Maxwell's verses) that defines the global state of the system. From this function, the set of "forces" acting on each point at every moment can be derived. Forces are no longer responsible for accelerations; rather, they are deducible from the structure of the dynamic system defined by the Hamiltonian; they are the effects of the global law of evolution which the Hamiltonian expresses.[12]

---

[9] Lewis Campbell and William Garnett, *The Life of James Clerk Maxwell* (London: MacMillan and Co., 1882), pp. 647-48.

[10] See Martial Guéroult, *Dynamique et métaphysique leibniziennes* (Paris: Les Belles Lettres, 1934).

[11] In "L'Evolution de la mécanique," which appeared in *Revue générale des sciences* throughout 1903, Duhem described the Leibnizian character of Lagrangean analyses. He showed the decisive nature of the change of representation at which Lagrange arrived when he replaced the description of a system in which real forces act on masses, some of which are linked by rigid constraints, with a canonic image in which fictive forces, redefined at every moment, act on masses free of constraint and produce on these masses the same accelerations as do real forces on constrained masses.

[12] There exist an infinite number of canonic representations in every given dynamic system, each of which can constitute much more than a simple geometric transformation of the "intuitive" description of the system. The canonic variables, in whose terms dynamic evolution is described in each of these representations, can in fact be very complex functions

We shall not continue along this path, which is accessible to any student of dynamics. What we would discover is deducible from the fact that the dynamic problem is henceforth posited in the same way that Leibniz posited it: movement is produced within a full world, an interdependent world in which nothing can happen that has not been made possible by the state of the set of bodies according to a harmony that determines and checks at every moment the unfolding of the different movements. What Leibniz thought of as a preestablished harmony translated at every instant by the conservation of energy the physics of Lagrange put to work through the study of movement as the succession of states of equilibrium, disrupted and reestablished at every instant, and Hamiltonian formalism transformed into an a priori syntax of the formal language in which every dynamic problem can be posited.[13] During the eighteenth century, in fact, physicists succeeded in inscribing Newtonian physics as a special a posteriori case within the a priori conceptual framework of Leibnizian physics.[14]

The Monadic World

We know that for Leibniz the physics of aggregates of bodies affecting each other had only an imaginary character. It is a dream (but a coherent one) to attribute the variations of force at each point to external factors. That is to say, in reality no longer from a physical point of view but from a metaphysical one, the world is composed of unextended substantial elements—monads—each of which displays a predetermined internal law:

> The monad automatically deciphers, both in itself and for itself, a universe that is at once its closed interior, its own account of it, and the extensive entirety of its exteriority. . . . The monad is full to an inaccessible extent of attachments that are sufficient for representing

---

both of the positions and of the measurable velocities of the points between which the "real" forces of interaction play. The variation from moment to moment of the canonic variables of position and of velocity is derived from the Hamiltonian, which is the sum of the kinetic and potential energies expressed in these canonic variables. The local description of the system and the evolution of each point reflect and express locally the law of global evolution as it is defined by the energy, the constant of this evolution.

[13] Maxwell's analogy between the movement of bodies and the liberty of the gods reproduces the constancy of Leibniz's concept of equilibrium among the theories of perception, of physical movement, and of decision. See, on this, the analyses of Serres, particularly in *Le Système de Leibniz,* 1:201-6, and *La Naissance de la physique,* pp. 43-44, 62.

[14] Yahuda Elkana made some interesting comments on this point in *The Discovery of the Conservation of Energy* (London: Hutchinson Educational Ltd., 1974).

a full and compact nature like itself: the inherence of all the numbers belonging to deciphering. Impressed and expressive but never impressionable.[15]

It is God alone in the Leibnizian system who can know monads as such; it is he who, at the origin, calculated each one's individual law so that the monads express each other, so that each one, through its internal law, translates every change that has occurred in another—that is to say, so that the universe described by physics is imaginary but not illusory.

But the jump from the imaginary point of view of the monad dreaming itself and dreaming of things affected from the outside to the point of view of God—from the physics of aggregates to monadology—has now received a purely physical translation: *every integrable system, every system whose equations of movement can be integrated, allows for a monadic representation.*

Let us first of all define what we mean by an integrable system. A problem put in the canonic language of dynamics is presented in the form of a set of differential equations that describes the following situation for every point: at every instant, a set of forces derived from a function of the global state (such as the Hamiltonian, the sum of kinetic and potential energies) modifies the state of the system. Therefore this function as well is modified: from it, a moment later, a new set of forces will be derived. To resolve a dynamic problem is, ideally, to integrate these differential equations and to obtain the set of trajectories taken by the points of the system.

It is evident that the complexity of the equations to be integrated varies according to the more or less judicious choice of the canonic variables that describe the system. That is why dynamic physics as it was formulated in the nineteenth century is a theory of transformations among canonic languages, among points of view on a system, each describing this system in terms of a different set of canonic variables and thereby placing it within a different space defined each time by these variables. More precisely, it is a theory that allows for the choice of the best point of view so that the system can be integrated and the trajectories calculated.

But what integration could be easier than that of the movement of an isolated body, with no interaction with the rest of the world? No external perturbation determines a change in velocity, which thus remains

---

[15]Michel Serres, *Hermès III: La Traduction* (Paris: Minuit, 1974), p. 131.

constant, while the position is a linear function of time. All the energy is kinetic; the value of "potential energy" is zero.[16]

The optimal point of view on a system, the best choice of variables, is therefore the one that cancels out the potential energy redefined in terms of these variables. And dynamic theory tells us that every *integrable* system can be represented in this way—can be redefined as a set of "units" evolving in a pseudo-inertial movement, without any interaction among the "units." Each "monadic unit" is no longer determined in each of its movements by interactions with the aggregate; each deploys its own law for itself, alone in a system which it reflects intrinsically, because its very definition supposes and translates this system in every detail. There is full passage between the local and the global.

Michel Serres has shown that Leibniz did not "speak of" science, did not "speak about" it from an external position;[17] he "spoke" science, and did so even when he "spoke" metaphysics. Thus, speaking the language of dynamics in a philosophical manner—moreover, a language which was based on his work in physics—Leibniz arrived at a conclusion which was only to be found by dynamics in its most abstract state. This is not an anachronism; Leibniz is not even a "precursor"; he introduces no new fact or concept. He simply undertakes—with the rigor for which he is criticized—an exploration of that internal coherence of the physical and mathematical language of his age which he contributed to creating. The point of view he attributes to God is a privileged point of view whose existence is affirmed by physics as soon as the system can be exactly integrated.

But—and this is how the difference between classical dynamics and Leibnizian metaphysics is now defined—we know that the class of integrable systems is extremely restricted (the theorem of Liouville). Moreover, our formalized science (we shall soon speak of this) is no longer limited to classical dynamics. The world described by the science of

---

[16]This kind of representation is called cyclic. The canonic variables to which it has recourse are in fact those variables of action and of angle which typically describe circular movement. A curious turn of events: Newton is considered, quite correctly, to have made decisive progress in treating circular movement as uniformly accelerating, thereby undermining the privileged position occupied by circular movement in ancient physics; not to have accepted this progress condemned Leibniz to the taint of being a pre-Newtonian (see, in particular, S. R. Westfall, *Force in Newton's Physics* [London: MacDonald, 1971]). Cyclic representation rediscovers the unique nature of circular movement on which Leibniz insisted, unique in implying no variation in kinetic energy. In his *Leibniz*, Michel Serres presents what will remain the definitive example of a method for exploring the properties of duality at play within fields like cosmologies, families of mathematical propositions, and mythologies (vol. 1, pt. 1, ch. 1, sec. 3a-b). See also the canonic pages of his book on Jules Verne (*Jouvence sur Jules Verne* [Paris: Minuit, 1974], pp. 74-78).

[17]*Hermès III: La Traduction*, pp. 152-57. The same problematic of the optimal site from which to judge without any risk is taken up in chapter 2 of the present volume.

irreversible processes, the world described by quantum mechanics, is a world in which interactions play an ever more important role. The Leibnizian exploration of classical style therefore allows us to identify precisely what is now at stake in science: the description of a world of processes, the definition of entities that participate in the becoming of the world.

Pretenses and Limits of Style

Let us leave Leibniz. We have not shown that the Leibnizian system could be entirely reduced to a theorem of dynamics, nor that the plurality of isomorphic languages could be reduced to one: the language of dynamics is only one model among others in the Leibnizian system. We have simply shown the pertinence of this model. In fact, for the past two centuries, there have been physicists who affirmed that the whole world could be described as if it were an integrable dynamic system: this is what we have called the Laplacean dream. We shall not enter into the discussion of this dream, which acted as a regulatory ideal, but rather content ourselves with noting that it seems to reappear in every generation, apparently without opposition from the scientific community, each time translating the continuity of a style as well as the individuality of its contemporary theoretical and cultural context.[18] We wish to show that such a pretense, which will be called "ideological," cannot be separated from the history of science as an active force.

Let us examine the properties of the dynamic world based on the model of integrable systems, which is also the world whose legality Lucretius's *clinamen* will undermine. It is a world of determinist and reversible trajectories whose definition presupposes two disparate kinds of information: knowledge of the law of evolution which syntax allows one to formulate a priori from the definition of the forces of interaction and the binds inside the system, and knowledge of the description of any state of the system. From this point on, "everything is given." The law will lay out the trajectory taken both toward the past and toward the future. The law is generality itself: it defines the limits of all the possible evolutions of the system and defines them as equivalent to each other, each reflecting the arbitrary particularity of an initial condition.

The property of reversibility is given in a very simple manner: the law of dynamics is such that the operation of instantaneous inversion $v \rightarrow -v$ of velocities at each point of the system is equivalent to the operation of

[18] In *La Naissance de la physique,* what Serres calls a return to things undoubtedly implies a more lucid and free relation to different styles.

inversion of the direction of the flow of time t→ −t. For any dynamic evolution it is thus possible to define an initial state (in fact, the one prepared by this operation of inversion of velocities) such that the system undergoes inverse evolution, "moving in reverse."

This property is an excellent illustration of the arbitrary and determinist character of dynamic evolution. Generally, for any given state, the law permits the calculation of the initial condition needed for the system so that it ends up "spontaneously" at a specified moment at that state. In this world of automata, both arbitrary and inflexible, to know is in fact to dominate; the most extravagant evolutions are deployed indifferently, translating the extravagance of an initial state. Among these extravagant evolutions, "moving in reverse" has the force of a symbol. Everyone knows the absurd impression provoked by movies shown in reverse: burning matches which become reconstituted; flowers which become buds; a wave of water in a swimming pool which projects a diver up onto the springboard. Dynamics describes and postulates this absurd world.

The notion of reversible and determinist trajectories does not belong exclusively to classical dynamics. It is found in relativity and in quantum mechanics; the evolution of the wave-function as defined by Schrödinger's equation also echoes the syntax of dynamics.

Rather unexpectedly, it is in quantum mechanics that the monadic character of every integrable system has been most evident. In Bohr's model of the atom each orbit is characterized by a well-determined energy level in which electrons are in steady, eternal, and invariable movement. The steady state of orbital electrons is the typical example of the monadic state. The orbits are defined as being without interaction with each other or with the world; it is as though they were isolated, alone in the world. This monadic description was absorbed in the modern formulation of quantum mechanics by means of Schrödinger's equation: this description becomes a privileged representation such that quantum evolution is reduced to the evolution of a set of isolated steady states without interactions which remain identical to themselves for an indefinite time.

One might object that we have not spoken of the second half of Bohr's model: electrons can jump from one orbit to another, emitting or absorbing a photon of energy corresponding to the difference of energy between initial and final levels. For that reason we can know that these levels exist; the electron without interaction is unknowable.

It is here that quantum mechanics decisively parts company from dynamics; quantum formalism does not define the determinist and reversible description as being complete. It associates a second type of evolution with it, one that is irreversible and discontinuous, the reduction of the wave-function that corresponds, for example, to the jump from one orbit to another with the recorded emission or absorption of a photon, or corresponds to any other interaction with an instrument of measurement, after which one can deterministically attribute a numerical value to one of the quantum parameters. Thus irreversibility of the measurement is necessary to the definition of the quantum phenomenon. Starting from quantum mechanics, the physicist knows that there are interactions in the physical world which cannot be eliminated by a dynamic transformation. The process that ends with the amplification and recording of a quantum phenomenon at the macroscopic level is one such interaction, as is the world of unstable sub-quantum particles.[19]

Quantum mechanics thus presents a reversal of perspective relative to classical style. It is no longer a question of looking for simplicity at the level of elementary behavior. Dynamic simplicity, as reflected by the possibility of a completely monadic representation, belongs, in fact, to the macroscopic world, to the world on our scale. Our physics is a science created by macroscopic beings, created with conceptual tools and instruments that belong to the macroscopic world. It is from that position, when we question the world of quanta, that we must choose what will allow us to express matters in terms of measurable, reproducible, and communicable properties. We can no longer allow ourselves, as far as the physical world is concerned, the privileged point of view which, when pushed to its limit, we once could have identified as that of God.

Change of Style

If dynamics is above all a science of the macroscopic world, the following question immediately comes to mind: in the natural world, where irreversibility seems to be the rule, what is the status of the reversible

---

[19]We can see how unfortunate was the widespread assumption that quantum mechanics "discovered" that the process of measurement disturbs the system measured, uncontrollably modifying the values of certain parameters in order to ascertain the value of others. Such an assumption in fact implies that only an arbitrary positivistic prohibition prevents us from speaking of "hidden variables," that is to say, prevents us from affirming that the system in question is, at every moment, defined by the set of physical parameters, even if all of them cannot be known simultaneously.

The actual situation is entirely different. The real discovery of quantum mechanics, as it is expressed by the inseparable character of reversible evolution and irreversible reduction, is not that the process of measurement disturbs, but rather that it participates in the definition of the measured parameter, so that this parameter cannot be attributed to the quantum system "in itself" and one cannot speak of "hidden variables." As Niels Bohr repeatedly said, quantum mechanics discovered the necessity of choice, choosing what question to ask, in other words, choosing both the instrumental framework of the question and one of the complementary descriptions articulated among themselves by formalism but irreducible to a single description.

descriptions of dynamics? Two solutions have often been proposed, and the ground common to both is denial of the existence of the problem. According to the first, reversible description is only an idealized and partial model that must be abandoned or "completed" adequately as soon as it is no longer valid. According to the other, irreversibility is only an illusion; we are dream-like automata "swimming" in one direction in the sea of an eternal and legal world.[20]

Neither of these solutions, too simple and especially too sterile, has ever really taken hold. The first amounts to the acceptance of a strict separation of disciplines and to the idea that a style is never more than an inflated paradigm. The second, in contrast, brings us back to a pseudo-Leibnizian style, telling us that the irreversible world is only a well-fabricated illusion determined by our subjectivity, and that objective reality is reversible, legal, and determinist.

But a style is not abandoned in the name of prudence and plausibility. Like the Laplacean dream, repeatedly declared defunct, it regroups and deploys, changes arenas, rises again under different theoretical guises. On the other hand, our style is no longer the classical style: from Laplace to Du Bois-Reymond, the nineteenth century, which made dynamics the basis of a conception of the world, was also the period in which a new history and culture arose, and thus a new style of science.

> What is the Industrial Revolution? A revolution operating on *matter*. It takes place at the very sources of dynamics, at the origins of force. One takes force as it is or one produces it. Descartes and Newton, crowned by Lagrange, chose the first alternative: force is there, given by the biotope, the wind, the sea, and gravity. It is beyond our control except insofar as men and horses are subject to it, but it is not under our dominion when it is a question of heavy bodies, of air, and of water. With it one produces motion, work, by using tools. . . . Then a sudden change is imposed on the raw elements: fire replaces air and water in order to transform the earth. . . . Fire finishes off the horses, strikes them down. The source, the origin of force is in this flash of lightning, this ignition. Its energy exceeds form; it transforms. Geometry disintegrates, lines are erased; matter, ablaze, explodes; the former color—soft, light, golden—is now dashed with

---

[20] The metaphor of swimming seems particularly attractive to theoreticians of general relativity. See, for example, D. Williams, "The Myth of Passage," in *The Philosophy of Time: A Collection of Essays*, ed. R. M. Gale (London: MacMillan, 1968). It is remarkable that parallel solutions were proposed in quantum mechanics to resolve the problem of the relation between Shrödinger's equation and the irreversible reduction of the wave-function. See, in particular, the notable analysis of B. d'Espagnat, *Conceptions de la physique contemporaine* (Paris: Hermann, 1965), revised and enlarged in *Conceptual Foundations of Quantum Mechanics* (Reading, Mass.: Benjamin, 1976).

bright hues. The horses, now dead, pass over the ship's bridge in a cloud of horsepower.[21]

From mechanics to thermodynamics, changes of style and society have occurred. And, in parallel fashion, dynamics developed and reached a point of formal perfection. For the last century we have been faced with an original scientific problem, that of the articulation of styles and of reversible and irreversible time. We no longer live in Leibniz's time: to speak the language of dynamics, and conclude from it that we are dreamt monads, is for us not to speak "science" but to speak "a science," not only against the style of the age and against eventual personal beliefs, but also against another science.

We have spoken of the fertility of scientific style and of the questions it raises. The problem of the relation between thermodynamics and dynamics has not been given a simple solution such as the eighteenth century would have offered.[22] Both the failure of simple solutions and the continued confrontation are the occasion for a renewal of physics. We must, and we can, as Leibniz wished, calculate.

There is a prerequisite to this calculation. If the limits of dynamics coincided *de jure* with those of the science of monads, it would be useless to calculate; simple logic would be sufficient to demonstrate the irreconcilable character of the two descriptions. In fact, Henri Poincaré thought that the best way to refute Boltzmann's assumptions was by logic alone: beginning with reversible premises, Boltzmann attempted to arrive at irreversibility; thus his reasoning *had to be* specious. What then is the value of integrable systems, with their reversible and determinist trajectories? Is the field of dynamics homogeneous? Does dynamic description always call for the image of the great calculator as the limiting case —Laplace's demon with his sharpest senses and with the mathematical powers necessary to calculate exact trajectories?

---

[21] See chapter 5 of the present volume.
[22] The rational mechanists like D'Alembert and Lagrange knew that the language of dynamics supposes an idealization, that it implies that a noise be neglected (cf. chapter 6 of the present volume). In fact, from the end of the eighteenth century on, the question of irreversibility as an approximation was asked in a remarkable way, in the context of discussions about the status of a term to be added to the equations of dynamics in order to take into account the losses produced when collisions occur between hard bodies and hydrodynamic turbulences. See W. L. Scott, *The Conflict between Atomism and Conservation Theory, 1644-1860* (London: MacDonald, 1970). The point at which the losses begin to create problems is the point at which physics becomes idealist. The elimination of noise then no longer appears as an inevitable, rational strategy. A more fundamental, non-noisy physical truth is invoked. Thus the conflict becomes possible and is made even more dramatic by the discovery of the constructive role played by irreversibility in nature. The science of irreversible processes is the science of the processes of auto-organization and of bifurcating evolution.

A New Theorem of Impossibility

Michel Serres has often cited Leon Brillouin's response to the claims of dynamics: a dynamic description is only determinist if the description of its initial state is completely accurate—and accuracy is expensive. All the energy in the world could not pay the energetic debt of a completely determinist description on a global scale.[23] In this form, the argument is perfectly correct: no description actually produced will be perfectly determinist. However, determinism stands out as a *limit*, perhaps an inaccessible one in practice but one which nevertheless defines the series of increasing precision: style resists the argument of plausibility.

However, dynamics has discovered today that as soon as the dynamic system to be described is no longer completely simple, the determinist description cannot be realized, even if one dismisses questions of cost or of plausibility. In other words, we now know that there are dynamic systems of different sorts. There are the rare ones in which determinism exists as a limit-state, costly but conceivable, in which extrapolation is possible between the approximate description of any observer and the infinitely precise one of which Leibniz's God is capable. And there are systems in which the idea of determinist prediction conflicts with the laws of dynamics and in which the idea of determining the initial conditions becomes unthinkable. In certain cases, the passage between local, dynamic descriptions and global vision is impossible.[24]

We have said that integrable systems are rare, and only their fascination could make dynamics seem a closed and perfect science, without a history. Since the end of the nineteenth century, dynamics has had a new history, born of two necessities: one, coming from astronomy, the need to define exactly the trajectories that determine the interactions among more than two bodies, and the other, the need to derive from dynamics the description of irreversible evolution, typically defining the increase

---

[23] In "Point, plan (réseau), nuage" (*Hermès IV: La Distribution* [Paris: Minuit, 1977], p. 35) Serres associates the criticism of determinism with Brillouin and Don Juan: "When he must pay his debts, the law given by the determinist falls apart. The law only exists in the interest of someone, someone who wants to take everything and give nothing, someone who kicks Monsieur Dimanche out the door." Don Juan cheats as does Laplace, wants to take without paying, thereby breaking the law of exchange that regulates our communication with nature: "Yes, we give orders to nature, but in the sense that we send it an order, or ask it to give us something for which we pay. . . . This supposes that nature can answer, that nature can hear. This supposes that we can answer nature, that we can and wish to hear nature" (ibid., p. 34). That is the prime lesson of quantum mechanics.

[24] Thus dynamics rediscovers, along with topology, just what myths revealed to us: the difficult passage (not always possible) between spaces in the sense explored in chapter 4 of the present volume. The theorem of impossibility finds, in its own language, the dangerous path strewn with obstacles and prohibitions.

in entropy tending toward a maximum. The first led to non-integrable systems, the second, to research on complicated dynamic systems which would not a priori exclude complicated evolutions (ergodic systems, mixing systems, etc.). The history of dynamics has therefore been marked by the coexistence of the two styles; the fruit of this coexistence, the formulation of a broadened dynamic theory in which an "operator" of entropy can be defined, does not belong to history but rather to current research in physics.[25]

In fact, dynamics here encounters the mixture: the systems which, since Poincaré, have been known not to be exactly integrable and the systems which are studied by statistical mechanics cloud the view of the observer, even the demon. The science of analysis and of separation must henceforth, as Serres says, *becalm itself, feminize itself, erase itself,* with observation disappearing in favor of relation: "The world as it is is not the product of my representation; my knowledge, on the contrary, is a product of the world in the process of becoming. Things themselves choose, exclude, meet, and give rise to one another."[26]

The systems which aim for the theorem of impossibility of which we are speaking are called unstable systems. In order to understand what an unstable dynamic system is, let us describe a stable system. A rigid pendulum can have two kinds of movements that are qualitatively distinct: oscillation and rotation. The behavior of a pendulum is predictable and depends on the initial conditions. There is only one case of uncertainty; it occurs when the initial acceleration is such that the pendulum attains the vertical with zero velocity. In that case, a perturbation "as small as one wishes" will be sufficient to determine which side it will fall to and thus what kind of movement it will adopt. The pendulum is thus the type of system for which, with the exception of these individual rare cases of uncertainty, an approximate description is sufficient to avoid any unexpected evolution and for which a determinist description is the limit. An unstable system, on the other hand, is a system in which the initial conditions determining various qualitatively distinct behaviors are not clearly separated but are, on the contrary, as close as one might wish. We are all familiar with this sort of intimate mixture—it is described by number theory: every rational number is surrounded by irrationals, and every irrational by rationals. Similarly, whatever the neighborhood defined for an initial state, one always finds at least one other state giving rise to a qualitatively different behavior, just as oscillation and rotation are qualitatively different.

---

[25] See Ilya Prigogine, *From Being to Becoming* (San Francisco: Addison Wesley, 1980).
[26] Michel Serres, *Hermès IV: La Distribution* (Paris: Minuit, 1977), pp. 158, 157.

Under these conditions, in order to predict deterministically the type of behavior the system will adopt, one would need *infinite* precision. It is of no use to increase the level of precision or even to make it *tend toward* infinity; uncertainty always remains complete—it does not diminish as precision increases. That means that divine knowledge is no longer implied in human knowledge as its limit, as that toward which one might tend with increasing precision; it is something other, separated by a gap.

For the third time in the twentieth century, physics finds itself defined by the fact that we cannot observe and measure with positively infinite precision, no more than we can communicate faster than the speed of light or measure with instruments that are not macroscopic. Just as the demonstrations of impossibility in relativity and in quantum mechanics are tightly linked to the opening of a new conceptual field, the impossibility of conquering the indeterminacy essential to unstable dynamic systems is not an epistemological discovery which only concerns the relation of our knowledge to the world; rather, it offers a new method of positing problems of physics: the possibility of positing the problem of irreversibility within dynamics. It is not a question of recognizing that we are incapable of calculating such trajectories; rather, it is a question of realizing that the trajectory is not an adequate physical concept for these systems. Henceforth the field of dynamics will appear larger: systems described in terms of trajectories with their determinist and reversible properties are only a particular class within that field.

Parallel Flows and *Clinamen:* How Things Are Born

Where monadic physics ends and trajectories become unstable, the world of the irreversible begins, the open world in which, through fluctuations and bifurcations, things are born, grow, and die. The instability of trajectories, their irreducible and essential indeterminacy, have as a global result the heavy, macroscopic irreversibility of the self-organizing processes that make up nature.

To speak of unstable trajectories is to use the language of classical dynamics to introduce non-classical physics; it is to use the determinist and reversible model to construct the description of the irreversible; it is to invoke monads to describe interactions that cannot be reabsorbed in the monadic interior. In short, it is to repeat Lucretius's procedure, "starting" with the inflexible and legal order and then introducing disturbance and indeterminacy. Things are born where the law is not sufficient to exclude disturbance or to prevent the dynamic monads from interacting.

> Without the declination, there are only the laws of fate, that is to say,
> the chains of order. The new is born of the old; the new is only the
> repetition of the old. But the angle interrupts the stoic chain, breaks
> the *foedera fati*, the endless series of causes and reasons. It disturbs, in
> fact, the laws of nature. And from it, the arrival or life, of everything
> that breathes; and the leaping of horses.[27]

The model of falling atoms, parallel flows in an infinite void, eternally
identical to itself, constitutes an exact image of the monadic evolutions of
classical dynamics, parallel as well, without interactions, in a reversible,
that is to say, in an indifferent, world. The fall is nothing but the universal without a memory whose every instant is the integral repetition of
the preceding instant. Classical dynamics was the mathematico-physical
effectuation of this ordered world, directed by a law.

But the parallel flow is only one of the models of the primitive base
from which things are born. The second is that of the cloud, of stochastic
chaos, closer to reality, Serres says. Here, atoms go in all directions and
collide randomly; it is an immense, tumultuous population, a "disor-
ganized, fluctuating, brownian mass composed of dissimilarities and oppositions."[28] Here as well one must note the exactness. This is a description of another physical situation, a purely macroscopic one but one
which also is integrally subject to a law: statistical equilibrium within a
population in which all the processes and their opposites are produced
simultaneously and compensate for each other. At this macroscopic level,
just as at the microscopic level of the description of atomic trajectories,
the apparent absurdity of the *clinamen* is repeated. Statistical disorder
should not produce a difference, any more than a disturbance should
occur in the established trajectory, for disorder is the state in which all
differences are abolished in the indifferent, senseless tumult in which
they all coexist.

Yet non-classical science has taught us that trajectories can become
unstable and that stochastic chaos can become creative. In certain circumstances, evolution bifurcates, the homogeneous disorder is no longer
stable, and a new order of organized functioning is established, with
amplified fluctuation. For example, laminar flow in parallel sheets "spontaneously" becomes turbulent; that is to say, we now can calculate it. In
this realm of the bifurcation, in which *turba* becomes *turbo*, rather a
strange tumult reigns, the complete opposite of indifferent disorder.
Creative chaos is illegality itself, for its description dissolves the distinction between the macroscopic state and the microscopic fluctuation; cor-

---

[27] See chapter 9 of the present volume.
[28] Serres, *La Naissance de la physique*, p. 42.

relations can appear among distant events; local deviations echo through-out the system—the matrix-state in which fluctuations are amplified and from which things are born.

And thus Serres is correct: the question is reversed. It is no longer necessary to ask where the *clinamen* comes from or how one might justify the disturbing of laws. All laminar flows can become unstable past a certain threshold of velocity, and that was known just as the productive nature of organized forms, of bifurcating evolution, of what we call dissipative structures, was known. One must ask how an abstraction of this knowledge could have been made to describe the world in order, subject to a universal law. We already know one answer given by Serres. Classical science is a science of engineers who knew, of course, that their flows were never perfectly laminar, but who made the theory of laminar flow perfectly controllable and directable, the only flow for which know-ing is controlling.

> The technological model is in place. It is a physics of water mains. Our physics was first of all a physics of fountain-builders, of well-diggers, or of builders of aqueducts. . . . Hence this physical world where the drainpipe is essential and where the *clinamen* seems to be freedom because it is precisely the turbulence that refuses enforced flow. Incomprehensible by scientific theory, incomprehensible to the hydraulic engineer.[29]

The history of science particularly repeats itself when it is a question of mastery or control. We could rewrite the same text with irreversible replacing *clinamen* and the builder of thermic machines replacing the well-digger, with matter transformed by fire and heat replacing flowing water. This text would tell of the birth of the thermodynamics of equi-librium, the classical science from which will later be born the study of irreversible processes. It would tell how Clausius and his followers, seeking the ideal output of thermic machines, developed the theory of the "perfect" motor, functioning reversibly, that is to say, in a completely controllable way—subject, of course, to the impossibility of perpetual motion of the second sort (you cannot make a motor work as a creator of mechanical differences without the consumption of a thermic difference), but within a conservative world. The ideal thermic machine turns in perfectly completed cycles in the world of the eternal return of dif-ferences. It came into being when Carnot, in a founding gesture, "gave" himself two sources and in one fell swoop stilled the furnaces where, irreversibly, fire devoured matter and created difference. For it is only for a given difference that an ideally reversible function can be imagined and irreversibility relegated to a secondary status as a source of loss, a waste that, theoretically, can be canceled out and that occurs only through a lack of control. Carnot's gesture extended the classical division between the universality of the law and the imperfections of human applications that the new style of science, the affirmation of the irreversibility of natural processes, was to subvert almost immediately.

Today we are discovering the limits of laws, the limits of the realm in which nature can be controlled, that is to say, in which it is indifferent. We are rediscovering this truth, announced a long time ago by Serres and on which *Lucrèce* is a meditation: "Nature does not code the universal. . . . there is no code at the equilibrium point."[30] Everything that exists, all the individual bodies that come into being, coded circumstances, tablets of their own law, do so by distancing themselves from the law without a memory, the law of the dynamic "fall," the stable and infinite interlinking, or the law of evolution toward thermodynamic equilibrium, the forgetting of the specificity of initial states.

A scientific style does not die if the limits of the questions it implies or the specificity of the questions it brings to the fore are uncovered. It remains the witness to a successful dialogue with nature. Serres's work helps us understand that our questions no longer can be asked of a world without friction or holes—the world of Leibniz. After all, our physics was never capable of truly understanding the Leibnizian harmony of the thousands of voices translating each other in a universal code.

[30]Serres, *La Traduction*, p. 62.

Permissions

The essays in this volume which were originally published in the *Hermès* series by Editions de Minuit, Paris, are translated here by permission of the publisher. They are as follows: from *Hermès I: La Communication* (Paris: Minuit, 1968) comes "The Apparition of Hermes: *Dom Juan*" ("Apparition d'Hermès: Dom Juan") and "Platonic Dialogue" ("Le Dialogue platonicien et la genèse intersubjective de l'abstraction"); from *Hermès II: L'Interférence* (Paris: Minuit, 1972) comes "Mathematics and Philosophy: What Thales Saw . . ." ("Ce que Thalès a vu au pied des pyramides"); from *Hermès III: La Traduction* (Paris: Minuit, 1974) comes "Turner Translates Carnot" ("Turner traduit Carnot"); from *Hermès IV: La Distribution* (Paris: Minuit, 1977) comes "Language and Space: From Oedipus to Zola" ("Discours et parcours"), "Knowledge in the Classical Age: La Fontaine and Descartes" ("Le Jeu du loup: *Le Loup et l'agneau*"), and "The Origin of Language: Biology, Information Theory, and Thermodynamics" ("Origine du langage"); from *Hermès V: Le Passage du Nord-Ouest* (Paris: Minuit, 1980) comes "The Origin of Geometry" ("Origine de la géométrie, 5"). "Lucretius: Science and Religion" was originally published as "Conditions culturelles. Violence et contrat: Science et religion" in *La Naissance de la physique dans le texte de Lucrèce: Fleuves et turbulences* (Paris: Minuit, 1977).

"Michelet: The Soup" originally appeared in *Clio* 6, no. 2 (Winter 1977), and is reprinted by permission. The translation of "Knowledge in the Classical Age: La Fontaine and Descartes" originally appeared as "The Algebra of Literature: The Wolf's Game" in Josué Harari, ed., *Textual Strategies: Perspectives in Post-Structuralist Criticism* in 1979 and is reprinted by permission of Cornell University Press. The translation of "The Origin of Geometry" originally appeared as "Origin of Geometry IV" in *Diacritics* 8, no. 1 (Spring 1978) and is reprinted by permission. All other translations were made for this volume and are copyrighted by The Johns Hopkins University Press.

Name Index

Subject Index

Complex: in Freud, 72; in Listing and
Maxwell, 53, 72; of an organism, 75-
76
Crisis. *See* Sacrifice
Criticism. *See* Strategy

Determinism, in physics, 150-52
Dialogue: aporetic, 67, 69; and dialectics, 69; philosophy of, 70; Platonic,
65-70; and third man, 67
Diarrhesis, 74
Discourse: as constitutive of mythical
itinerary, 48-49; of Lagrange, 56; of
mathematics, 50, 79; of nineteenth-
century science, 73; philosophical,
72; and representation, 62; and space,
48-49. *See also* Myth; Space
Dynamics: classical, 144-46; history of,
150-51; Leibniz's, 139-45; Poincaré's,
149, 151; reversibility in, 145-48; as
theory of motion, 55. *See also* Mechanics; Physics

Electrology, 33
Empiricism, 69, 70
Encyclopedia, in nineteenth-century
sciences, 29-38
Entropy, 73-76; and death, 100; in information theory, 81; law of, 18, 71;
in Lucretian world, 116; and negentropy, 74; in physics, 115. *See also*
Equilibrium; Thermodynamics
Equilibrium: and *clinamen*, 51; and exchange, 8-11; of forces, 55 n, 61; and
hereditary flaw, 41; and homeostasis, 73; laws of, 102; in mechanical
systems, 71; in an organism, 74; in
physics, 115-16; and psychology, 118.
See also Physics; Thermodynamics
Esthetics: Bach's and Leibniz's, 46; Kant's,
44; and music, 46; Serres's, 44
Exchange: in *George Dandin*, 13; in *The
Gift*, 13; and Hermes, 13; in *The Miser*,
13; natural, 9; and profit, 10; rupture
of, 6, 8-11; simulacrum of, 11; struc-

ture of, 5-9, 13. *See also* Circulation;
Communication

Feast, 3; and death, 12-13; and exchange,
5-6, 12, 14; as festive meal, 40-41; Master Jacques's, 13. *See also* Comedy
Flaw. *See* Equilibrium

Game, 16-28; and circulation, 42; and
jeu de l'oie, 40-42; martial, 27-28; as
model of exact knowledge, 27; -space,
19-21. *See also* Strategy
Genesis: and chemistry, 34; and feminine principle, 30; and mechanics,
32; and spherical geometry, 31-32;
and thermodynamics, 33-34
Geometry: and abstract idealities, 70;
Aristotle's, 130; and the art of drawing, 54-62; and communication, 50-
53; Comte's, 23; double writing of,
127-28; of the *Fighting Téméraire*, 57;
and Greek reason, 111; history of,
128; measurement in, 85-97; and mechanics, 55; origin of, 44, 52, 87, 91, 93,
125-33; perspectival, 92; Plato's, 94-
96; pyramid as object of, 84-97; representation in, 92; and sacrifice, 129-
30, 133; as strategy, 87; Thales's, 84,
91. *See also* Nature; Reason, Strategy
Gift, law of, 4-5. *See also* Communication

Heterogeny, 29-30, 36
History: and atomist physics, 118; as
event, 115-17, 120; Plato's, 95; as symp-
tom, 116-17. *See also* Mathematics; Pol-
itics; Science; Thermodynamics
Homeomorphism, 52, 68
Homeorrhesis, 74-76, 82, 120
Homeostasis, 73-74, 78
Homoiothermy, 76
Homothesis, in mathematics, 89, 91
Hylozoism, 29; as synthesis of mechan-
ism and vitalism, 35

166 / *Subject Index*

Mythical (*continued*)
42; narrative, 52; operators, 50; text, 45-46

Nature: Baconian, 21, 23; contract with, 104, 119; Galilean, 23; and science, 155. *See also* Geometry; Science
Negentropy, 73-74. *See also* Entropy
Neptunism, 29-30, 36
Noise, 76-81; in communication, 66-70, 73, 126-27; as empirical portion of message, 70; figures of, 67; in information theory, 73, 76; organism as rectifier of, 78; and Platonism, 70. *See also* Communication; Information theory; Language
Numbers: irrational, 131-33; prime, 131; rational, 50-51; theory of, 151. *See also* Communication; Reason; Strategy

Object, in science, 122-23
Observer: in information theory, 76-83; in physics, 152
Ontogenesis, 74-75
Order. *See* Numbers; Physics; Reason; Thermodynamics
Organism: and circulation, 75; in classical philosophy and psychology, 78; as converter of time, 75-76; cybernetic vs. mathematical model of, 77; and homeorrhesis, 74-75; stability and imbalance of, 74-75; as thermodynamic system, 71-83. *See also* Information theory
Origin. *See* Geometry; Myth; Physics

Painting: and mechanics, 54-56, 60; stochastic disorder in, 58, 61; and thermodynamics, 56-62
Philosophy. *See* Geometry; Mathematics; Metaphysics; Myth; Nature; Physics; Reason; Strategy
Phylogenesis, 74-75
Physics: Archimedean, 103, 107; atom-

ist, 113-20; and catharsis, 124; of death, 98-101; declination in, 99-102, 119-20; Epicurean, 112-13; history of, 139-45; and hydraulics, 101; laminar flow in, 75, 99, 101-2, 118; Laplacean, 140, 145; laws of conjunction in, 113-20; Leibnizian, 139-41; local vs. global in, 138, 141; Lucretian, 99-124; of Mars, 98-107; Newtonian, 139-41; principle of constancy in, 119; and sacrifice, 124; stochastic phenomena in, 103; turbulence in, 99-102, 121; of Venus, 98-107; vortex in, 100-102. *See also* Dynamics; Mechanics; Science
Plague, and violence, 100, 108-10, 123
Platonism. *See* Dialogue; Geometry; Reason; Science; Strategy
Politics: and metaphysics, 105; in science, 104-6, 110, 112, 116-17, 123. *See also* Sacrifice; Science; Strategy
Psychoanalysis. *See* Information theory; Organism; Repression, Unconscious
Pyramid: and knowledge, 91-92, 94; as mnemonic device, 88; as original geometric object, 84-97; and time, 86-87; as tomb, 127. *See also* Geometry; Mathematics; Strategy

Reason: Baconian, 21; Cartesian, 17-18, 21, 24; and death, 100-101; Greek, 84, 111, 121; and myth, 46-53; and nature, 100, 104-5; and order, 99-101; Platonic, 69; as ratio, 52; as repetition and identity, 100-101; Rousseauian, 22-23; as strategy, 105. *See also* Myth; Numbers; Strategy
Representation: and geometry, 92; idealism of, 94; and imitation, 131; and myth, 95-96; optical, 86-87; origin of, 92; philosophy of, 91, 97; in Plato, 93
Repression: in Freud, 79-80; in information theory, 79-80
Reservoir: as analytical concept, 37; and circulation, 36-37, 72; in thermodynamics, 35-37, 71-72

Reversibility. *See* Irreversibility

Sacrifice: and crisis, 108-10, 121-22; and murder, 108-10; and origin of geometry, 130, 133; and physics, 124. *See also* Physics; Science; Violence

Science: and agonistics, 23; Baconian, 21; Cartesian, 21; classical, 104, 137, 154; conditions of possibility of, 105-6; and encyclopedia, 36; as game, 21-22; history of, 29, 39-40, 94, 97, 103; and Leibnizian metaphysics, 144; martial, 99, 101, 104; and metaphysics, 27; and myth, 41-53; natural, 29; and nature, 155; paradigm of, 102-3; and political power, 110; and politics, 23, 104-6, 112, 116-17, 123; and religion, 109; and social contract, 108-9; as text, 37-38; violence in, 124. *See also* Geometry; Mathematics; Physics; Strategy; Thermodynamics

Shadow. *See* Knowledge; Pyramid

Space: and communication, 49-52; cultural, 45; Euclidean, 44, 52-53; in Kant, 44; mythical, 48; projective, 44; Riemannian, 43; and time, 86-88; topological, 44, 47-48; of touch, 48-49; varieties of, 42-53; visual, 49. *See also* Communication; Myth

Spatial operator, 40-53; bifurcation as, 47; body as, 44-45; bridge as, 40-43, 46; category of *between* as, 45; crossroads as, 46-47; incest as, 46-48; labyrinth as, 40, 49, 53; Sphinx as, 47; well as, 40-43

Statics: and geometry, 60-61; as theory of rest, 55

Strategy: Baconian, 21, 105, 107, 121; Cartesian, 21-27, 105, 107, 121; as cartography, 111; of criticism, 38; Einstein's, 27; Epicurean, 111; geometry as, 84-87, 90-91; Greek, 111; of history of science, 40, of interpretation, 37-38; La Fontaine's, 15-20; Lucretian, 111; of majorant/minorant, 19-21; martial, 27-28; in *Meditationes* of Leibniz,

24-25, 27; in *Metaphysical Meditations*, 23-27; mythical, 48-49; Pascalian, 28; Platonic, 95, 121; of reason, 110-12; in *Regulae*, 24; in science, 21-28, 104-23. *See also* Geometry; Mathematics; Myth; Nature; Reason; Science

Structure: biological, 16; causal, 17; definition of, 16, 37; ethical, 17; etymology of, 24; invariance of, 17, 42-43; models of, 16-19; ordered, 16; parental, 18; political, 18; social, 18; temporal, 18; topographical, 17. *See also* System

Style: Carnot's, 155; in classical physics, 145; in mechanics, 148; from mechanics to thermodynamics, 148-49; in scientific thought, 137; in thermodynamics, 148-49

Symbol, nature of, 67-69

Syrrhesis, 74-75

System: hypercomplex, 74; Laplace's, 138; living, 103; notion of, 71; open, 74; organism as, 71-83; in thermodynamics, 73-74; three types of, 71-72; and time, 76. *See also* Information theory; Thermodynamics

Text, and scientific models, 37-38

Thermodynamics: birth of, 154-55; Carnot cycle in, 34, 36, 57; Carnot's, 59; and circulation, 33-35; in Freud, 72; furnace in, 61; and history, 58-59, 61; and information theory, 73, 81-83; as interpretive grill, 40; of open systems, 74; and ordered structure, 18; and painting, 56-62; reservoirs in, 35; in *Rougon-Macquart* novels, 39-43; second principle of, 59, 71, 74, 118; as science of fire, 62; and steam engine, 57-59; technologies of, 39; and time, 116; Turner's, 57-62; waterfall in, 62. *See also* Circulation; Entropy; Information theory; Irreversibility; Science

Third man: in communication, 126; as demon, 67; in dialogue, 67; and em-

Third man (*continued*)
piricism, 70; exclusion of, 67, 69; and prosopopeia of noise, 67. *See also* Communication; Dialogue

Time: Bergsonian, 116; convergence of, 75; irreversibility of, 71-72, 74, 118, 120; Lucretian, 115-16; Newtonian, 115-16; notion of, 71; in systems, 76; in thermodynamics, 72, 75-76, 116; variety of, 75, 81. *See also* Irreversibility; Space; Thermodynamics

Topology, 51-53; as *analysis situs,* 46; and the category of *between,* 45; Euler's, 43; in Freud, 72. *See also* Geometry; Space

Tragedy, origin of, 123

Trial, as process, 16-20

Unconscious, in organism, 79-81. *See also* Repression

Violence: and communication, 122; figures of, 100, 108-10; in history, 122-24; and plague, 123; and science, 124. *See also* Sacrifice

Weaver: as connector of spaces, 45, 49-52; as geometer, 133; mythic figures of, 49-50; Plato's Royal Weaver, 49

World: as furnace, 61; scientific models of, 35; as steam engine, 59

Writing: alphabetic vs. ideographic, 125-28; as drawing, 65; and information theory, 73; and logic, 67

THE JOHNS HOPKINS UNIVERSITY PRESS

This book was composed in Baskerville text and Palatino display type by David Lorton from a design by Lisa S. Mirski. It was printed on S. D. Warren's 50-lb. Sebago Eggshell paper and bound in Kivar 5 by The Maple Press Company. The manuscript was edited by Jean Owen and Mary Louise Kenney.